Sex, Race, and God

Sex, Race, and God

Christian Feminism in Black and White

Susan Brooks Thistlethwaite

Crossroad · New York

1989

The Crossroad Publishing Company
370 Lexington Avenue, New York, N.Y. 10017

Printed in the United States of America

Library of Congress Cataloging-in-Publication Data

Thistlethwaite, Susan Brooks, 1948–
    Sex, race, and God : Christian feminism in black and white / Susan
Brooks Thistlethwaite.
        p. cm.
    Includes bibliographical references.
    ISBN 0-8245-0969-2
    1. Feminist theology. 2. Black theology. I. Title.
BT83.55.T45   1989
261.8′34—dc20   89-36219
                                                                          CIP

Grateful acknowledgment is made to St. Martin's Press for permission
to reprint "with no immediate cause" from *Nappy* Edges by Ntozake
Shange. Copyright © 1972, 1974, 1975, 1976, 1978 by Ntozake Shange.
Reprinted by permission of St. Martin's Press.

Contents

Acknowledgments

Acknowledging the gifts of time, energy, and ideas of others is a true joy of feminist scholarship. Carol Christ gave me the tremendous gift of her honesty. Cheryl Townsend Gilkes gifted me with her rigorous attention to the real study of black women's lives. Virginia Mollenkott helped give me courage to go ahead and publish this book. Faculty colleagues at Chicago Theological Seminary, Bonnie Miller-McLemore, Dorothy Bass, Bill Myers, and Dow Edgerton helped with their interest and willingness to discuss. The Hyde Park Women's Faculty Reading Group discussed Chapter One to my great advantage. Mary Potter Engel listened to me muddle around in a philosophy of nature and, as always, had insights to share.

This acknowledgment would not be complete without the names of black women students at Chicago Theological Seminary, past and present, who insisted on their own vision: Verda Beach, Margaret Neal, Mae Wilson, Wanda Jefferson, Francina Parrett, Janice Hodge, Precious Mays-Dixon, Yvonne Morey, Marsha Thomas, and Linda Parrish. White women students such as Lorollee Brown, Linda Noonan, Deb Baxter, and the students of my theology classes who were willing to listen to me work things through also have my heartfelt thanks.

My thanks to Max Havlick for his careful typing of the manuscript. I'd also like to acknowledge with gratitude Frank Oveis, editor and friend.

But I must thank last, first and always, my husband, Dick, and our boys, James, Bill, and Douglas, whose love makes me believe I can do anything.

Introduction

This book began as another project entirely. I have for some years been engaged in writing a book that was to be entitled "God and Her Survival in the Nuclear Age."[1] This study is the product of work in the peace movement both in the United States and abroad. In conversations I had while working on that book, however, I began to get an inkling that there were directions I had not explored. When I mentioned to black colleagues that my approach so far had been to read the memoirs and biographies of Holocaust survivors, their replies were instructive and went something like this, "That's typical of you white people. Whenever you want to know anything, the only place you look is Germany." I decided this was quite true. In looking for additional source material I began reading the novels and essays that black women in the United States have written, figuring that they too knew something about survival. They do.

I wrote an essay for *Christianity and Crisis*[2] describing my struggles with this literature and the changes it was precipitating in my work in feminist theology. I received an enormous amount of mail, some of it quite critical. One letter from Carol Christ and my reply were published in a subsequent issue.[3] The subject of debate in this correspondence was my contention in the article that the experience of white and black women is so different that I as a white woman, given our history in the exploitation of black women, cannot ignore that gap.

Difference as a theoretical issue in white feminist theology has become central for me, primarily in reading Audre Lorde's work. Her essay "The Master's Tools Will Never Dismantle the Master's House" was a critical transition. This essay was originally an address presented in 1979 during a panel discussion, "The Personal and the Political," at the Second Sex Conference. Of the women present, who were overwhelmingly white, Lorde asked:

If white american feminist theory need not deal with the differences between us, and the resulting difference in aspects of our oppressions,

1

then what do you do with the fact that the women who clean your houses
and tend your children while you attend conferences on feminist theory
are, for the most part, poor and third world women? What is the theory
behind racist feminism?[4]

Recognizing and responding to the differences between black and white
women is the challenge Lorde poses. Over the years it has been the
genius of patriarchy to deal with difference by obliterating it, by projecting a white male face onto the definition of humanity. If white
feminism replicates this process of obfuscation/suppression, it will
never deal with patriarchy at its most fundamental level.

Lorde goes on to say that a shift in method is critical if white
feminists are to meet her challenge.

> [S]urvival is not an academic skill. It is learning how to stand alone,
> unpopular and sometimes reviled, and how to make common cause with
> those others identified as outside the structures, in order to define and
> seek a world in which we can all flourish. It is learning how to take our
> differences and make them strengths. For the master's tools will never
> dismantle the master's house. They may allow us temporarily to beat him
> at his own game, but they will never enable us to bring about genuine
> change. And this fact is only threatening to those women who still define
> the master's house as their only source of support.[5]

This book, then, is an attempt to ask the questions, What happens in
white feminism if we begin to give up all the master's tools and not just
some? What happens when the differences between black and white
women become the starting point for white feminist theology?

A number of feminists are already asking these questions, and some
theoretical shifts have emerged. For example, God's Fierce Whimsy, the
work of seven feminists who make up the Mudflower Collective, contains an exchange of letters between Katie Cannon and Carter Heyward
on the question, "Can we be different but not alienated?"[6]

The force of their conversation on the difference that color makes
and the common bond of all women is to turn attention to liberalism
and the problem it poses for feminist theology. One response this
collective makes to Lorde's question about the theory behind racist
feminism is liberalism. Liberal theory has several key elements that
allow accommodation to racism and preclude the emergence of radical
critiques. One of the goals of this book, therefore, is to explore the
limitations of liberalism and to posit alternatives to liberal theory. (The
role of liberalism in white feminist theory in the nineteenth century is
discussed in Chapter Two.)

Black and White Women

The question may be asked, Why deal exclusively with black women in this book? Hispanic women, Asian women, Native American women, and women of other racial minorities have also had experiences that differ profoundly from those of the dominant white culture in the United States. In truth, I began this book with the intention of trying to include the experience of minority women other than black women. I realized in fairly short order, however, that I was continuing to make the same mistake: this time universalizing the experience of all nonwhite women. The unreflective sense of oneself as the definition of humanity and of all others as a deviation from that norm is what is meant by the term "first world" as it is used to describe white-dominated North Atlantic cultures. The term "third world," by logical extension, then becomes a legitimate description of other cultures. As Shiva Naipul argues, the term "third world" itself exhibits imperialism, for it is a term of bloodless universality that robs individuals and societies of their particularity. In the spirit of clarity, a hallmark of liberal objectivity, we go forth and denude others of their particular differences. "Third world," then, is "a flabby concept," even "an ideological instrument of the West."[7]

This book, then, is particular. It is an examination of the history of the differences between black and white women in slavery, in subsequent American history, and on the contemporary scene. It makes a proposal for a feminist theory based on the embrace of these differences and applies this theory in a preliminary fashion to some aspects of feminist theology.

Fiction as a Source

One of my primary sources for encountering differences between black and white women is the fiction of black women. There has been nothing short of an explosion of fiction writing among black women during the past decade, but a long and tortuous track of earlier writings precedes this period.[8] Until very recently, this literature provided almost all the source material available in print on the lives of black women.[9] Because black women have been excluded from the various guilds of history, theology, philosophy, sociology, anthropology, law, medicine and so forth—the main shapers and chroniclers of dominant culture—fiction writing and poetry have often been the only public channels through which they could express their creativity.[10] Audre Lorde has stressed, "Poetry Is Not a Luxury."[11]

For black women who are struggling with the demands of these various guilds (theology, for example), the fiction of their sisters is like coming home to a fully stocked pantry: Here, for a change, they are not starving. Katie Cannon makes the work of Zora Neale Hurston the basis for her development of a black womanist ethics.[12]

White women, too, have sought in women's fiction an articulation of their experience denied by the same guilds. Judith Plaskow's *Sex, Sin and Grace* is a study that contrasts the three theological constructs in the writings of Reinhold Niebuhr and Paul Tillich with "Women's Experience" as she establishes it from the novels of Doris Lessing.[13] In *Diving Deep and Surfacing,*[14] Carol Christ draws on the works of Lessing and other women writers, including Ntozake Shange, in her quest for an alternative canon of women's religious experiences.

Yet since difference is a subject of this book, I have attempted to explore the ways in which the writing of black women functions as an articulation of not only black women's experience but of their theological, political, sociological, and anthropological viewpoints as well. In general, black women's fiction contrasts with white women's fiction because it accents public perspectives as much as or more than private life. Given the closure of the guilds to black women writers, as has been pointed out, these writers have often used their fiction as a vehicle to present the black community's alternative worldviews under the guise of fiction.[15] Barbara Christian writes:

> Stories do occur in place, but what the women writers emphasize is the importance of place and community as a character. By confining their landscapes of action to the community and examining the routines of daily life and feelings under a magnifying glass, black women writers accomplish two things: They highlight the art of daily living and give back to the community a mirror of itself; and in that mirror, they can correct the stereotypes about black life that seem to proliferate so irresponsibly in our society.[16]

Black women writers also articulate the difference between the experience of black women and that of the larger black community—the "small, dark enclosure" inside the "narrow space" that white society allows black life, as Gloria Wade-Gayles writes.[17] Theirs is a fiction wired into a community that is on the edge of survival.

I believe that, as a white feminist, I cannot use the fiction of black women as a source in the same way I have been able to use the fiction of white women as a resource for white feminist theology. In approaching the literature of black women I must be aware of difference. For example, the element of psychological interiority of white women's fiction

(Lessing is an excellent example) takes on a different resonance in the literature of black women because it is almost always linked with community survival. In an essay on her fiction, "Salvation Is the Issue," Toni Cade Bambara writes:

> One, we are at war. Two, the natural response to oppression, ignorance, evil, and mystification is wide-awake resistance. Three, the natural response to stress and crisis is not breakdown and capitulation, but transformation and renewal to. The question I raise from "Gorilla" to "Sea Birds" to *Salt* to "Faith of the Bather" is, is it natural (sane, healthy, whole-some, in our interest) to violate the contracts/covenants we have with our ancestors, each other, our children, our selves, our God?
>
> In *Salt* most particularly, in motive/content/structure design, the question is, do we intend to have a future as sane, whole, governing people? I argue then and in "Faith" as well that immunity to the serpent's sting can be found in our tradition of struggle and our faculty for synthesis. The issue is salvation. I work to produce stories that save our lives.[18]

White women, too, work to save lives. As I said to Carol Christ in our exchange of letters in *Christianity and Crisis,* "Many white women owe their sanity to your work and I, for one, am one of them." Hers is valuable and important work when we consider how often (more than 50 percent, or so the FBI estimates) women are subjects of male violence in their most intimate relationships. Further, one of the strengths of Christ's work is that she has referred to the literature of black women and has not respected the artificial barriers erected between the experience of black and white women.

Yet I have come to believe that *my* task as a white feminist at this time is to signal the differences between the works of black and white women and to construct my feminist theology in light of these differences.

In the essay in *Christianity and Crisis,* I quoted from Christ's widely read chapter "Why Women Need the Goddess." Christ herself is quoting Ntozake Shange:

> At the close of Ntozake Shange's stupendously successful Broadway play "For Colored Girls Who Have Considered Suicide When the Rainbow is Enuf," a tall beautiful black woman rises from despair to cry out, "I found God in myself and I lived her fiercely." Her discovery is echoed by women around the country who meet spontaneously in small groups on full moons, solstices, and equinoxes to celebrate the Goddess as symbol of life and death powers and waxing and waning energies in the universe and in themselves.[19]

What Christ talks about in her chapter is acceptance of female power, female will, female bodies, and their connection to nature and female bonds—critical themes in the work of many white feminists. The situation of white women in a patriarchal culture is one of learned self-hatred, to be sure, and the love of self and other women, as Christ rightly points out, is a critical transformation.

While Shange also addresses similar themes in her work, this is not the whole meaning of her statement about finding god in the self and loving her fiercely. *for colored girls . . .* is, as Shange says, "a black girl's song." This song is not only about affirming femaleness but also about affirming blackness, as Christ herself notes.[20] The "carin'/struggle/hard times" of what life is like uniquely for black-American women, I believe, must be allowed to stand on its own. It must count for the survival of these women and their people and not for someone else's survival. "I cdnt stand being sorry & colored at the same time it's so redundant in the modern world," says one of the women characters in Shange's "coreopoem." It is precisely that being of blackness in suffering and struggle, defeat and resistance to the thousand indignities of being black and female in a racist and sexist society that the lady in red finds in herself and loves so fiercely. Shange herself does not universalize this discovery. The full passage from *for colored girls . . .* reads:

> i found god in myself
> & i loved her/i loved her fiercely
> & this is for colored girls who have considered
> suicide/but are movin to the ends of their own
> rainbows[21]

Shange was distressed by the mainstream accolades of her work and finally distanced herself from the Broadway production, stating that "*for colored girls . . .* is either too big for my off-off Broadway taste, or too little for my exaggerated sense of freedom. . . ."[22]

The title clearly states *for colored girls* and, at least at this point in my history, I am finding that it can be a strength for white feminist theology to respect that difference. This is a new insight for me, and one that shapes this book. It is an insight I have gleaned from my personal struggle with black women and their literature. I am offering it as a suggestion and not as the last word on all directions for white feminist theology, and certainly not for *thealogy*. It was, after all, Carol Christ who taught me to use the first person when I write.[23]

Social Analysis

Fiction is a central resource for this work, but it is well to remember, and I must continually remind myself of this, that fiction is *fiction*. Fiction can evoke truths that are obscured by social analysis, but sociology, anthropology, and economics are becoming, for me, key resources for a white feminist theory seeking ways to grapple with the cloying hands of class and race privilege. While many sections of this book use black women's fiction to evoke some truths of the experience of black and white women, these fictional evocations will be buttressed, where possible, by data from the social sciences.

As a white feminist I find I have too often been seduced into an exclusive interiority by an alliance with psychology as my only analytical tool. This alliance aggravates the tendency I have toward interiority and social passivity as a result of my own socialization as a white woman. For me the solid, unromantic data of the social-science disciplines has become an invaluable corrective, especially where these data have been submitted to a feminist critique of the presumed objectivity of science.

Guilt and Paralysis

There are a number of risks involved in making the argument that as a white woman I must apply what I have learned about critical consciousness from the white women's movement to the race and class condition of middle-class white women. One of my greatest fears is that in putting forth this argument certain proof-texts will be abused to further the liberal guilt of white women or, even worse, as an undeserved put-down of post-Christian feminism. In traveling around the country to speak on the subject of the difference race makes for white feminist theology, I have been struck by how difficult it is to own one's own racism as the *inevitable* product of socialization in a racist culture. Moreover, the struggle to bring the consequences of this socialization to consciousness often appears to have a paralyzing effect. During the late 1960s, Hannah Arendt observed:

> We all know, for example, that it has become rather fashionable among white liberals to react to Negro grievances with the cry, "We are all guilty." . . . Where all are guilty, no one is; confessions of collective guilt are the best possible safeguard against the discovery of culprits, and the very magnitude of the crime the best excuse for doing nothing.[24]

Further, many in traditional religions are made profoundly uncomfortable by the deep challenges post-Christian and post-Jewish feminism pose for white male patriarchy. They search for and use any intrafeminist debates for their own divide-and-conquer purposes. All feminists are not of one mind, however; in their individual creativity they give off the sparks of difference Audre Lorde so frequently addresses in her writings. As a white Christian feminist, seeking to understand the experience of black women, my thesis is that the boundaries of difference must be respected. I must also extend this to feminists who work out of other paradigms. Yet as feminists we spark off of one another because we take each other's work seriously. These tensions are not easily reconcilable, nor are they completely resolvable. They do, however, model an alternative to the divide-and-conquer mentality.

Overview of the Book

This book is my attempt as a white feminist to pay close attention to the way in which black women articulate their experience and to make a methodological shift in light of their statements. The first chapter, "Experience in White Feminist Theory," begins with the assertion by black women, or womanists (the term, coined by Alice Walker, means "black feminist or feminist of color"[25]) that white women who take women's (sic)[26] "experience" as their premise in critiquing patriarchal perspectives have always ignored the differences in the lives of black and white women. Some white women have attempted to respond to this critique, notably by using poststructuralist theories to examine the uncritical use of the term "experience." But poststructuralist theories are themselves mired in patriarchal perspectives. I argue that they must be counterbalanced by some of the truths experienced by white women in their lives, notably in the movement to end violence against women. Hence a white feminist theory that is sensitive to the difference race makes must be "conceptually unstable."

This theoretical elaboration concludes with the role of anger in feminist theory. If the contrived and manipulative distortions of racism do not make white women sufficiently, explicitly angry, they will not, as their suffrage foresisters did not, be able to generate the energy to break with the alliances of race and class.

Chapter Two, "Slavery: A White Feminist History," explores the differences of race, sex, and class as lodged in the "peculiar institution" of American slavery. This is the history of white women as well as black women and men. To understand the alienation of black and white women, it is important to examine the separation of black slave women into the despised laboring and reproductive body and of white mistresses into the repository of nonfunctional values as the soul of culture. This division aggravated the systemic violence of the hierarchical relationship of white mistress/black woman slave and turned it toward the physical violence of white women slave owners toward black women slaves.[27]

Beyond the separations of sex and race are those of race and class. Slavery was, above all, an economic system, and for this reason black exploitation must be subject to economic analysis. Enlightenment liberalism, the foundational theory of white women abolitionists, had no resources to enable these white women to either analyze the causes of their own anger at slavery or to examine its economic base. White women activists who labored for emancipation believing in the cause of equal rights for all were shocked and disaffected by the passage of the Fourteenth and Fifteenth Amendments after the Civil War. This left them vulnerable to arguments of racial supremacy.

Chapter Two concludes with an examination of sex and class, and extends the critique of liberalism to its doctrine of the solitary individual. White women suffragists ignored and finally betrayed the Northern union women struggling for economic justice.

Chapter Three, "Class and Creation," explores two specific points of focus for the differences between black and white women: housework and motherhood. I argue that taking these differences seriously requires a nonunitary approach to the nature of women's existence and ultimately demands an articulation of difference as a primary representative of the intricate relation of creation and destruction in the nature of existence itself.

Audre Lorde's writings on difference are juxtaposed with Mary Daly's as a means of beginning to construct a theory of difference that is specific. Difference must be located in particular dwellings. These locations must be subject to a social analysis that reveals the role difference can be made to play in exploitation. The roots of Western intolerance for difference are found in artificial and abstract notions of unity that do not, in fact, exist.

Chapter Four, "Creating and Destroying Grace: Nature and the Fall," is an exploration of nature and creation, especially with regard to evil in the writings of black and white women. Chapter Five, "The Self and Sin," troubles the waters of white feminist definitions of sin and grace, the waters already churning from the encounters with traditional Christian misogynist definitions of women. Chapter Six, "Jesus and Christa," explores the difference race makes in the way in which white Christian feminists and black womanists approach Christology. Chapter Seven, "God the Father, God the Mother, and the Goddess," seeks the real roots of the differences in God language used by black and white women in the relative tolerance for diversity in black and white Christianity. Chapter Eight, "A Difference in Common: Violence," articulates the structural interconnection as well as difference of sexual violence in the lives of black women and white women, with particular attention to the history of racism as a factor in understanding the systemic violence of American society. This is a violence that must be examined within as well as without.

This exploration has shown me the extent to which I have turned away from my own class and race context in examining personal experience. After reading the works of Bell Hooks and Angela Davis, I remembered, and realized that I had deliberately "forgotten" the ethnicity and economic status of my own family history. I am the grandchild of Hungarian immigrants who came to this country in the early part of this century as children sent by their parents to escape the Kaiser. My grandparents on both sides of the family worked in the sweatshops of the garment district in New York City as children. My maternal grandmother lost her eyesight while doing fine beading work in poor light over long hours. She was legally blind by twenty-five. My great-aunt, who recently died at ninety-five, became a labor organizer for the International Ladies Garment Workers Union. Raped by a shop steward, beaten by scabs, she remained a radical social iconoclast until her death. My paternal grandfather was a labor organizer for the auto workers in Detroit. My parents did not go to four-year colleges. My father was a building contractor; my mother a secretary and housewife. Their chief aspiration, however, was to be *middle-class*. It is that "truth" about my life that I have lived until I began this research project, not that of my immigrant, labor background. Why is it that my parents turned their backs on the American labor movement and its struggles for a socialized American economy? This question has now become for me a central question of white feminist experience as I now define it.[28]

1

Experience in White Feminist Theory

Without community, there is no liberation. . . . But community must not mean a shedding of our differences, nor the pathetic pretence that these differences do not exist.

Audre Lorde, *Sister Outsider*

The more the separateness and differentness of other people is realized, and the fact seen that another . . . has needs and wishes as ɔ ːmanding as one's own, the harder it becomes to treat a person as a thing.

Iris Murdoch, *The Sovereignty of Good*

Many black women writers call attention to the origin of the modern white women's movement in Betty Friedan's *Feminine Mystique*. What Friedan refers to as "the problem that has no name," the disaffection of millions of women with the 1950s definition of what it meant to be a woman—mother, housewife, and helpmate to their husbands' careers—was in fact predicated on the experience of college-educated, white middle-class married women who wanted "something more."[1] Considering that fully one-third of American women were in the work force at the time she wrote *The Feminine Mystique*, Friedan never questioned, and continues not to question, whether her experience and that of women like her was adequate to describe the experience of all women.[2] Bell Hooks, in her chapter on "Shaping Feminist Theory" in *Feminist Theory: From Margin to Center*, quotes Rita Mae Brown's statement that "class is much more than Marx's definition of the relationship to the means of production. Class involves your behavior, your basic assumptions about life. Your *experience* validates those assumptions. . . ."[3]

Given that the genesis of the modern genre known as "feminist theology" lies in claiming women's *(sic)* experience as human experience,[4] this is particularly important. In an excellent essay entitled "The Limits of the Appeal to Experience," Sheila Greeve Davaney makes exactly this point. In recent years, Davaney points out, women of color

11

have "asked whose experience is meant when white feminists refer to 'women's experience' and have argued that white women have made a mistake parallel to that committed by white men—the assumption of common experience and hence the false universalization of what is in fact only the experience of a particular group."[5] The appeal to experience as the cornerstone of feminist theology and thealogy[6] has been the source of much alienation between black and white women. Finding a way to describe the difference race makes in an appeal to experience is now, for me, a key agenda for white feminist theology.

The Epistemology of Sojourner Truth

I am increasingly struck by the methodological soundness of Sojourner Truth's self-chosen name. The need to *sojourn*—that is, to live for a while with a new reality before we can say we have found the *truth*—seems to describe the way in which people really do come to have knowledge of the world and, more importantly, change their ideas of the world.[7]

This section could have been subtitled "We Don't Yet Know What Freedom Looks Like."[8] There is an epistemological shift that is necessary. The struggle to change a racist, classist, sexist society ("Mama, I'm walking to Canada and I'm taking you and a bunch of other slaves with me") creates the conditions of liberation and opens our eyes to possibilities whose existence is hidden by the pervasive character of the current system. We cannot begin to know what it means to be recovering from racism[9] without the ongoing struggle to change the conditions of a racist society.[10] This is the sojourn.

But the question of the truths that follow the sojourn is not itself easy. Like many academics, I have been nurtured in the postcritical movement of recent years and have tuned a fine hermeneutic of suspicion. Currently, academics are increasingly suspicious of truth claims. Sharon Welch's *Communities of Resistance and Solidarity: A Feminist Theology of Liberation*[11] articulates the postcritical spirit in feminist theory via the work of Michel Foucault. Yet I have come to believe that Welch has not realized the potential that her focus on *community* has for the possibility of truth-in-action, the definition of truth I find in the writing of many black women.

The Truths of Women's Experience and the Conceptual Instability of White Feminist Theory

If Sojourner Truth is an epistemological model, how can I as a white "recovering racist" rely on the *truths* of white women's experience?

When Davaney contends that the appeal to experience must have limits, she does so because those who have made the appeal to experience have been "predominantly white" and black women have "asked whose experience is meant when white feminists refer to 'women's experience.'" These black women, Davaney observes, contend that "white women have made a mistake parallel to that committed by white men—the assumption of common experience and hence the false universalization of what is in fact only the experience of a particular group."[12]

Davaney explores the work of three white feminists—Elisabeth Schüssler Fiorenza, Rosemary Radford Ruether, and Mary Daly—for the role experience plays in each. She concludes that each has securely anchored the heuristic category of experience in a safe haven that is beyond critique: Schüssler Fiorenza and Ruether in the God-validated experience of the struggle for liberation; Daly in the essential biophilic tendency of women-identified women.

Experience cannot be kept out of the contradictions of society and history in either of these ways, Davaney contends. Taking a postcritical perspective as her premise, she argues that it is necessary to reject the notion that "any human perspective has a privileged access to ontological reality."[13]

Daly, Ruether, and Schüssler Fiorenza assume "that there is, in the words of feminist theorist Andrea Dworkin, a distinction between 'truth' and 'reality.'" While reality may be socially constructed, behind reality there is a discoverable truth—the "way things really are." Whether because of their privileged relation to nature (Daly) or to social struggle (Ruether and Schüssler Fiorenza), those white feminists claim to have access to knowledge of the truths of existence that the patriarchs lack. (Though Davaney details the ways in which each of these women accounts for diversity among women, she asserts that the claim to ontological truth has priority for each of them.)

Many white feminists have been influenced by the postcritical movement; I have already mentioned Sharon Welch. Welch, Davaney, and other white feminists have turned to such thinkers as Michel Foucault precisely in order to find a way to understand how it is possible for white feminism to have been so blind to its class and race biases for so long. The basis of Foucault's theoretical work is an analysis of the relationship of power and knowledge. According to Foucault, there is a "politics of truth"; different political regimes have structured truth differently. There is no truth in itself for Foucault.[14]

I believe that Foucault's so-called "anti-humanism" is a distinct danger we run in considering his work. Poststructuralism is considered antihumanist in that it removes human subjectivity from the individual, a cardinal tenet of liberalism; it denies that there is an essential female nature.[15] Given the argument of this book, these two objections can easily be dealt with. But more important, there is the broad-based challenge poststructuralism poses for the forms of legitimate authority; today these are usually science, God, and experience. Feminists have routinely, as we have seen, used the last to undermine the first two. But if the truths we know from experience are wholly relativized, I believe there are tremendous dangers—and particularly for women, both black and white.

A concrete example of the dangers of removing all supports for the truth claims of experience (especially when taken beyond individualism to the broader analyses offered by sociology or economics) may be found in Foucault's *The History of Sexuality*. From a descriptive standpoint this work is extremely useful, especially on the subject of how bodies have been perceived and how they have been valued or devalued. Further, it illumines the ways in which sexuality has become a central focus in the contemporary exercise of power. But as Chris Weedon, a white feminist philosopher, writes, for Foucault, "Sex has no essential nature or meaning" which, in relation to power, can mean, finally, that there is no place to stand to absolutely condemn sexual violence against women, or even the sexual abuse of children."[16]

In a recent article, Sandra Harding greatly illumined the problems of feminist theory, particularly in relation to poststructuralism. One of Harding's arguments is that since feminist theory is usually developed from or in reaction to patriarchal theory, we need to treat patriarchal theories very lightly and at a good distance. "The patriarchal theories we try to extend and reinterpret were created to explain not men's experience but only the experience of those men who are Western, bourgeois, white, and heterosexual."[17] As a result, feminists who share some of these characteristics, even when they are critically conscious of some of the limitations of these theories, may miss oppressive elements from other directions. This is a live risk in using theoretical categories of any kind, as I argue below.

Harding also contends that the use of postcritical thought should vary for dominants and nondominants. For dominants it solves the problem of different interpretations of reality in different social locations. On the other hand, "for subjugated groups, a relativist stance expresses a false consciousness. It accepts the dominant groups' insistence that their right to hold distorted views . . . is intellectually legitimate."[18] What concerns me is that as I employ poststructuralism to loosen the absolutist hold on "women's experience" that I have held as a white feminist (that is, as a dominant), I may be opening the door to a denial of the truths of my experience in the movement to end violence against women (as a nondominant). I find that postcritical theory does not always allow me to declare that violence against women is wrong in all circumstances.

Harding further contends that feminists need to skip around, be "conceptually unstable" if you will, because of the origins of many of the theories we employ. I myself am beginning to see that I usually have one foot in class and race dominance and one foot in the important and valid oppressions of white middle-class women. (Keep in mind that many white women know that white middle-class patriarchy batters and kills white middle-class women.) I may therefore need to apply the suspicions of poststructuralism to my experience as a dominant, as well as make the truth claims of my experience of violence against women as a nondominant.

The conceptual instability of white feminism means that some of what white women know from the truths of their experience as women needs to be kept in tension with the critical suspicions generated by poststructuralist theory.[19] All experience is not an unmediated category, an immediate source of access to the "truths" of reality; yet the experiences of some white women have a high correspondence to the criterion of truth-in-action. This means that white feminist theory that takes account of the difference race makes needs both a poststructuralist critique of ideology and an affirmation of some of the truths of white women's experience.

The Need for a Poststructuralist Critique

One of the most important contributions Mary Daly has made to the development of white feminist theory is her interpretation, drawn in part from Simone de Beauvoir, of women's (sic) situation as Other in a patriarchal culture. Furthermore, Daly has realized the profound limitations of de Beauvoir's continued adherence to the definition of freedom as transcendence of physical reality.[20] The limitation of Daly's work is that she does not apply her analysis of women's (sic) otherness to women (sic) themselves as a means of exploring the otherness of black women in white women's consciousness. She uncritically assumes that women-identified women have access to what she calls "true being," which is an undifferentiated fund for the truths of women's experience (sic).

Daly's basic method, which she has sustained through *Gyn/Ecology: The Metaethics of Radical Feminism, Pure Lust: Elemental Feminist Philosophy,* and *Websters' First New Intergalactic Wickedary of the*

English Language, is to turn the definition of reality given by culture against itself in order to reveal or uncover the nature of true being. Women's lives, in particular, are subject to the reversals of patriarchy: Adam gives birth to Eve, Zeus to Athena, and so on.[21] These reversals are turned back upon themselves for what they reveal of the mechanism of patriarchal culture and its systematic distortions. Daly is perhaps best known for her work in reclaiming the pejorative terms of patriarchal false naming: Crone, Hag, Witch, Nag, Scold, Shrew, Spinster, Wanton. Through lexigraphic work she has redefined these terms, among others, and through new uses bespeaks a new reality. She has also coined new terms to describe the elements that characterize the reality of women in patriarchal culture: plastic passions and virtues; and the patriarchal state itself: phallocracy, clonedom, Gynocidal Society, foolocracy.[22] The power of these new words is to enable women to pass out of the world as defined and ordered by patriarchy and into the world of authentic women's being. Each of Daly's books reflects this process of movement out of patriarchy: In *Gyn/Ecology,* there are three passages in the journey of exorcism; in *Pure Lust,* there are foreground and background sections in each of the three realms; in the *Wickedary,* there are three phases with between three and five "webs" in each phase.

Daly exhibits the influence of the several forms of modern philosophy and theology—including this clear dialectical pattern, a pattern not often discerned as being influenced by such figures as Heidegger or Tillich due to the striking difference between her rhetoric and theirs. But Daly should have attended to Harding's warning that feminists who are sensitized to gender issues in patriarchal theories they employ can be ideologically blind on issues of race and class. Daly herself has imported into her feminism assumptions of racial superiority along with this dialectical method.

Racism has been defined as the uncritical appropriation of what is normative to only one race, the one deemed dominant.[23] Joel Kovel has remarked that "in a racist society, the oppressor assumes the power of definition and control, while the oppressed is objectified and perceived as a thing."[24]

Unlike de Beauvoir, Daly identifies true being with the forces of nature, "when true to our Originality, we are Elemental, that is, 'of, relating to, or caused by great force of nature.' "[25] Reversing the reversals, Daly identifies authenticity not with transcendence but with immanence. This makes differentiation among women in the realm of true being impossible. A significant section of *Pure Lust* on "the Elemental Race" makes this clear.

> A basic thesis of this book, implied in the title, is that women who choose biophilic be-ing belong to the Race of Lusty Women, which participates in the Race of Elemental be-ing. For we are rooted, as are animals and trees, winds and seas, in the Earth's substance. Our origins are in her elements.[26]

The role of patriarchy, according to Daly, has been to keep women from recalling their racial oneness—race dynamically interpreted to mean "the act of rushing onward: Run," "a heavy or choppy sea; especially one produced by the meeting of two tides. . . . This definition indeed applies, for the Race of Women is Wild and Tidal, roaring with rhythms that are Elemental, that are created in cosmic encounters."[27]

But this dynamic tide of oneness also has the effect of crashing over the racial differences among women. Daly quotes Virginia Woolf:

> "As a woman I have no country." And together with her we may add: "As a woman I want no country. As a woman my country is the whole world." . . . "the whole world" [Daly elaborates] is the country, the homeland of the Race of Women.[28]

Daly has not really left behind dualistic, oppositionalist interpretations of existence but has exchanged them for an undifferentiated immanentism in which the races of women *make no difference* and opposed them, in an absolutist fashion, to phallocracy.

Daly's goal is to find a way to locate human imagination in nature and to identify the legacy of violence that comes from the alienation of consciousness from the "tides." "Elemental/tidal imagination" leads women into "Metabeing."[29] The "Metamorphic process" is the weaving together of transcendence and immanence that have been sliced apart by patriarchy. It is therefore ironic that Daly's views are, in fact, a sexual ontological dualism in which women's experience *(sic)* is undifferentiated access to "true being" and men's experience is undifferentiated alienation from true being. In practice this means that Daly is unable to turn her suspicions of the projections of patriarchy as a racist phenomenon on herself and her definition of experience. The person who gave white women a language with which to name their own experience has denied black women this same right because of her emphasis on the unitary character of "women's experience." This ironic reversal of Daly's intention illustrates Harding's point that any theories imported by feminists into their views carry with them unexamined freight—in this case the racial oneness of white-dominated Western society. Daly has failed to be sufficiently suspicious of the racial and class connotations of "true being."[30]

Audre Lorde on Difference

In May 1979, Audre Lorde wrote to Mary Daly thanking her for sending a copy of *Gyn/Ecology: The Metaethics of Radical Feminism* and detailing her reactions to the book. When she had not received a reply from Daly after four months, Lorde published the letter in *Sister Outsider: Essays and Speeches.*[31]

Lorde wrote that while she was excited about the passages through the myths and mystifications that obscure the Goddess, she was increasingly troubled that the only goddess images were "white, western european, judeo-christian." Having concluded that Daly had decided to limit her explorations to the "ecology of western european women," Lorde writes that she was astounded to find the "inclusion of African genital mutilation" in *Gyn/Ecology*. While consideration of this practice is "an important and necessary piece in any consideration of female ecology," why, Lorde asks, is there this marked "absence of any images of my foremothers in power?" "Where was Afrekete, Yemanje, Oyo, and Mawulisa? Where were the warrior goddesses of the Vodun, the Dahomeian Amazons and the warrior-women of Dan?" (p. 67) African women are portrayed by Daly as victims, not victors.

Lorde's analysis of the dismissal of African women's power is instructive: It "does not essentially differ from the specialized devaluations that make Black women prey, for instance, to the murders even now happening in your own city." In the spring of 1979, twelve black women were murdered in the Boston area. From the brutal facts of black women's lives a method of difference emerges: Black and white women die at different rates from the gynocidal practices of patriarchy (p. 70).

Beginning from the differences in the lives of black and white women is not what leads to separation among women. What leads to separation and perhaps will ultimately lead to "war between us" is the obliteration of difference. "Assimilation within a solely western european herstory is not acceptable" (p. 69). There is no realm of metabeing directly accessible to the imagination; what is accessible is always fraught with class, race, and even sexual differences that, when obliterated in the name of true being, return as classism, racism, and sexism.

The "Mythical Norm"

What are the "isms" of class, race, and sex? Lorde's answer to this question is developed in *Sister Outsider*: "*Racism, the belief in the inherent superiority of one race over all others and thereby the right to dominance. Sexism, the belief in the inherent superiority of one sex over the other and thereby the right to dominance. Ageism. Heterosexism. Elitism. Classism."*[32] The "isms" do not constitute difference itself, but the institutional organization of difference for the purpose of exploitation.

> Institutionalized rejection of difference is an absolute necessity in a profit economy which needs outsiders as surplus people. As members of such an economy, we have *all* been programmed to respond to the human differences between us with fear and loathing and to handle that difference in one of three ways: ignore it, and if that is not possible, copy it if we think it is dominant, or destroy it if we think it is subordinate. But we have no patterns for relating across our human differences as equals. As a result, those differences have been misnamed and misused in the service of separation and confusion.[33]

Like most black women, Lorde begins with an economic analysis: Difference organized as prejudice facilitates economic exploitation. A market economy, which characterizes Euro-American society, requires a surplus labor force that can be expanded or contracted depending upon the competition of market forces (which are managed by economic interests).

Lorde pictures what she calls "a *mythical norm,* which each one of us within our hearts knows 'that is not me.' " The Other. In American society, the 'that is not me' is usually "white, thin, male, young, heterosexual, christian, and financially secure."[34] Those who stand outside one or more aspects of the norm (and, this spurred me to think, that is the majority experience: most people, even the supposedly most successful, doubt that they "measure up") focus only on their own exclusion and not on the ways in which they exclude. "By and large within the women's movement today, white women focus upon their oppression as women and ignore differences of race, sexual preference, class and age. There is a pretense to a homogeneity of experience covered by the word *sisterhood* that does not in fact exist" (p. 116).

Lorde contends that human difference is "a springboard for creative change" and that "[U]nacknowledged class differences rob women of each others' energy and creative insight." But when "white women ignore their built in privilege of whiteness and define *woman* in terms of their own experience alone, then women of Color become 'other,' the outsider whose experience and tradition is too 'alien' to comprehend" (pp. 116–17).

Praxis as an Orientation

Yet even among white women who have been attuned to the radical ontological dualism of Daly's interpretation of women's essential being, there has not been an adequate articulation of the otherness of black women. Rosemary Radford Ruether is among those white feminists who have been most attentive to the fact that race does make a difference in feminist theology. Ruether's basic interpretive paradigm is that the dualistic oppositions of patriarchy—mind/body, spirit/matter, God/nature, male/female—are illustrative of the "male ideology of transcendent dualism" and "the model for the inferiorization of other subjugated groups, lower classes, and conquered races."[35] But in addition, Ruether has found in the economic analyses of the theologies of liberation a means of articulating more precisely how it is that race and class enter into the examination of patriarchy. Furthermore, Ruether has understood, primarily from the Latin American theologians of liberation, that liberation begins when oppressed peoples who have internalized these dualistic categories bring them to consciousness and critically reject them.

The development of critical consciousness in oppressed peoples is called *conscientization,* a term coined by the Brazilian educator Paulo Freire.[36] The rise of critical consciousness enables the oppressed to cease being an object and to become a subject, an actor in history.

This is the Marxist theoretical contribution to much feminist theory (as well as, of course, other modern theories of human liberation). The "consciousness-raising group" is a partial realization of some of Marx's ideas.

For several reasons this semipraxis process of reenvisioning a feminist future has proved inadequate to enable white feminists to become sufficiently suspicious of the white connotations, the class connotations, of "women's experience." Some of the inadequacies lie within the manner in which white feminists are socialized. Some lie within inadequacies in Marxism itself. An examination of these debilities is critical to the understanding of the differences and *distances* between black and white women. I need to understand why the praxis solution offered by some white feminists, such as myself or Ruether, has brought black and white women no closer together than Daly's elemental philosophy.

Marx argued that the proletariat had absorbed the worldview of the dominant culture: this he called "false consciousness." According to Marx, the proletariat gets out of false consciousness by "revolutionary activity," which amounts to "the changing of oneself [which] coincides with the changing of circumstances."[37] This may be called acting oneself into a new way of thinking. (Sojourner Truth, if you will.)

White women's consciousness-raising groups, however, have depended equally, if not more so, on the hegemony of psychological theory among white women. Euro-American culture has responded to Nietzsche's critique of religion (as the neurotic denial by humankind of their own power and the projection of that power onto divinity)[38] by turning to Freud, not Marx, to explain the human situation. In their efforts to topple the idols of traditional religion, white Western women, too, have turned to psychology, though they have also been very critical of Freud. But it is certainly the case that white feminists have not differed significantly from the Western assessment that change occurs primarily in the mind and not in the material conditions of reality.

This focus on the human mind fits naturally with liberal assumptions of human rationality. While liberals have profound faith in human reason and the progress of human history, the same cannot be said for Freud, who was profoundly pessimistic about human nature. Yet the paradox of liberal feminists adopting the paradigms of psycho-therapeutics as their own can be understood when the commonality of the role of reason in each is assessed. Peter Gay, author of a recent definitive biography of Freud, has written:

> Freud, the man who above all others is supposed to have destroyed the justification of Enlightenment rationalism, was the greatest child of the Enlightenment which our century has known. His fundamental assumption was that the search for truth must never stop, that only knowledge allows reason to function, and that *only reason can make us free*.[39]

White feminism has been highly responsive, though critical, to psychology as a mode of analysis.[40] This is antithetical to the way the black community has perceived the process of change. Black women seminarians, I have observed, are reluctant to attend designated women's [sic] organizations at their schools, not because they are unaware of the oppression of black women but because the primary method employed by these organizations is consciousness-raising groups. Intrapsychic self-examination is not a black woman's first impulse when confronted with the need for social change. One black woman seminarian put it to me this way, "We're more likely to start a feeding program for the neighborhood." Black women have consistently been more attracted to the fields of social work, sociology, and ethics than to psychology or pastoral care.[41] This is the communitarian approach to the healing of the community found in black women writers.[42]

Another central idea of Marxism is historical materialism, the belief that ideas are the products, not the producers, of social, political, and economic arrangements. According to Marx, "the mode of production of material life conditions the social, political and intellectual process in general. It is not the consciousness of men [sic] that determines their being, but, on the contrary, their social being that determines their consciousness."[43] The material conditions of white women, Marxists would contend, will therefore determine white feminist ideas. In other words, the social being of the majority of white feminists has been middle-class and therefore their theories will not challenge the economic system that sustains their status. While Marx may be right in his description of the manner in which white feminist views have emerged, the Marxist analytical perspective of historical materialism is not useful for fabricating a theory that can build alliances among women of different social classes. In fact, Marxists do not perceive these alliances as being possible.

The inadequacy of Marxism in accommodating those with dual states of oppressed/oppressor is one factor among many that sustains the continued patriarchalism of socialist societies. Christine Delphy defines patriarchy as "the exploitation of wives' labor by their husbands."[44] Therefore the exploited male worker (or happy socialist male worker) is exploiting the labor of his wife. As Zillah Eisenstein writes, "The sexual division of labor as the sexual division of roles, purposes, activities, etc., had no unique existence for Marx." The sexual division of labor is "natural." Men's control over women's labor power is not addressed in Marxist views of the emergence of class consciousness.[45] Marxism does not allow for the existence of persons (socialist male worker or white American feminist) who are both oppressor and oppressed to bring both of these factors to consciousness.

Like the male socialist, as a white feminist I, too, am unable to find within my experience alone the means to uncover our separate roles as oppressors. There is no impulse from within to change a system from which one is benefiting (the logic of class conflict applies here). Change in the Marxist view can only come from without when, as an oppressor, one is confronted by anger and rebellion on the part of the oppressed. This places the onus for systemic change on the oppressed, and many black womanists have written that they are sick of informing white women about racism. Has Marxist theory missed theoretical possibilities that would enable white feminists themselves to structure a consciousness of racism into their theories?

Anger as a White Feminist Theoretical Base

White women are socialized by the dominant Euro-American culture to avoid conflict. As the bearers of the affective aspects of private life, their role is to affiliate, to foster dependence, to bond with males for harmonious family lives, to create a resting place from strife and competition in a capitalist society. In the numerous studies of [white] women's psychology that have emerged from the white woman's movement, these tendencies are frequently observed. Jean Baker Miller and, more recently, Carol Gilligan have both pointed out this tendency.

White women have therefore sought to *bond* with black women as they have bonded with other white women, calling this sisterhood. This is what Lorde calls "pretence to homogeneity." It is also the impulse that drives white women to see in nature a harmonious locale of further bonding, nature being looked upon as the exploited sister.[46] It has further precluded an examination of the differing social classes of white women, the engagement of white feminism by working-class women, and the perception of the dramatic increase in poverty among *all* women during the past eight years. The best that the general white liberal feminist consciousness has produced is a resistance to the lack of "compassion" perceived by many women during the Reagan administration.[47]

In her essay "The Power of Anger in the Work of Love," Beverly Harrison analyzes the seductive invitation of love as a mode of moral activity for white women that plays on all the characteristics of social powerlessness to which white women have been socialized: "effete gentility, passivity, and weakness." Anger is not the opposite of love when love is understood as the capacity to actually create the other in relationship. Anger "is better understood as a feeling-signal that all is not well in our relation to other persons or groups or to the world around us." Anger is a form of connectedness that seeks not an undifferentiated bonding but a different kind of social relationship. It is "a sign of some *resistance* in ourselves to the moral quality of the social relations in which we are immersed."[48]

For the white feminist, anger is the energy that excites the hermeneutic of suspicion. That all is not well in the social relations between black and white women is the understatement of the year. As a white woman, socialized to harmony, my first impulse has been to try to smooth over the disharmony between us. But below this passion for bonding is the dis-ease, the real knowledge that this relationship is seriously damaged. I believe that as I gain the capacity to touch this feeling of disruption it can emerge full-blown as anger, the anger that signals the need for change. This anger is a recognition that racism is a system from which, in fact, I as a white woman am and am *not* benefiting—a system that rewards me materially but functions to limit and distort my understanding of my gender, my race, and my social class.

Anger turned inward upon the self becomes depression. Anger turned outward does not always become the energy for social change unless it is combined with a social analysis of the conditions that generate the injustice. For example, I have often observed that women who have been battered are extremely angry and that they turn this anger inward (usually because it is literally dangerous to turn it out= ward) and become seriously depressed. As they come to a critical consciousness of their situation as unjust, battered women can get in touch with this anger and turn it outward. Most studies of battered women who kill their battering spouses identify this initial period during which a battered woman gets in touch with her anger as extremely dangerous.[49] When the battered woman can be both supported in her expression of anger and helped to analyze her options for change (move into a shelter, obtain a restraining order, divorce) she does not lose her anger but is energized by it. The origins of the shelter movement are found in the lives of women who were battered but managed to change their situations and became passionately committed to changing the social conditions of other women in battering relationships.[50]

In this way the anger Harrison describes could be named passion, the passionate commitment to work through the causes of injustice toward greater justice. Yet Harrison's use of the bald term "anger" is, in my view, necessary particularly in the complex relationship between black and white women, because it does evoke the strong and often negative feelings typical of this situation.

Experience and the Criterion of Truth-in-Action

In the beginning of this chapter I said that I am resistant to eschewing the category of truth for white feminism because there are truths in the experience of white women, particularly their experience of sexual violence. Speaking on the need to begin exploring a poststructuralist suspicion in regard to class and race analysis, I have observed that many white women tend to harbor an undifferentiated sense of guilt for all the problems of the world while denying their own victimization.[51] Through my work in the battered women's movement I am aware that as many as 50 percent of all women are victims of sexual and domestic abuse by males, often by males with whom they live or work.[52] Rape, incest, battering—all of these crimes of violence claim black women, Hispanic women, Asian women, Native American women, white women—all women every day. It is very important for all women, including white women, to be able to trust the truth of their experience that this violence perpetrated against them is always and everywhere wrong and must be stopped.

One of the reasons white women can rely on the truths of their experience that the violence against them is wrong is that the understanding of truth that emerges from this recognition is that of truth-in-action, a definition of truth I often find in the writing of black women as well. Here again, Sojourner Truth's hard-won philosophy is instructive. Truth contrasted her vital experience of the truths of black women's lives with abstract discussions of "women's true nature" in suffrage meetings. Her criterion of truth-in-action mitigates against an abstract, fixed understanding of the nature of truth. As articulated by her, the true definition of women's nature is that

> nobody ever helps me into carriages, or over mud-puddles, or gibs me de best places. And ain't I a woman? Look at me! Look at my arm! I have ploughed, and planted, and gathered into barns, and no man could head me! And ain't I a woman? I could work as much and eat as much as any man when I could get it, and bear de lash as well. And ain't I a woman? I have borne thirteen children, and seen 'em mos' all sold all off to slavery, and when I cried out with a mother's grief, none but Jesus heard me! And ain't I a woman?[53]

This understanding of truth-in-action must be applied to the relationship of black and white women. In a lecture at Chicago Theological Seminary, Ada Maria Isasi-Diaz was asked by a black woman in the audience, "How can women of color trust white women?" She replied that she had learned to trust white women who would "cover your back."

The notion of community that Isasi-Diaz's comment raises is relational, but it is neither captive to notions of community as mental process nor to specific economic or political theories; that is, it is neither liberal nor Marxist. It is, I would argue, uniquely feminist. This is the correction that feminist practice adds to postcritical theory. Among its male practitioners, postcritical theory has the well-deserved reputation for elitist unintelligibility, an ironic critique for what is primarily a theory of human intelligibility. It is also highly individualistic.[54]

Critiques of the category of experience in white feminism have ranged over a wide area. On the one hand, there is the critique of the assumption that women's experience, especially when limited to white women, is the source of a true knowledge of being and the basis for feminist politics. This may be viewed as the patriarchal remnant of liberal-humanist assumptions that human subjectivity is an authentic source for discovering the meaning of "reality." On the other hand, experience as the political practice of "consciousness-raising" has been equally limited by liberal-humanist assumptions that the nature of subjectivity resides in mental process. But even when a more material basis for human existence is posited, as in Marxism, white feminists are left without a full identification with the social forces of racism and classism that are so essential to the energy within the proletariat if it is to initiate change.

Anger is a means of gaining access to the recognition that class and race do deform and distort white as well as black women. This provides the passionate energy for the conflict that is so necessary in the pursuit of changing the world rather than merely understanding it.

But the insights of the white women's movement, particularly the movement to end violence against women, do not need to be disregarded. In a white feminist theory that is "unstable," the truth-in-action of the white women's movement can be combined with the hermeneutics of suspicion generated by poststructural critiques of the category of experience. This truth is profoundly communitarian and must remain so if it is to be applied to the movement to effect changes in race and class as well as gender hierarchies.

As a communitarian practice, truth-in-action is distinct from the harmonious connotations of bonding. The truth-in-action of the white women's movement in regard to race and class will or will not be found as white women seek to "cover the backs" of black women, to find black women capable of their own self-definition, and to change their own practice and theory in light of that work.

To begin to construct another praxis between black and white women, I need to explore the origins of the alienation and separation between them. This alienation has its beginnings in the history of slavery.

2
Slavery: A White Feminist History

Baby, you could be Jesus in drag—but if you're brown they're sure you're selling.

> Lorraine Hansberry, *To Be*
> *Young, Gifted and Black*

The most important location of the genesis of black women's role as "other" in the consciousness of white women is found in the history of slavery in the United States. It is striking that, almost uniformly, black women writers have made the slave experience central to their fiction, social and political analysis, theology, ethics, and poetry. This trend can be observed in the fiction of nineteenth-century black women writers such as Frances Harper as well as in the more contemporary works of Zora Neale Hurston, Alice Walker, Toni Morrison, and many others;[1] in theology and ethics, there is Katie Geneva Cannon and Jacquelyn Grant;[2] in social and political analysis, Angela Davis and Bell Hooks; and in poetry, Audre Lorde. Yet the experience of slave-owning is alarmingly absent from white-authored histories of the period. White authors examining the history of slavery have typically done so only to note the activities of white female abolitionists and to relate their work to the origins of the women's suffrage movement.[3] Barbara Andolsen's recent study of racism and American feminism and Elizabeth Fox-Genovese's interdisciplinary work on the plantation household are ground-breaking exceptions.[4]

In developing an adequate white feminist theory it is essential to comprehend the reasons why white women in the South, far from identifying with the exploitation of black women as women under slavery, often blamed these women for their condition. And during abolition it is necessary to examine both the remarkable dedication of white women abolitionists to black emancipation and the racism involved in much of the theory of women's suffrage that emerged following emancipation.

The Fox-Genovese study of plantation households demonstrates that white women in the South depended on the rigid hierarchical structures

27

of their society for self-definition. They did not oppose slavery, but rather were persuaded of its beneficient aspects.[5] Most studies of women *(sic)* in the nineteenth century have been of Northern white women, especially those in the New England area. The white women who opposed slavery did so on the basis of the Enlightenment ideals that were becoming a cultural influence in the North. When Southern women such as the Grimké sisters opposed slavery this was after they left the South and had reshaped their *gender identity* through Northern, Enlightenment ideals.[6]

The sexual exploitation of black women during slavery needs to be understood both as an example of the psychological projection of evil onto women, compounded by race (sex *and* race), and as political terrorism having some connection (in both instances) with the Salem witch trials (sex *and* class). Our feminist theories must include some means of understanding how changes in the economy of the North led to the Salem witch trials as well as some means of comprehending the extent to which this developing industrial economy was intricately connected with the stresses on the more agricultural South.

Sex and race are intricately interwoven into the class tensions that existed during the rapid industrialization of the United States. Because their Enlightenment liberalism allowed no scope for economic analysis, white liberal feminists like Elizabeth Cady Stanton had no rubric under which to analyze the failure of the Republican party to actively support the vote for women after the Civil War. White women such as Stanton believed that the Civil War was waged over the principles of human rights, and they ignored the fact that it was a war largely generated by economic competition between the North and the South. Their disillusionment with the postwar politics of the Republican party left them vulnerable to the white supremacist ethos of the rest of the country when black men received the vote. The failure of white women to examine the coalition between white supremacy and the suffrage movement is at the root of much of the alienation between black and white women today. So, too, does the involved relationship between the sexual exploitation of black women that began under slavery and has continued to the present impinge on the sexual identity of black and white women today.

The Difference Race Makes: Sex and Race

It was years ago that I read the *Grimké Sisters from South Carolina: Rebels Against Slavery,* yet the image of the physical brutalization of black women under slavery depicted by Sarah Grimké remains with me to this day. In this book she tells the story of a black woman whose repeated efforts to escape from slavery had earned her so many whip-pings that "a finger could not be laid between the cuts." Because this slave took every opportunity to leave the plantation, a heavy spike collar was eventually placed around her neck and a front tooth ex-tracted for purposes of identification. Grimké writes that although her owners were known as a good Christian family,

> This slave, who was the seamstress of the family, was continually in her mistress' presence, sitting in her chamber to sew, or engaging in other household work, with her lacerated and bleeding back, her mutilated mouth and heavy iron collar, without, so far as appeared, exciting any feelings of compassion.[7]

Only recently have I listened accurately and *heard* that this woman did her household work not in the midst of her male owners but among the white women of the family. Why, as Grimké herself wonders, were these *women* blind to her suffering? Why did they even inflict it?

Bell Hooks quotes from *Once a Slave,* a collection of slave nar-ratives, that a white mistress returned home unexpectedly and found her husband raping a thirteen-year-old slave girl. The white mistress's response was to beat the girl and lock her in a smokehouse. The child was whipped daily for several weeks. When the older slaves pleaded the child's case, saying that she had been forced, the mistress simply replied, "She'll know better in future. After I've done with her, she'll never do the like again through ignorance."[8] Whipping—par-ticularly of naked slave women, including the pregnant and the nursing mother—was another form of sexual terrorism employed against black women. White mistresses would send their female slaves to be publicly stripped and flogged for the slightest offense, such as when the bread did not rise or the breakfast was slightly burned.[9]

In the dominant Christian teaching prior to and during the early period of slavery, women (*sic*) were portrayed as evil sexual temp-tresses who brought sin into the world. The Puritan theology that met the frontier was fearful of its expanse, of the lack of constraint this wild, unstructured land represented. Andrew Sinclair comments:

> The terrible liberty of isolation and the wilderness made some of the first settlers discard their European moral restraints. Cases of bestiality, ac-cording to Cotton Mather, were not unknown. . . . As the first mission-aries of the West were told, barbarism was the first danger to the pi-oneers. "They will think it no degradation to do before the woods and wild animals, what, in the presence of a cultivated social state they would blush to perpetrate." Until a stern public opinion could govern the habits

of a scattered and immigrant society, small governments tried to do what
they could to keep up the standards of civilization.[10]

Fear of the uncharted possibilities of the wilderness aggravated mis-
ogynistic tendencies already resident in a Christianity that had declared
sin and death to be the fault of women. Stringent regulation of women's
chaotic sexual behavior was the ministerial prescription for the threat of
the encroachment of the wilderness. Sex was a symbol of that which
threatened man's rational control over his environment.

This rabid fear of women's sexuality was not unknown to white
women. It was preached to them for hours on end. What the black slave
woman provided, therefore, was a buffer against the hatred of all women
built up on the American frontier. She could become the bearer of the
stigma of the physical, the carnal and the excess of women's lust that
threatened the rationality of Christian civilization. The thirteen-year-old
child is not too young to tempt the Christian man to perdition, so it is
she who must be punished. At some level white women must have
known that were the black women not punished, the fault for men's
carnality would return to rest at their doors.

Fox-Genovese notes the views common in "Southern theologians
and proslavery ideologues" who, like the famous Thomas Dew, argued
that the Southern slave system *improved* the lot of [white] women. "The
introduction of slavery, according to Dew, rescues woman from her
misery by substituting 'the labor of the slave . . . for that of the
woman.'" Men like Dew or William Harper of South Carolina saw
slavery and this supposed improvement in the lot of Southern white
women as the "march of civilization."[11] Yet this civilization imposed
on the chaotic wilderness was markedly hierarchical, white man over
white woman; the white race over all others: "The self-evident subordination of women to men confirms the legitimacy of slavery."[12]

Sexual terrorism during slavery was developed as a means of dealing
with the psychological tension created by the taming of an uncharted
frontier (the underside of the so-called civilizing impulse), while it also
contributed to the maintenance of the South's agricultural structure.
Slavery as a system could not be maintained without psychological and
physical threat. Rape, as Susan Brownmiller has documented, is an
established method of the subjugation of conquered peoples.

Rape in slavery was more than a chance tool of violence. It was an
institutionalized crime, part and parcel of the white man's subjugation of
a people for economic and psychological gain.[13]

In their antislavery tracts white female abolitionists appealed for an
end to the brutal rape of black women. But they did so from the

perspective of the changing status of the nineteenth-century white woman. The increasingly industrialized North dramatically altered the lives of white women in the rising middle-class by separating them from the manufacturing sites. The colonial home had been the site of the manufacture of many goods such as candles, soap, beer, wine and so forth—production that was the direct responsibility of the wife. But the rapid industrialization of the North moved the location of production to the factory, leaving the white woman isolated at home. This shift has been called the "disestablishment" of women.[14]

In the more densely populated nineteenth-century, Northern white women were no longer needed to resolve the tensions that resulted from the unstructured wilderness experience: They came instead to serve as the shelter and nurture required by the factory worker after his long day. It was during this period that the white woman became the "angel of the home" and the "Cult of True Womanhood" became firmly entrenched.[15]

The antislavery tracts distributed by white women reflected the increasing strength of the image of woman *(sic)* as gentle, kind, religious, and intuitive: White women's horror at slavery lies in its mistreatment of black mothers. Harriet Beecher Stowe transfers this stereotype in her remarkably effective antislavery novel *Uncle Tom's Cabin* to the slave woman Eliza, who embodies all the female virtues the popular press attributed to white women. It is Eliza's "natural" maternal instinct that drives her to pursue her heroic deed of escape from slavery. Prior to her master's threat to sell her child, she is quite compliant under the slave system and frightened by her husband's desire to flee slavery. But when her child is threatened, Eliza is able to bound across ice floes; her armor of Christian womanhood protects her from harm.[16]

On several levels the appeal to the "natural" source of heroics for both black and white women precluded a more complex and penetrating view of the resistance of both groups to the institution of slavery.[17] The Grimké sisters do not discuss it, but surely the fact that their brother had sired several children by a black female slave formed some part of their anger at the slave system. Of her white mistress and slavery, Linda Brent wrote:

> I was soon convinced that her emotions arose from anger and wounded pride. She felt that her marriage vows were desecrated, her dignity insulted; but she had no compassion for the poor victim of her husband's perfidy. She pitied herself as a martyr; but she was incapable of feeling for the condition of shame and misery in which her unfortunate helpless slaves were placed.[18]

The Enlightenment theories of liberalism that informed much of the Grimkés' work, particularly Sarah Grimké's, divided human experience into the rational and the irrational, with the dominant faculties of the rational mind the superior. Like Mary Wollstonecraft (1759–1797) or Francis Wright (1795–1852) before her, Sarah Grimké in her *Letters on Equality* (1838) argues that women and men are intellectually equal as "intellect is not sexed";[19] and she claims that women are moral equals. Men and women are ontologically the same.

> According to the principle which I have laid down, [that] man and woman were created equal, and endowed by their beneficent Creator with the same intellectual powers and the same moral responsibilities, and [that] consequently whatever is *morally* right for a man to do, is *morally* right for a woman. . . .[20]

Grimké had arrived at this assertion as she and her sister Angelina attempted to speak against slavery throughout the North and were routinely ridiculed and even prevented from speaking, especially when the site of the speech was to be a church pulpit. After a pastoral letter of "The General Association of Massachusetts (Orthodox) to the Churches Under Their Care" denounced the behavior of females "who so far forget themselves as to itinerate in the character of public lecturers and teachers," becoming "unnatural,"[21] both Grimkés became far more aware that their commitment to abolitionism also involved an assertion of women's *(sic)* rights.

Given the later history of the distance between and even antipathy toward the movement to attain the rights of citizenship for freed black men *(sic)* and the movement for white women's rights, it is important to understand two other hallmarks of liberal feminism. In addition to its faith in human rationality and its assertion of men's and women's ontological identity, liberalism was further predicated on a view of the human being as isolated individual who seeks truth and whose dignity depends on the freedom to pursue this search. Closely related to this is the doctrine of natural rights, the view that each individual has certain inherent or "natural" rights. This latter is consummately represented in the American Declaration of Independence: "We hold these truths to be self-evident. . . ."

These four hallmarks of liberalism: faith in human rationality, the ontological identity of men and women, the human being as isolated individual, and the natural rights doctrine all had pernicious consequences for an alliance between black and white women. The first two, rationality and identity, relate more to the theme of this section— namely sex and race. The latter two, individualism and natural rights, are more aptly related to the next section, race and class.

Their excessive faith in human rationality did not allow abolitionist white women to analyze their own anger at the misogynist division of black and white women into body and soul. Sarah Grimké wrote that "it is an occurrence of no uncommon nature to see a Christian father sell his own daughter and the brother his own sister."[22] Something like this may have taken place in the Grimkés' own family, as has been noted. But in their writings, the Grimkés' appeals to end this untenable situation are predicated on an assumption of white women's "enlightened" minds coupled with their "moral purity." This leads them into an ideological blindness to the dependence of this purity on the black woman's sexual degradation and its inaccessibility to objective analysis alone.

In her letter on sexual equality Sarah Grimké goes on to quote the "Circular of the Kentucky Union."

> To the female character among our black population, we cannot allude but with feelings of the bitterest shame. A similar condition of moral pollution and utter disregard of a pure and virtuous reputation, is to be found *only without the pale of Christendom*. That such a state of society should exist in a Christian nation, claiming to be the most enlightened upon earth, without calling forth any *particular attention* to its existence, though ever before our eyes and *in our* families, is a moral phenomenon at once unaccountable and disgraceful.

Grimké's next line is, "Nor does the colored woman suffer alone: the moral purity of the white woman is deeply contaminated."[23] Grimké equates the physical assaults against black women in slavery, as well as the psychological deprivation resulting from their lack of control of their own persons, with the white slave mistresses' psychological pain at their husbands' behavior.[24] But such analyses did nothing to chip away at the real failure of white women to grasp the white supremacist underpinnings of the social and psychological parameters of the "Cult of True Womanhood." Purity in this context not only means moral rectitude but should be read as racial purity. Grimké is outraged at miscegenation, though she is unaware of it. The uncritical appeals to the "enlightened" nature of their views prevented white women from seeing either their own situation or that of black women in slavery. On the subject of Harriet Beecher Stowe, Angela Davis has written that actual black women,

> unlike Eliza, were driven to defend their children by their passionate abhorrence of slavery. The source of their strength was not some mystical

power attached to motherhood, but rather their concrete experiences as slaves.[25]

Davis refers to the slave woman who kills her child rather than have it returned to slavery, an incident that inspired Toni Morrison's contemporary novel *Beloved*. The actual guerrilla warfare that black women practiced against the slave system, was, as previously cited from Fox-Genovese, considerable.

> Resistance was woven into the fabric of slave women's lives and identities. If they defined themselves as wives, mothers, daughters, and sisters within the slave community that offered the positive images of themselves as women, they were also likely to define themselves in opposition to the images of the slaveholders for whom their status as slave ultimately outweighed their identity as woman. The ubiquity of their resistance ensured that its most common forms would be those that followed the patterns of everyday life: shirking, running off, "taking," sassing, defying. The extreme forms of resistance—murder, self-mutilation, infanticide, suicide—were rare. But no understanding of slave women's identities can afford to ignore them, for, if they were abnormal in their occurrence, they nonetheless embodied the core psychological dynamic of all resistance. The extreme forms captured the essence of self-definition: You cannot do that to me, whatever the price I must pay to prevent you."[26]

White female abolitionists had no intellectual framework for understanding such acts on the part of black women.

As a result of the ontological identity of women and men in liberalism, the *woman* (white)/*slave* (male) analogy was frequently used by white women in the suffrage and abolitionist movements. This idea had actually been briefly suggested by Mary Wollstonecraft and was also used by Margaret Fuller. In her *Appeal to the Women of the Nominally Free States,* Angelina Grimké may have written that "they [black women slaves] are our countrywomen—*they are our sisters;* and to us as women, they have a right to look for sympathy with their sorrows, and effort and prayer for their rescue. . . ." But she goes on in that appeal to make a comparison between white women and black *men*.

> Women *[sic]* ought to feel a peculiar sympathy in the colored man's wrong, for, like him, she has been accused of mental inferiority, and denied the privileges of a liberal education.[27]

The ontological equality argument flattened all perceptions of genuine difference in human situations: White women and men are the same in the realm of being; so, too, are white women and black men. And following the great chain of being, what is true ontologically is suddenly also true existentially.

This argument was frequently used by Elizabeth Cady Stanton, who, like the Grimkés, was an Enlightenment feminist. Cady Stanton, for example, did extended analyses of the deprivations suffered by both white women and male slaves: (white) women have no name of their own, neither do slave men; (white) women cannot own property, neither can slave men; (white) women do not have disposition over their own children, neither do slave men; (white) women have no legal existence, neither do slave men, and so forth. Cady Stanton pointed out that (white) women and slaves can be legally beaten by their respective husbands or slave owners. She even went so far as to claim that the rights of black male slaves *exceeded* those of white women.[28]

It was Sojourner Truth, not particularly burdened by white liberal ideology, who exposed both the difference between the situation of black and white women and the need for a distinct, separate analysis of the two. Perhaps her most famous statement, uttered to quiet a heckler at the 1851 women's rights convention in Seneca Falls, went to the heart of the social separation of black and white women. Black women's children are sold.

> I have borne thirteen children, and seen 'em mos' all sold off to slavery, and when I cried out with my mother's grief, none but Jesus heard me! And ain't I a woman?[29]

For Sojourner Truth, existential reality had priority over ontological truths. This, in fact, is the logic of the name she chose for herself. After the Civil War, Truth observed that "there is a great stir about colored men getting their rights, but not a word about the colored woman" and warned that "if colored men get their rights, and not colored women theirs, you see the colored men will be masters over the women, and it will be just as bad as it was before." This was in fact the result, for, as Bell Hooks notes, the result of the focus on the rights of black males was the subservience of the black female.[30]

When we turn to the next section on race and class in order to examine the interrelationship of race and economic change, it is critical that this separation of sex and race discussed above be recognized as the artificial treatment it is. I have separated these issues only for purposes of analysis in such a complex and interrelated subject. In actuality, they are not at all separate, but layered, each reinforcing the other.

The Difference Race Makes: Race and Class

It is critical to remember that slavery was first and foremost an integral component of the agricultural system that developed in the South. Throughout human history, slavery has been principally an economic system legitimized by ideologies of the superiority of the slaveholder (hence the role of sex in relationship to race in American slavery). Slavery has often been found in agricultural economies. I have come to believe that the legitimation of slaves' obedience to their masters and its link to the subordination of wives and children addressed in Eph. 6:5–6 is the response of Christian apologists to the widening appeal their religion had for landowning farmers in the Greco-Roman world.[31] Eph. 6:5ff. certainly figured prominently in the proslavery preaching of the nineteenth century.[32]

It is no secret in the late twentieth century that the Civil War was fought not over the human rights of black Americans but was in fact a struggle between the economic interests of the increasingly industrialized North and the agricultural system of the South. The Republican party, the party of Abraham Lincoln, was controlled by the new Northern capitalists, young men who expressed their desire for economic control over the entire country thorough its politics.[33]

At the war's end, the chief agenda of the controlling Republican party was increasing the number of Republican votes in the South. This they could do by extending suffrage to black men; should they include black and white women, the white Southern woman would surely vote Democratic. The Republican Senate leader Charles Sumner had often been vocal in his support of women's suffrage before and during the war, but the postwar period found him backpedaling. The vote for women was "inopportune," or rather, as Miriam Gurko observes, ". . . the Republicans wanted nothing to interfere with winning two million black votes for their party."[34]

Women's suffrage leaders such as Elizabeth Cady Stanton and Susan B. Anthony had no framework in their political and social philosophy for understanding these forces. Having believed that the war was the result of "enlightened" minds seeking to restore human dignity to those enslaved in the South, they saw the betrayal of white women's suffrage in favor of the black male as nothing less than a male plot. The moral to be drawn from these years was, according to Cady Stanton, that woman should never "labor to second man's endeavors and exalt his sex above her own."[35]

Because the human rights perspective of liberalism identified the true end of human existence as freedom, and because the natural rights doctrine made it possible for the situation of white women without suffrage to be identified with that of slavery, Cady Stanton and other feminists were prone to see the enfranchised black male as having attained "the kingdom" while they were being left out. This left the white female suffragist vulnerable to the all too prevalent racist atmosphere of the postwar period. In a letter to the editor of the *New York Standard* on December 26, 1865, Cady Stanton illustrates this coalescence of ideas.

> Although this may remain a question for politicians to wrangle over for five or ten years, the black man is still, in a political point of view, far above the educated white women of the country. The representative women of the nation have done their uttermost for the last thirty years to secure freedom for the negro; and as long as he was lowest in the scale of being, we were willing to press his claims, but now, as the celestial gate to civil rights is slowly moving on its hinges, it becomes a serious question whether we had better stand aside and see "Sambo" walk into the kingdom first.

"In fact," Cady Stanton concluded one of her more unedifying pieces of prose, "it is better to be the slave of an educated white man, than of a degraded, ignorant black one. . . ."[36]

To subvert Republican plans for new votes in the South, the Democratic party jumped on the train of votes for (white) women. In a move she later regretted, Cady Stanton with Anthony joined forces with George Francis Train, whose motto was "Woman first and Negro last. . . ."[37] Train financed a speaking tour for the three and together they published a journal called, at Train's insistence, *Revolution*. On its masthead the paper claimed, "Men, their rights, and nothing more; women their rights, and nothing less."[38] A widening gap between a more narrowly defined "women's *(sic)* rights" and racial justice was evident in this perilous alliance.

At the last meeting of the joint organization between suffrage and black rights leaders, the Equal Rights Association, the Fourteenth Amendment had already been passed. This amendment had added, for the first time, the word "male" to the Constitution. Endorsement of the Fifteenth Amendment, which was designed to prohibit disenfranchisement on the basis of race, color, or previous condition of servitude but not on the basis of sex, was on the agenda. White female suffragists were adamantly opposed to the passage of this amendment as written.

Frederick Douglass, who has been a longtime advocate of women's rights, tried, in a final appeal, to sketch the dramatic ways in which the existential condition of a terrorized black population in the South differed from that of the white women present.

> When women, because they are women, are dragged from their homes and hung upon lamp-posts; when their children are torn from their arms and their brains dashed upon the pavement; when they are objects of insult and outrage at every turn; when they are in danger of having their homes burnt down over their heads; when their children are not allowed to enter schools; then they will have [the same] urgency to obtain the ballot.[39]

There were major barriers in liberal theory that impeded the white suffragists' understanding of either the economic forces that underlay both slavery and the Jim Crow system of social terror that replaced it or the actual differences these forces made in the lives of white women and former slaves. Consequently, the divide-and-conquer tactics of both the Republican and Democratic parties were successful in shaking apart a potentially radical coalition of oppressed Americans. Some of these barriers have already been mentioned: the Enlightenment emphasis on "human rights" as certain political freedoms and the "natural rights" doctrine that underlined the objective rationality of human freedom and dignity.

The Difference Race Makes: Sex and Class

Some aspects of liberal theory precluded the development of even the rudiments of a social analysis or the implementation of strategies for social change. One of the central tenets of Cady Stanton's liberal theory, which is probably most convincingly expressed in her last address, the "Solitude of the Self," is that every person is isolated. The human being, and woman as human being, is essentially the isolated individual. Women need only to be granted the basic human right to stand on their own, then they will be able to act in all things with freedom and dignity. In her final address Stanton argues that because every person is an isolated individual, women must learn to take responsibility for their own lives. The doctrine of natural law enters the argument as Cady Stanton images each woman as "an imaginary Robinson Crusoe with her woman Friday on a solitary island." She is "in a world of her own, the arbiter of her own destiny. . . . Her rights . . . are to use all her faculties for her own safety and happiness."[40]

The analogy is telling. The isolated woman who is free and responsible is also, like Crusoe, white. She does not acknowledge, as Crusoe did not, her dependent relationship with her "Friday," who was also a person of color. Furthermore, this arrangement is ultimately justified as "natural." This philosophy had a direct impact on such documents as the Seneca Falls Declaration, which argued that when some seek to "assume among the peoples of the earth *a position different from that which they have hitherto occupied,* but one to which *the laws of nature and of nature's God entitle them*" then they should present their reasoning for changing course. Except for the addition of the one word "women," the reasoning was almost a verbatim statment of the Declaration of Independence: "We hold these truths to be self-evident: that all men and women are created equal. . . ."[41]

The Seneca Falls Convention, taking place before the Civil War (1848), was radical for its time but did not succeed even in winning unanimous ratification of Cady Stanton's proposed suffrage amendment. Its focus was on the lives of the majority of white, educated, married middle-class women who attended. It articulated their grievances at the loss of women's property rights in marriage, their lack of rights to their own person, and the inequality of the laws of separation and divorce. But Seneca Falls ignored the different conditions of black women, for whom the liberal philosophy of freedom of choice was nonsense.[42] It was also nonsense for the majority of white working-class women, whose worsening economic condition in the Northeast was likewise ignored.

Two direct consequences of the liberal emphasis on the self as solitary, free individual, was to hide from white feminists the social forces that underlay the differences in the actual life experience of different women and to preclude the social solidarity that might have forged an alliance among black slave women, freed black women, white middle-class women, and white working-class women.

Some factory women had given strong support to the abolitionist cause.[43] During the abolitionist period (1831) there were 38,927 women in the major textile industries of the Northeast as compared with 18,539 men.[44] Conditions for these women workers were from the beginning exploitative—with twelve, fourteen or even sixteen hours daily, little time for meals, crowded, unsanitary working conditions, fines for infractions, poor food, and no provision for illness—but they actually worsened as the century continued. From the surrogate families provided by the Waltham and Lowell systems for women factory workers, the lives of the "mill girls" deteriorated.[45]

These women organized strikes as early as the 1820s, rocking the foundations of female exploitation. Barbara Wertheimer has documented the struggles of the working-women's movement in the United

States. Several years before Seneca Falls, the Lowell Female Labor
Reform Association petitioned the Massachusetts State Legislature
(1843 and 1844) to investigate labor conditions for women in the Lowell
textile factories. In their campaign for the ten-hour day, these women
obtained the first government investigation of labor conditions in the
United States. By the summer of 1848, when the Seneca Falls convention began, working conditions at the New England factories had
worsened to such an extent that the farmers' daughters were fast being
replaced by cheap immigrant laborers, the new industrial underclass in
the United States.[46] These immigrant workers, organized for their very
survival, were by the 1840s "in the leadership of labor militancy in the
United States."[47] Yet the Seneca Falls Convention largely ignored the
conditions and achievements of these women. Wertheimer notes a final
irony of history: Of all the women present at the Seneca Falls Convention, only one lived long enough to actually vote. Charlotte Wood-
ward was a working woman who voted for the first time when she was
more than seventy years old.[48]

There were some who, like Sarah Grimké, had a glimpse of the
working woman's situation and argued:

> There are in the poorer classes many strong honest hearts weary of being
> slaves and tools who are worthy of freedom and who will use it worth-
> ily.[49]

Yet Grimké is clearly operating from the same perspective as Cady
Stanton in her emphasis on "freedom." Echoes of the natural rights
doctrine resonate from the rhetoric of "honest strong hearts" and the
analogy with the conditions of Northern poverty and slavery.

Mill workers also described their situation as one of "slavery."
Northeastern textile factory workers marched and sang:

> Oh, I cannot be a slave
> I will not be a slave.
> Oh, I'm so fond of liberty,
> I will not be a slave.[50]

While they had more insight than most into the actual conditions of
slavery, these factory women had no resources for comprehending that
it is not by homogenizing the conditions of the oppressed that political
coalitions are formed, but by their clear identification.

The latter years of the nineteenth century saw a widening gulf between women's rights advocates, labor leaders, and activists on behalf

of racial justice. Susan B. Anthony turned Frederick Douglass away from suffrage meetings in the South rather than risk offending Southern women. Of her decision to ask Douglass not to attend a meeting of the suffrage association in Atlanta, Georgia, Anthony wrote, "I myself asked Mr. Douglass not to come. I did not want to subject him to humiliation, and I did not want anything to get in the way of bringing the southern white women into our suffrage association."[51] Ida B. Wells was increasingly critical of both Anthony and the National Women's Suffrage Association for capitulating to racism in order to win support for suffrage.

The mob violence against blacks throughout the South at the turn of the century—lynchings and beatings on a mass scale—failed to turn the association from its "neutral" policy on the "color question."[52] At the association's 1895 convention, held in Atlanta, a prominent advocate of women's suffrage "urged the South to adopt woman suffrage as one solution to the negro problem."[53] This represented no great strides over the resolution passed just two years earlier.

> RESOLVED. That without expressing any opinion on the proper qualifica-
> tions for voting, we call attention to the significant facts that in every
> State there are more women who can read and write than the whole
> number of illiterate male voters; more white women who can read and
> write than all negro voters; more American women who can read and
> write than all foreign voters; so that the enfranchisement of such women
> would settle the vexed question of rule by illiteracy, whether of home-
> grown or foreign-born production.[54]

The 1893 resolution stated in no uncertain terms that the white women of the suffrage movement had chosen for their allies the middle-class white male and his system of industrial exploitation of foreign workers. If white middle-class women could obtain the vote, the resolution argued, their numbers would be more than enough to subdue the black and immigrant worker.

This alliance has in fact alienated white middle-class women from those with whom they most need to work in gaining an understanding of their history of separation and division, and with whom they needed to form coalitions. Their emphasis on the ontological identity of women and men did not allow these suffragists to explore either their own differences as white women of different classes or the differences in the situation of white and black women. The theoretical priority of existential differences was never even a question; it was assumed that difference, wherever it existed, was accessible to rational choice.

Women as Nature/Women as Culture

Rationality is the hallmark of liberalism, as has been said repeatedly. Rationality governs the world; the rational mind can discern the "natural" and logical order of the world. Rationality is the realm of the subject, the realm of the male. Women and nature, as the nonrational, must be ordered and checked. For liberal feminists, freedom has always meant access to the male world of reason and subjectivity.

In her work *The Death of Nature: Women, Ecology, and the Scientific Revolution,* Carolyn Merchant has correlated the witch crazes that swept Europe and New England with the ascendance of the Newtonian scientific worldview. The witch was the distillation of the dangerous irrational elements of the universe. She was the symbol of the "other" that the rationalists so feared and felt they must control. Merchant shows us that through the eyes of scientific rationality "the witch, symbol of the violence of nature, raised storms, caused illness, destroyed crops, obstructed generation, and killed infants. Disorderly woman, like chaotic nature, needed to be controlled."[55]

Francis Bacon in particular is cited by Merchant for his attempts to impose scientific rationality and order on "passive nature." During this period, she suggests, women became identified with recalcitrant nature, resisting scientific order. Bacon in fact used the analogy of witch interrogation to explain the scientific method of extracting "truth" from nature. He wrote: "For you have but to follow and as it were hound nature in her wanderings, and you will be able when you like to lead and drive her afterward to the same place again."[56]

But Merchant and other feminist theorists such as Sherry Ortner would do well to appreciate more fully the role of racial and economic forces for this dynamic. As Bacon elaborated his theories of the subjection of nature, the American slave trade was at its height. Slaves, too, were considered unruly nature that must be subdued. From its theoretical infancy, the modern technological worldview has been at the service of economic exploitation of nondominant peoples. In fact, I believe a more nuanced theory needs to be developed. The effect of the "peculiar institution" of slavery in U.S. society was to divide black and white women, not to identify them both as undifferentiated "nature." From the time of slavery black women were the symbol of the exploitable body (see Hansberry quotation at beginning of chapter), as all slaves represented "nature" to some degree. White women became the symbol of the soul of *culture*. This is evident in analyses of the "Cult of True Womanhood" and well argued in *The Feminization of American Culture*. White women in the United States are culture, not nature. Hence black womanists have chosen to examine their condition as body and nature through cultural analysis; while white women, laboring under another stereotype—that of the soul of culture—have directed their analysis toward reclaiming the nature side of this dichotomy.

The Difference Race Makes: Sex, Race, and Class

White feminist Enlightenment theory did have within it some radical possibilities, especially the attribution of women's *(sic)* subjection to patriarchal systems. This led white feminists to critique the domestic sphere, marriage, and its legal and social mores. But the emphasis on legal redress of these inequalities did not, as Zillah Eisenstein has put it, cause them to recognize that because of the duties assigned to women as a whole, they would necessarily start "the race of life" from a different (and inferior) place.[57]

The white feminists' emphasis on the ontological identity of women and men did not allow them to explore either their own differences or those that existed between the situation of white and black women. Difference is assumed to be the result of rational choice. White feminist liberals, therefore, do not include analyses of existential difference *a priori* in their analyses.

Whether in the nineteenth or the twentieth century, then, white feminist theory is badly in need of an analysis that allows for the range of divisions among women. Women are subject to sex and race divisions, as black and white women have been pitted against each other as exploitable body and exploitable soul. Women are subject to sex and class divisions, as the disproportionate exploitation of working-class women is not included in white bourgeois feminist theory. And women are subject to sex, race, and class divisions, as these are interfaced with the cultural presumptions of science and technology.

Yet the liberal humanist assumptions of ontological identity, harmony and progress, and, to a lesser degree, individualism have continued to plague white feminism. The fact that these assumptions have endured, though revised and transformed in the twentieth century women's movement, prevents a real appreciation of the *priority* of women's existential difference over their biological similarity (their "essential nature"); of the conflicts of social existence over unity with nature; and of political solidarity over "sisterhood."

3

Class and Creation

A cold November wind "announces the . . .
discord between man and nature."
                          Ann Petry, *The Street*

Ann Petry's novel *The Street* (1946) opens with a devastating scene of
the tragic disharmony that exists between human life and nature.[1] An
evident difference that race makes in the writing of black and white
women is that, especially in theology and thealogy, white women have
found in nature a sister and a source of reunification of the separations
they experience as women; while black women have taken the conflicts
of urban civilization as their point of departure.

Compare Petry with Carol Christ's words in the introduction to her
book of reflections on her journey to the Goddess, *Laughter of Aphrodite*. Christ writes: "My theology, or rather thealogy, reflections on the
meaning of the Goddess, is rooted in my experience. Two intuitions
nourish this thealogy. The first is that the earth is holy and our true
home. The second is that women's experience, like all human experience, is a source of insight about the divine."[2] This is true for me as
well. In "God and Her Survival in the Nuclear Age," I have written that
"the survival of God is the survival of nature: the earth and all its
splendors, including but not limited to human beings."[3] In *The Street,*
however, nature is the enemy, conspiring with the urban jungle of
violence and despair to destroy initiative. When the main character,
Lutie, is finally driven to murder, it is because she does not understand
"the street" and the forces of filth and poverty ranged against her.[4]

In examining the writing of black and white women, there is, first, the
difference of race and class. The black woman writer begins with her
experience, but it is an experience of conflict and alienation from the
basic necessities of life in urban America. Sometimes the contrast
between the crisis of black urban life and a more rural, steadied existence in the South before urban migration is made plain. But this
Southern existence is always presented as one of conflict as well; the
pain-stained years permeate the landscape.[5]

44

Social analysis, therefore, is far more prominent in the writing of black women than in that of white women. Wade-Gayles begins *No Crystal Stair,* her book on images of sex and race in black women's fiction, with a discussion of capitalism: "American capitalism is an oppressive system that divides people into groups on the basis of their race, sex, and class." This economic analysis forms the outline of the book. She envisions capitalist American society as a group of circles in which whites, the largest circle, experience the greatest influence and power. "Far away from it there is a smaller circle, a narrow space, in which black people, regardless of sex, experience uncertainty, exploitation, and powerlessness." But, almost invisible in this small circle, there is "a small, dark enclosure in which black women experience pain, isolation and vulnerability."[6]

The failure to make class analysis a primary constituent of feminist theology and thealogy is a source of tremendous conflict between black and white women. In her essay "Black Women's Literature and the Task of Feminist Theology," Dolores Williams writes that feminist theologians need to claim "racial history" as "an important source for Christian theology . . . if tensions are to be eased between black and white women in church and society."[7] Bell Hooks is even more blunt. She attributes the failure of white feminists to analyze "class privilege" to their desire "to project an image of themselves as victims and that could not be done by drawing attention to their class."[8]

As I concentrate on the relationships of black and white women, I am beginning to get a glimpse of how deep-seated and historically entrenched this relationship of victim and victimizer is when subjected to class and race analysis. White and black women are bound by the history of slavery in this country. American society as a slave society has almost from its founding divided women by race for purposes of social control.[9] Black women were designated the body and sexuality; white women were designated the "angel of the home," the soul and spirituality. The history of slavery and the complex interrelationship of black and white women in the history of sexual exploitation is a critical interpretive starting point.[10]

In this chapter I have chosen to focus on class and creation in exploring the difference race makes. In the Combahee River Collective statement there is the line, "We also often find it difficult to separate race from class from sex oppression because in our lives they are most often experienced simultaneously."[11] The absence of an analysis of class and race in white feminist thought is due not to the fact that white women have no experience of class and race along with their sex, but to the fact that they have not allowed their consciousness of the interconnections among these social forces to become central. I have come to believe that class and race solidarity have been a source of the bonding among white women, and that what is often labeled sisterhood is in fact sometimes economic and ethnic solidarity.

When a black woman joins an all-white women's consciousness-raising group the tension, the awkwardness, the sense that as a white woman one has to be careful not to offend, not to "say the wrong thing," is evidence of the unconscious bonding through class and race that white women experience. I have begun to ask myself, "What is being hidden in this class and race solidarity?" Gustavo Gutiérrez once said that he is suspicious of anyone who is not in the liberation struggle for themselves.[12] I am not in this exploration of the difference race makes *for* black women; nor am I in it *on behalf* of black women. I want to know *for myself* what is being hidden and carried along unexamined in the class and race solidarity of white women. Herbert Marcuse has written that "the success of the system is to make unthinkable the possibility of alternatives."[13] When we consider that "sexism and racism are systems of societal and psychological restrictions," as Barbara Christian writes,[14] then it seems eminently probable that these restrictions are of tremendous significance for white women as well as black women, making even the possibility of another relationship among all women unthinkable.

Class Vs. Creation as Starting Points

The following sections focus on three themes selected from the works of representative white and black women in making the case that there are significant and largely unexamined differences in the starting points of black and white women. The first theme, housework, is seldom given priority, and is often not even considered, in the writing of many white women. When it is, as in Kathryn A. Rabuzzi's presentation of a "theology of housework," it is interpreted as a symbol of "women's rituals." Black women writers, by contrast, find housework to be a symbol of the economic exploitation of black women.

In the second theme, motherhood, I extend the case for difference to the exploration of the very common starting point of both white and black women: the biological function of motherhood. Here white women have chosen to focus on the reclamation of the "natural" rhythms of women's biological function of reproduction. Black women, by contrast, have included political and social struggles such as civil rights in their examination of motherhood.

In the last section, "Unity with Nature," I consider Mary Daly's work again. Her work figures largely in the reexamination of white feminist thinking here because her views are so influential and so representative of long-standing positions taken by white feminists. Daly has argued for the essential, life-affirming reintegration of matter and spirit that characterizes women's being in order to overcome the death-seeking separations of patriarchy. Separation and alienation from nature is what traditional Christian theologians would call the Fall. In choosing to place all women's essential nature prior to the Fall, Daly, in my view, offers no resources for understanding the alienations that continue to exist between black and white women. This theme of "unity with nature" leaves white women blind to the absence of class and race unity among women.

The Difference Race Makes: Housework

Housework deserves primary treatment in the consideration of sex, race, and God because it is a significant theme in black women's treatment of class. Angela Davis published *Women, Race and Class* during the early 1980s. Primarily a historical text, Davis's work traces the relationship of class and race (though she focuses far more on race than on class) from the early nineteenth century, with particular attention to the intertwining of the suffrage and abolitionist movements.[15] In the latter chapters of her book Davis applies her analysis of a "working class perspective" to the subjects of rape, reproductive rights, and housework. In "The Approaching Obsolescence of Housework: A Working Class Perspective," Davis argues that "the industrialization of housework, along with the socialization of housework, is becoming an objective social need."[16] She tends to agree with Engel's well-known thesis that the invention of private property was simultaneously the invention of sexual inequality.[17] Yet with the far from peripheral addition of race to her analysis, Davis digresses from the standard Marxist analysis of housework to argue that the housework of *black* women is not merely a hidden cog in the capitalist means of production but a *precondition* in a capitalist, racist society—the means to a "body of exploitable workers."[18]

As a result, the housework of poor black women must be treated substantially differently from that of middle- and upper-class white women because black women constitute this pool of exploitable workers: "Proportionately, more Black women have always worked outside their homes than have their white sisters. The enormous space that work occupies in Black women's lives today follows a pattern established during the very earliest days of slavery."[19]

While not all black women would agree with Davis that a socialization of housework is the best corrective to the exploitation of American black women as domestic workers, most agree that the issue of housework warrants primary attention. Contrary to Davis's view, in a review of *Women, Race and Class* that appeared in *The Nation,* Jacqueline Jones contended that freedom from housework is the beginning of liberation, that "to care for one's own family without interference from slaveholders, welfare bureaucrats or 'workfare'-minded politicians is the freedom that black women have struggled for throughout their history in America." According to Jones, Davis's "contention that housework is rapidly becoming 'obsolescent' indicates that, among American Communists, hope continues to spring eternal."[20] Nevertheless, for both Jones and Davis, housework is pivotal to an understanding of the situation of black women.

Housework as Ritual Enactment

There is a striking difference between Davis's analysis of housework as an exploitative pattern established during slavery and the treatment of housework in a book by Kathryn A. Rabuzzi, *The Sacred and the Feminine: Toward a Theology of Housework.* The thesis of Rabuzzi's book is that what has been fictionalized as the happily ever after ending of fairy tales, the dream of being married and having two children,[21] is a possible *source* for constructive feminist (*sic*) theory, as well as an object of critique. I have noted the universalized use of the adjective "feminist" in this regard because there is no nuance of either class or race analysis in Rabuzzi's argument. What emerges is amazing in its ideological blindness to the difference race makes in any consideration of housework. Rabuzzi maintains that the sacred is "ritually enacted" through housework. She derives her definition of the word *sacred* "partly from my own experience, partly from writers like Rudolph Otto, Mircea Eliade, and Paul Tillich, who speak of numinosity, the contrast with the profane, order in contrast to chaos, mystery, otherness, centeredness, ultimate concern, and Being to describe sacrality."[22] At this point it should be noted that in drawing on her own experience and that of Otto, Eliade and Tillich, Rabuzzi has illustrated very nicely the "limits of the appeal to experience" Sheila Greeve Davaney has delineated.

This becomes particularly evident when one recognizes that the treatment of housework is made exclusively from the perspective of one who could choose to hire someone for this work. In a statement taken from the December/January 1980–81 issue of *National NOW Times,* Rabuzzi quotes Diana Silcox, whose major recommendation for women (*sic*) is "the acquisition of hired help in the home, even for women who can't afford it yet," in order to "get rid of the attitude that a woman must do everything herself."[23] The operative word here is "yet." Silcox operates from an Enlightenment feminist point of view in which increased education and hard work enable one (male or female) to progress toward greater economic reward. The goal of feminism, therefore, is to make access to this system of economic rewards possible for women (*sic*).[24]

This is not Rabuzzi's goal. She aligns herself with the woman who does *not* want to hire someone to take care of her home. Such a woman would regard another caretaker as an intruder. To illustrate the "hierophany" that can occur in housework Rabuzzi uses an experience of the poet Rainer Maria Rilke recounted in *Lettres à une musicienne*. "*Because his cleaning woman was absent,* he had polished his piano . . .*" is Rabuzzi's lead-in to the rhapsody the poet comes to find when he grabs a dust cloth and cleans his piano, like "an emperor washing the feet of the poor, or Saint Bonaventure, washing dishes in his convent."[25]

While Rabuzzi is not an Enlightenment feminist, neither does she examine the character of housework from any perspective other than her own. The universalizing perspective is so hegemonic that it fails to give her any interpretive categories with which to distinguish the experience of a German poet on his cleaning lady's day off from that of black women who, as a class, clean for a living. This perspectival hegemony has the classical ideal as one of its roots. Rabuzzi places the figure of the goddess Hestia, whose name means "hearth," at the center of this cultic ritual. She subscribes to the Jungian archetypal interpretation of the various gods and goddesses of the Greco-Roman tradition, finding them "names for certain modes of being." Hestia, then, is the name for a certain type of patterned behavior associated with housework that evokes sacred space. (There is a lot of Victor Turner lurking in the background of this book.) Like Hestia, who has the most obscure image of all the Olympian divines, the housework celebrant is "like a prelapsarian Eve, inhabiting Paradise," without awareness.[26]

The choice of a Greco-Roman goddess to symbolize the content of this approach is significant. In his book *Prophesy Deliverance!*, Cornel West has argued that the origins of racism are many, but one that is often overlooked is the Greek ideal of beauty that has dominated North Atlantic culture.[27] The physical characteristics of the Greek gods and goddesses are not separate from their "archetypal" characteristics. Though Jung does not explore racism as an archetype, one might say that identification of the Greek ideal of beauty with the white race is carried along as a "race memory."

One other area of Rabuzzi's work can contribute to an examination of the difference race makes. This is the "cosmic viewpoint," the creation

of "a world of perfect order, one envisioned, perhaps, from fragmen-
tary memories of a grandmother's lovingly ordered home."[28] While
Rabuzzi claims that the concern for order can be taken too far and
become demonic, her argument presents a troubling contrast to Audre
Lorde's perception, in *Sister Outsider,* that difference or, I would say
disorder, is a creative spark. Order is often a code word that for
oppressed peoples signifies maintenance of the status quo. When applied to class, the ordering function becomes classism; when applied to
race, it becomes racism, the suppression of conflict and change.

The point is not that Rabuzzi may have illumined a rarely examined
aspect of the lives of white middle-class women who do not work
outside their homes, but that she projects from this limited experiential
pool to make sweeping claims for "women's lives."

Housework as Exploitation and Destruction

Some tremendous differences emerge when we compare Rabuzzi's
work with Toni Morrison's. *The Bluest Eye,* Toni Morrison's most
wrenching novel, until *Beloved,* is the story of a black girl's desire for
blue eyes. Pecola Breedlove is poor and black. Her family despises
themselves for their poverty and their blackness. Their storefront house
is ugly and depressing, a vivid contrast to the beautiful house in which
Pecola's mother, Pauline, works as a maid. Pauline is the mammy cum
housekeeper for the blonde girl-doll who is the daughter in the beautiful
house. In her critical essay "The Concept of Class in the Novels of Toni
Morrison," Barbara Christian describes the vivid scene in which
Pecola is expelled by her mother from the beautiful house because she
has dropped a pan of blueberry pie on the clean floor. Pauline rushes to
comfort the girl-doll, who was upset by the spill; not her daughter, who
was burned.

> This scene is beautifully constructed to contrast the extremes of class
> positions in terms of what is desirable. For Pauline hates the ugliness of
> her house, her daughter, her family, herself and blames her sense of
> unworthiness on being black and poor. Instead, she aspires to the pol-
> ished copper and sheen of the kitchen she works in where everyone is
> clean, well-behaved, and pretty. For her, any violation of that paradise by
> anyone, even her daughter, is paramount to a crime.[29]

The Bluest Eye underlines the contradictions that class and race
introduce. Housekeeping, which functions as symbolic enactment for a
white middle-class woman such as Rabuzzi, is for Pauline a double
source of destruction and self-hatred. The very orderliness of this white
middle-class home is an imposition on her blackness, a statement that

she is profane, if you will. And her failure to find her own home beautiful and worthy of care (in the same way she fails to find her daughter worthy) is the psychological consequence of the economics of racism. Left unexplored, these normative class distinctions breed alienation and despair.

For Morrison there can be no separation of sex, race, and class. Because their survival depends on alienated work, her female characters can neither claim a female world of home and hearth for themselves nor choose to move beyond alienation and join the white male world of economic success. The black woman is more alien in a racist culture than in nature itself: She is, as the character Nanny says in Zora Neale Hurston's *Their Eyes Were Watching God,* "de mule uh de world."[30]

In *The Bluest Eye* the contradictions of class, race, and sex finally drive Pecola into madness. Claudia, the narrator, explains the tragedy of Pecola:

> All of our waste which we dumped on her and which she absorbed. And all of our beauty, which was hers first and which she gave to us. All of us—all who knew her—felt so wholesome after we cleaned ourselves on her. We were so beautiful when we stood astride her ugliness. Her simplicity decorated us, her guilt sanctified us, her pain made us glow with health, her awkwardness made us think we had a sense of humor. Her inarticulateness made us believe we were eloquent. Her poverty kept us generous. Even her waking dreams we used—to silence our own nightmares. And she let us, and thereby deserved our contempt. We honed our egos on her, padded our characters with her frailty, and yawned in the fantasy of our strength.[31]

In housework the black woman writer sees a clue not to the ways in which women order the world for themselves but to how they are doubly exploited as beasts of burden for both white and black society.

As in fiction, so too in nonfiction. It is, as I have said, important for me as a white woman to check my interpretation of black women's fiction against other sources in order to guard against the dangers of interiority and romantic identity. In her famous volume *Like One of the Family* Alice Childress details in ironic and biting prose how her perception of herself as a domestic had to be won over against the perceptions of her white employers and their subtle (and at times not so subtle) exploitation of her as a black female.[32]

The Difference Race Makes: Motherhood

Motherhood is of particular relevance for this discussion of class and creation because it has been interpreted as women's biologically determined function, whereas fatherhood has been seen as a learned cultural role. White feminists have sometimes followed this interpretive split, looking to motherhood for themes of women's values that have been ignored or distorted by the dominant culture. Helen Caldicott, for example, appeals to women's "natural" capacity for nurture in her analysis of nuclearism: "Women are nurturers. They are generally born with strong feelings for nurturing of the life process."[33]

But even where white feminists have been critical of the inversion of women's oppression inherent in the naturalism thesis of someone like Caldicott, they have continued to interpret motherhood intrapsychically and have rarely placed mothering within a class and race context.

Motherhood as a Growth Experience

Two short examples will suffice. In her widely read book *Becoming Woman: The Quest for Wholeness in Female Experience,* Penelope Washbourn has argued that one can learn a tremendous amount about religious questions and the meaning of the holy by looking at the rhythms of women's (*sic*) life: menstruation, sexual maturity, pregnancy and birth, menopause, and so on. These are times of crisis, and in times of crisis the individual must summon old and new resources to meet the challenge. For women (*sic*) the "most significant life-crises are associated with having a female body."[34]

One of the strengths of Washbourn's work is that she does not always wax euphoric about these various changes in women's physiology. In discussing motherhood, for example, she tries to avoid seeing the mother as a goddess who is instantly, by virtue of her biological function as mother, all-knowing and all-wise. Washbourn wants to help women understand that they are people apart from their biologically determined selves. She approvingly quotes Mary Daly's critique of the "Eternal Woman" who is "not recognized as a genuine human person."[35]

But her analysis of motherhood reaches only into the mind of a particular type of woman who has become a parent, claiming that what motherhood affords women (and men) is a "unique opportunity to understand themselves." In watching and helping children grow, the mother comes to understand that "like gardeners we are part of an inherently mysterious process." This process is one of "growth" toward the "future." "Children therefore represent a distinct opportunity for psychological and spiritual growth for women and for men."[36]

Washbourn is directly parallel to Ann Belford Ulanov in the limits of her analysis. Ulanov identifies the "female [*sic*] elements of being" as vulnerability, interdependence, and personal continuity. These she further identifies with "God's action in our lives." The mother/child relationship is a religious experience because it is "*inward and personal.*"[37]

These women have assumed that the woman of whom they speak will be able to feed the child she bears. They have unreflectively assumed that she will see its growth toward the future in positive terms. The social security that envelopes these analyses is like a cocoon surrounding the conclusions: warm, sticky, and obfuscating. Personal growth is the spiritual luxury of those with money and time.

Motherhood as Survival

Audre Lorde writes of her son: "For survival, Black children in america must be raised to be warriors. For survival, they must also be raised to recognize the enemy's many faces."[38] In the chapter "The Happy Mother," which appears in her novel *Meridian,* Alice Walker writes that her main character, Meridian, considers suicide because she cannot become the exemplary young mother.

Meridian is Walker's exploration of the times and contradictions of the 1960s through the life of one black woman who is driven almost to madness by racism and sexism in black and white society. That she does not go mad but eventually survives in a purified and focused version of herself is one of Walker's first statements of the possibilities as well as the debilitations of black women. It prefigures the triumphs of *The Color Purple.*

The teenage Meridian has become pregnant and married the forever boy-child who made her pregnant. It took "everything she had to tend to the child." Numb with fatigue, she figures this "is what slavery is like." She begins to dream of murdering her baby and, in guilt, of killing herself instead. When she dreams of suicide she is calm and is told by everyone around her that she is "an exemplary young mother, so mature, so calm." This pleases her because of its irony: The way to be a good young mother is to be dead from the neck up.[39]

Meridian gives her son away, "believing she had saved a small person's life," but she feels "condemned, consigned to penitence for life" because she has committed the ultimate sin against Black Motherhood: She has decided to be free.[40] Of Walker's depiction of motherhood in *Meridian,* Barbara Christian writes that what she has done

is to present in a succinct way the essence of Afro-American motherhood as it has been passed on. At the center of this construct is a truth that mothers during slavery did not have their natural right to their children and did everything, including giving up their lives, to save them. From

this truth, however, a moral dictum has developed, a moral voice that
demands that Afro-American mothers, whatever the changed circumstances of their lives, take on the sole responsibility of children.[41]

As Meridian sinks into madness she is living out this history of dying
for her child. She knows the horror of Black Motherhood, its terrifying
responsibility. It is only another mother, her music teacher, who can
absolve her and allow her to live.[42]

Once she has been freed from the burden of guilt imposed by Black
Motherhood, Meridian is able to move into the social movement of her
time, the Civil Rights Movement, and become a spiritual leader for her
people. She has reinterpreted the meaning of the word *mother* to
include those who nurture the possibility of a decent life, not only
physically but psychologically and spiritually.

Elsewhere I have written that in *Meridian* Walker

> explores the spiritual truth of her conviction that the source of creativity
> in life and the wellspring of change lie in the connections to the heritage
> of black women. Meridian, the chief character, seeks her identity through
> the legacy left her and other Southern black women in the life of, for
> example, Sojourner Truth and Ida B. Wells. Meridian believes in the
> sacredness and continuity of life, the African spirituality of animism,
> the spirit that inhabits all life. She discovers, against impossible
> odds, "the societal forces that, in a perverted and distorted racist society,
> *inhibit the natural growth of the living creation toward freedom.*"[43]

I have emphasized the last phrase to draw a comparison between
Walker and Ulanov or Washbourn. The difference between Walker and
these two writers does not reside in their perception that there are
spiritual truths that are revealed to women through motherhood, and
that one of these truths is that the natural order of things is growth and
change. The difference race makes is evident in the fact that Walker's
angle of vision is focused through the divisions and distortions of class
and race as well as sex as these are constructed in America. The
conviction Meridian acquires at the end of the novel is that

> the respect she owed her life was to continue, against whatever obstacles,
> to live it, and not to give up a particle of it without a fight to the death,
> preferably not her own. And that this existence extended beyond herself
> to those around her because, in fact, the years in America had created
> them One Life.[44]

Walker's novel is based on the conviction that life is sacred, but that
this life is understood communally and socially rather than only indi-

vidualistically and intrapsychically. In juxtaposing the theme of the Civil Rights Movement and that of motherhood, Walker is saying that what is sacred about mothering human life is found within the struggles for justice that continue to be fraught with contradiction.

The fact that Jacqueline Jones, in her history of black women, work and the family, finds that a sociological study of black motherhood must be done *not only* within the context of the family but also within that of *work,* underlines the reality that the economic constraints of black women's lives have given considerable shape to their lives as mothers.[45]

This is the difference race makes in a consideration of class and creation. What I as a white feminist have considered "natural" is a condition constructed by particular social and economic relationships, and *never* in isolation from these conditions. What is critical for me as I delve into white feminist theology is to begin to explore the themes of nature in relation to social and political life. For this I need to examine feminist theoretical assumptions of nature as unitary and harmonious, and contrast them with a view of nature as conflicted and fraught with political and economic tension.

The Difference Race Makes: Unity with Nature

The term "Fall" is used theologically to describe the loss of unity with creation as it has been represented in the dominant religions of the North Atlantic. As Rosemary Radford Ruether argued very early in the development of feminist theology *(New Woman/New Earth: Sexist Ideologies and Human Liberation)*, patriarchal religions take their origins from the historical emergence of an ego-consciousness that differentiated itself from nature and community. Sexism is the correlate of the "war against the Mother" or nature, the desire of the ego to be free from bondage to material finitude. The religions created by this search for freedom from nature have been interpreted by white feminists as the transcendence and domination of the deity (and his followers) over women (*sic*) and nature.[46]

Women's (sic) Natural Biophilia

The hegemony of the transcendent God of "rape, genocide and War" . . . "the most Unholy Trinity," will be broken, according to Mary Daly, when women refuse to participate in their own objectification.[47] A creative refusal to be objectified, according to Daly, means "breaking down the barriers between technical knowledge and that deep realm of intuitive knowledge which some theologians [Tillich] call ontological reason."[48] This is a significant contribution white feminist thealogy has made to the process of overcoming the split between nature and history. But despite her creative analysis of the reintegrations that must transpire if the human mind is to be located in nature without romantic reductionism, Daly herself has so far failed to take seriously the difference race makes. In seeking a philosophical base for the essential biophilic nature of women (*sic*), Daly's work obliterates the class and race differences that exist among black and white women.

Daly has changed greatly since the early 1970s when she would quote Tillich, even obliquely, with approval. In *Pure Lust: Elemental Feminist Philosophy*, she describes the sadosociety, the culture that depends on abstractionist, nature- and female-despising works of sadoasceticism for its maintenance. Her point is that sadospirituality, the denial of the basis in nature of all life, prepares society to accept as rational (*sic*) the notion that destruction is a form of saving.[49]

"Patriarchy," according to Daly, is another word for *biocide*, degenerative and life-violating tendencies that are becoming more aggressive in the "aging and deterioration of patriarchy itself."[50] Biophilia, or love of life, is the opposite of the biocidal system of patriarchy. Women (*sic*), according to Daly, are intrinsically biophilic, but only when they are in touch with what she describes at length as the elements of the cosmos. Much of *Pure Lust* describes the transformation by patriarchy of the "elements" into the elementary. Elements could be described as the interconnections of spirit and matter in all of nature. "Elemental Feminist Philosophy," the subtitle of *Pure Lust*, is the effort to "name the philosophy of being concerned with ontological potency, knowledge, passion, virtue, creation, transformation."[51] Daly's agenda is to find a way through the mess of mind/body dualism to a philosophy of being that reunites spirit and matter and does not make a radical disjunction of the physical and the metaphysical: the origin of the so-called "Fall."

For Daly, even liberal alternatives to the radical mind/body dualism of traditional Christianity, such as Paul Tillich's "ground of being," are divided against themselves.[52] For Tillich reality has become a vacuum left by its split into two halves, one of which presumes to dominate the other but is in fact characterized primarily by its own alienation.

Reality, or the elements as the reintegration of spirit and matter, is in Daly's work not reduced to a substitution of female terms for a male transcendent deity; nor is the divine reduced to nature per se. The entire model for spirit/matter relationships has changed. Limiting the divine to a label instead of understanding the spiraling of metaphoric encounter with shifting images of radical otherness is a symptom, in Daly's view, of "the Standstill Society, the Stag-nation."[53] In her critique of the static views of reality that have predominated in Western patriarchal culture, she gives a profound glimpse into what it would mean to actually live in the physical world and the imagination, and not have to abandon the physical world for an abstractionist human consciousness. In her struggles with Tillich and pointing to the fundamental flaw in his alternative, Daly illustrates what poet and feminist Adrienne Rich proposes as women's agenda: a transformation of the nature/culture distinction that does not place consciousness as abstractionist, ontological reason over against technical reason and its handmaiden, the creation.

> We have been perceived for too many centuries as pure Nature, exploited and raped like the earth and the solar system; small wonder if we now long to become Culture: pure spirit, mind. Yet it is precisely this culture and its political institutions which have split us off from itself. In so doing it has also split itself off from life, becoming the death culture of quantification, abstraction, and the will to power which has reached its most refined destructiveness in this century. It is this culture and politics of abstraction which women are talking of changing, of bringing to accountability in human terms.[54]

Yet I want to go on to state that Daly has succumbed to some of the politics of abstraction that undermines her commitment to the reintegration of the nature/history split. A clue to this is her use of the term "pure" in the title *Pure Lust*. The journey of pure lust is a movement, a spiral, through "Metamorphospheres" of Wild Weird women who are purified in the Realm of Fire from the Plastic and Potted Passions and Virtues and are able to break out of these spheres and get in touch with Natural Grace. It is a movement of purification. It does not allow for the messy differences that exist in women's lives.

Apples and Oranges: The Otherness of Black Women

I find it significant that Daly has drawn on Alice Walker's book *The Color Purple* to illustrate the movement toward the inexhaustible "other." The philosopher (Daly) reads to a student from Walker's book:

> Don't look like nothing, she [Shug] say. It ain't a picture show. It ain't something you can look at apart from anything else, including yourself. I believe God is everything, say Shug . . . She say, My first step away from the old white man was trees. Then air. Then birds. Then people. But one day when I was sitting quiet and feeling like a motherless child, which I was, it come to me: that feeling of being part of everything, not separate at all.[55]

Daly continues: "Hearing these words, our Nag-Gnostic philosopher and Novice Nag must feel essentially in accord with Shug and Celie." But she adds in a note:

> It is essential to point out that Shug Avery and Celie are in no way responsible for the interpretations of their conversations and behavior presented in this section. I have assumed the Nag-Gnostic prerogative of having Nagging thoughts about them and expressing these. Any Nags—especially Shug and Celie—are, of course, free to disagree.[56]

What I read Daly as saying, however, is that in the realm of purity all differences dissolve. Daly includes black women in her reference to "Nags." Compare her words with what Dolores Hines has to say about the differences between the reality of black and white women.

> We are told that apples and oranges are the same, when we can see that they are not. You cannot easily substitute one for the other in a recipe. Their odors are different. They appeal to people differently. Even a blind person can tell them apart. Yet, a steady stream of rhetoric is aimed at convincing Black women how much alike their lives, experiences, wishes and decisions are to those of our stepsisters.[57]

Simply put, there are women who have no access to any of the spheres Daly describes because of their economic, social, and racial location. Daly's work remains a dualistic ontology because she has failed to find a way to confront the vast differences in the historical condition of women and to make a methodological shift in light of these differences.

Nature per se is not accessible to direct experience. What is called the natural world is always mediated by human consciousness and its social conditions. The fact that white women are objectified by a patriarchal consciousness does not free them from the internalization of these objectifications. Daly, of course, understands this quite well and refers to these objectifications as the "foreground." True enough. But racial and class distinctions among women *do not disappear* when one operates in the *background*. The social location of each woman is a primary constituent of her experience and is not directly accessible to the experience of women in other social locations. (To a great extent, for oppressed people in particular, the harsh realities of life on the margins of society alienate them one from another: The objectifications of the "foreground" culture are projected onto others who are similarly oppressed. Audre Lorde addresses this issue in "Eye to Eye," her wrenching address to other black women.)[58]

I am beginning to believe, therefore, that a white feminist treatment of the Fall should include an examination of the symbol of evil as the threat of the black woman as embodied "other." The consciousness of self as "other" to the world that is at the root of patriarchal religion is not sufficiently addressed by Daly and others who explore only their own objectification and the means to resist that objectification. Understanding oneself as a white woman means understanding the possibilities for idolatry resonant within the experience of white women. White feminism has given insufficient attention to the Fall as a symbol of the depth of human intolerance for difference. There are no prelapsarian possibilities in contemporary American culture, Rabuzzi or Daly to the contrary. Racist, sexist America is "fallen" and its address involves not a lapse into preconsciousness but precisely a consciousness of the depths of the alienations among women on the basis of race and class.

Traditional Christian theology has interpreted human difference as a consequence of the Fall and hence as wholly evil. It is possible to interpret human difference, and indeed the vast differences among all aspects of creation, as ambiguous. The ability of the "other" to speak reality to me in a different way is evidence of the freedom and independence of creation. It is when this original justice or righteousness is subverted and a hierarchical ordering of perceptions, valuations, and purposes is imposed that evil results. (But even there evil may be creative. I take up this ambiguity of evil in Chapter Four, where I discuss Maya Angelou's views on evil.)

Race and class make a difference in the way we interpret creation. White feminists, myself included, have assumed that they can know what is "natural" without recourse to social and economic analysis. But different racial locations (as well as class and gender locations) carry with them interpretive preunderstandings of what constitutes the natural. Theological categories such as sin and evil have been unhelpful to women, both black and white, when they have been employed in the service of patriarchy to blame women for finitude. But, divested of such patriarchal biases, theological reflection on sin and evil (as well as grace and salvation) can aid white women in a discernment of the conflicting moral values of not only sex, but also race and class. Uncritical appeals to the "natural" without such interpretation leads to an ideological blindness to the distorted freight of one's own social location.

4

Creating and Destroying Grace: Nature and the Fall

But like the earth, which is turned soggy by the blood of racism, he is maimed.

Barbara Christian,
Black Feminist Criticism

Another difference race makes is to intensify the question of the relationship of human beings with the rest of nature. In general many womanists, both in fiction and theology, tend to emphasize a conflicted relationship between human beings and nature. White feminists, by contrast, stress the interrelatedness of the two.

In examining the harmonies of nature, white feminism has taken its creative impulse not from white women's identification with nature and the body but from the legacy of denial nineteenth-century Victorianism has bequeathed them. The prevailing experience of many white women is one of alienation from their bodies.[1] In seeking to be whole, they endeavor to reintegrate with the body, often by reclaiming the natural processes of women's bodies.[2]

Black women, by contrast, have been cast as the exploited body and have seldom explored the theme of nature in isolation from the disruptions of racism and classism. Their work has been directed primarily toward the examination of culture (sociology); the development of a class analysis (economics); and a statement of the permutations of the experience of black Americans under a system of exploitation by class, race, and sex (fiction).

In 1974 Sherry Ortner wrote an article that has become pivotal in white feminist thinking. Ortner asked "Is Female to Male as Nature Is to Culture?"[3] Women (*sic*), she argued, together with nature, are considered "other" to the male subject, who is regarded as the creator of the civilizing impulse, or culture. I believe the question I need to ask at this point is whether I and other white feminists have not altered Ortner's thesis to read something like this: "Is white feminism to patriarchy as nature is to culture?" In other words, I am beginning to see that the white feminist's impulse to reclaim the body and nature has structurally precluded the development of social analysis because the creation of patriarchy has virtually been equated with the creation of culture. In practical terms, this means that white feminists have not pursued cultural analysis as vigorously as have black women.

But neither is this chapter designed to show that white feminists and black womanists occupy opposite ends of the same continuum and are merely moving toward a harmonious convergence at the center. Based on the difference race makes, different evaluations of nature and its relation to evil have emerged that are profoundly troubling and have, for me, stirred the waters of white feminism.

I have titled this chapter "Creating and Destroying Grace" in order to make the point that in the difference race makes, I have begun to question my unambiguous evaluation of nature (and her "sister" the feminine) as positive. The topic of the creation and nature includes destruction as well as creativity. On the other hand, I have learned from white feminists that the reductions of nature, an entity with its own teleology, to the creation, the work of a single god, is at the root of much of the destruction of the environment that is so visible today.

One of the aspects of patriarchal Christian theologies that feminists (*sic*) have identified and tried to eradicate is the emphasis (especially under Neoplatonic influence) on the divine as static. In patriarchal theology this emphasis has resulted in change and decay being denigrated and relegated to the realm of sin and evil. Although more modern white liberals have affirmed change, they generally see it in uniformly positive terms as growth toward greater harmony.[4] White feminists, even where they have challenged the Christian paradigm or left it behind, have followed this latter development by interpreting human beings as belonging to nature, and they see nature as a realm of "growth."

By contrast, the emphasis Latin American liberation theologians have placed on historical expressions of divine justice in nature has found a receptive audience among North American black liberation theologians such as James Cone. The fact that the Exodus narrative is central to this liberation perspective means nature is *reduced* to history. "Creation and liberation from Egypt are but one salvific act."[5]

According to many womanists, however, the creation is *fallen*, sin and evil are stunningly real and there is no (easy?) access to harmony. Further, and in apparent contradiction, I have heard womanists say that to know the evil of the creation is to know it more fully and that this mixed knowledge is creative. In addition, womanist writings reflect an awareness of the independence of nature, a theme of pagan feminists. In this respect black womanists differ from traditional Christian theologians, from many white feminists, and from many male liberation theologians (both black and Latin American).

In her chapter "Why Women Need the War God" (what she has learned from studying voodoo in the Caribbean) Karen Brown, a white feminist, has achieved a skillful grasp of this womanist theme of the complexity of good and evil in nature and culture. But it is the work of Maya Angelou that most vividly depicts the contradictory relationship of creation and destruction in the Fall, in the reality of evil.

Nature, Creation and History: Tiamat/Marduk

The defeat of the goddess is a theme in the Genesis narratives. The role of the serpent in Genesis 3, for example, represents an underlying struggle with goddess worship. The serpent is a well-known symbol that wound its way through the Near and Middle East, Crete and Mycenaean Greece as an integral aspect of the worship of a female deity. Cretan figurines of goddesses or their priestesses with snakes coiled about their arms or bodies are familiar. But in Genesis 3, female power is divided as it is destroyed. The etymology of the name Eve is open to dispute, but the Yahwist himself links her name, *hawwah,* with the Hebrew *hay* ("living"), calling her "Mother of All the Living." Bruce Vawter suggests a reading that reminds us of the snake-haired Gorgon of Greek mythology. "Not in the Hebrew preserved in the bible, but in the cognate Arabic and Aramaic languages a word related to *hawway* means "serpent."[6] Unable to completely destroy the symbol of the goddess, a tamed remnant remains in Eve.

In traditional Christian theology, the God of the Yahwist has been seen as a God of history who makes a covenant with the people of God. The goddesses and gods of the indigenous Canaanite religions (now interpreted as pagan) are rejected as the worship of the imminent, impersonal forces of nature. History is oriented toward events (wars, conquests, escapes from Egyptian slavery, etc.) and not toward the cycles of "repetitious nature." These incursions of God into history are sacred; nature is no longer considered sacred but is the creation, the work of the one god, sovereign over both history and creation.[7]

This traditional interpretation has been challenged by many white feminist thealogians and theologians who have pointed out that the Jewish and Christian religions have taken as their point of departure the defeat of the mother (Tiamat), symbolized in nature and the feminine. Social, political, and economic changes in Sumer during the fourth millennium, Carol Christ observes, began a period in which "male Gods begin to rise in prominence over the female Goddesses, often through murder, as is reflected in the story of Marduk's slaying of his Grandmother Tiamat in the Babylonian myth the *Enuma Elish* (first millennium C.E.)."[8] Rosemary Ruether identifies the splitting of Tiamat with the essential dualism of patriarchal religion.

> Patriarchal religion split apart the dialectical unities of mother religion into absolute dualism, elevating a male-identified consciousness to transcendent apriority. Fundamentally this is rooted in an effort to deny one's own mortality, to identify essential (male) humanity with a transcendent divine sphere beyond the matrix of coming-to-be-and-passing-away.[9]

Catherine Keller's new work *From a Broken Web* considers Marduk/Tiamat at some length and, I believe, sheds considerable light on the various problems that come together in a consideration of nature, creation, and history. What I have learned from reading Keller is that white women who have pursued the goddess traditions in feminist Christian or pagan spirituality are not "merely affirming immanence" over transcendence. They are trying to integrate the human capacity for imaginative self-transcendence with an affirmation of bodiliness and connectedness. Yet I believe that even in this impulse to connectedness, to wholeness, they have equated culture with evil and nature with goodness, reinventing the dualism. Both nature and culture are far more ambiguous than white feminism has allowed.

Keller observes that Tiamat "symbolizes something like the state of immanence, yet surely not as stagnation, but as an all-encompassing inwardness." When Tiamat mates with her spouse Apsu (the fresh waters), their union produces "the beginnings of difference itself." The coming together of these potentialities generates "form" and "consciousness," i.e., differentiation.[10]

This creative process produces the first *discord:* "Sibling rivalry, divine restlessness, new possibilities madly unleashed and competing for actualization. . . ." The final result of this surge of creativity and combativeness is that Marduk, the great-great-grandson of Tiamat, slays her and establishes patriarchal order.[11]

Keller points out that there is a lot of patriarchal jockeying going on in this epic. The sons wish to destroy the father and Apsu, far from pleased at the combative offspring he and Tiamat have produced, proclaims, "Their manners revolt me, day and night without remission we suffer. My will is to destroy them . . . we shall have peace at last and we will sleep again." Tiamat, too, is disturbed by her offspring's destructive ways: She is "stung, she writhed in lonely desolation, her heart worked in secret passion." But her response differs radically from Apsu's. "Why must we destroy the children that we made? If their ways are troublesome, let us wait a little while." Keller follows this outline of a critical passage in the *Enuma Elish* with the comment, "Not the maternal but the paternal uroboros shows itself intolerant of change and discord."[12]

But when the children kill Apsu, Tiamat turns monstrous. She conceives a whole generation of terrors, "serpents with cutting fangs," "snarling dragons" who have venom for blood. A peacemaking strategy fails because the rebellious sons cannot even look their mother in the face (Medusa?) in order to propose a cease-fire. At this dramatic moment Marduk appears and derides his uncles for their cowardice. "I will accomplish what you long for most in your heart. . . . *Only a female thing,* only Tiamat flies at you with all her contrivance. You shall soon straddle Tiamat's neck." With her emphasis in the text, Keller demonstrates the precise workings of the patriarchal mind: Cowardly and cringing, too "resourceless"[13] to find a negotiated settlement, they go for "the clean kill." Marduk not only kills Tiamat, he slaughters her and divides her conquered body. "The lord rested; he gazed at the huge body, pondering how to use it, what to create from the dead carcass. He split it apart like a cockle-shell; with the upper half he constructed the arc of sky, he pulled down the bar and set a watch on the waters, so they should never escape."[14]

The issue in the text is one of control. The ordering and control of the patriarchal culture of violence with its limited options (kill or be killed) contrasts powerfully with Tiamat's earlier "let's wait and see" approach to finding a way to deal with destruction.

But I often find (this is true in Keller) that the interpretations of the Marduk/Tiamat saga in white feminist writing underemphasize or ignore altogether that the *Enuma Elish* is a religiopolitical document. One of its primary purposes is to justify the violent aggression of the Sumero-Akkadian kingdoms over the indigenous peoples. In this way political violence is justified, as it almost always is, by the ordering of chaos.

Now, if in attending to the patriarchal redactions of the Tiamat/Marduk epic, white feminists appropriate *only* the notion that the guiding philosophy of feminism should be the return to a precreation harmony, I believe we have missed one of the lessons of that epic. Its construction is a political as well as a religious legitimation of totalitarianism, and the challenge is to move to a more just *civilization.* The creation of culture is not the "fall" or the "origin of patriarchy" so that redemption equals a return to the precultural garden. The civilizing impulse is profoundly ambiguous. Nature does not exist as an entity over against which patriarchal culture reigns. Nature is interpreted only through different cultural paradigms; there can be no return to a pre-cultural harmony.[15]

Chaos and Cosmos: Starhawk

Starhawk's new book *Truth or Dare* gives considerable space to the treatment of difference among white feminists as well as those of racial and ethic minorities. The knowledge derived from her political actions in the peace movement provides tremendous insight into how groups and individuals experience conflict and change. It is her firsthand knowledge of ambiguity, of conflict and difference, that she brings to this book. It is only when she deals macrocosmically that she advocates harmony and order, a curious contrast that I find instructive. Despite her profound knowledge of cultural ambiguity, when Starhawk talks in other than concrete, political terms she returns to the harmonies of an undifferentiated nature.

Truth or Dare is subtitled "Encounters with Power, Authority and Mystery." The analysis of power is divided into structures of "power-over," which is equated with war, and alternatives to violent, hier-archical forms of power labeled "power-from-within" and "power-with." Starhawk seeks nondominant sources for her exploration of the latter two forms of power but is very adamant in her decision to have nothing to do with "spiritual colonialists" who mine "the Third World (*sic*) for its resources of symbols and shamans, giving nothing back, in a way that cheapens both the traditions we seek to understand and our own spiritual quests."[16]

In a section on "building alliances across the barriers of difference," Starhawk examines the anger and fear that reside in the encounter with difference: anger by the nondominants "when they are attacked, ren-dered invisible, symbolically or actually annihilated, relegated to the ranks of those who have no value" and the fear that comes "when we are asked to shift perspective, when we encounter difference. . . ."[17] Throughout the book she constantly looks for racial difference and names it. For example, she examines the role of white supremacist ideologies held by white women during Reconstruction.[18] She has clearly spent a lot of time with women of color trying to hear them and trying to be heard.[19]

Starhawk's book is laced with firsthand accounts of the political actions and incarcerations involved in various peace demonstrations.

She effectively uses this political experience to posit the need to establish boundaries (who is in the group and who is excluded), the need for laws, rules and hierarchies, the realities of power, safety from attack, taking power, and many other issues that arise when groups act politically. The world of her political actions is filled with conflict, and meeting conflict head-on instead of avoiding it is the way political change comes about.[20]

Yet she does not extend this embrace of conflict to posit that political work is a way of acting oneself into a new way of thinking; the reverse remains true. One thinks oneself into a new way of acting. "This book is a text of magic, a liberation psychology."[21] Consistent with the interiority of the psychological approach to liberation is the macrocosmic affirmation of the status quo in creation.

> Power-from-within stems from a different consciousness—one that sees the world itself as a living being, made up of dynamic aspects, a world where one thing shape-shifts into another, where there are no solid separations and no simple causes and effects. In such a world, all things have inherent value, because all things are beings, aware in ways we can only imagine, interrelated in patterns too complex to ever be more than partially described. . . . For we are, ourselves, the living body of the sacred. This is what Witches mean when we say, "Thou are Goddess," and also what mavericks and heretics have always read into the biblical account of the creation of the world in the image of God.[22]

Here I find I must part company with Starhawk, though I have learned a tremendous amount from her political wisdom. But I believe that I must now be more attentive to the fact that there *are* "solid separations," though they are not, as she helpfully says, simple. I contend that a changed action reveals the conflicts resident within the nature of existence itself and not exclusively a patterning, however fluid and changing.

In their reclamation of the body and nature, white women have paid insufficient attention to the ambiguities of both nature and culture. Nature is not free of the distortions of class and race.

Displacement

Bell Hooks has written:

> *The formation of an oppositional world view is necessary for feminist struggle*. This means that the world we have most intimately known, the

world in which we feel "safe" (even if such feelings are based on illusions) must be radically changed. Perhaps it is the knowledge that everyone must change, not just those we label enemies or oppressors, that has so far served to check our revolutionary impulses. Those revolutionary impulses must freely inform our theory and practice if feminist movement to end existing oppression is to progress, if we are to transform our present reality.[23]

I, as a white feminist, must stop trying to belong to nature and its harmonies and begin to see myself as an "other" in order to transform society.

Displacement, the sense that all is not harmony, is the dominant motif one finds from Ann Petry, with her sense that even the pavements of the city are ranged against her protagonist, to Toni Morrison in her evocation of the house "palsied by the baby's fury at having its throat cut. . . ."[24] The alienation that has taken place between the land and the black community is evoked in all its complexity in Morrison's writing, for the land and nature as a whole is also a sustaining factor in the survival of the community.

In *Sula,* this complexity emerges in the image, the bitter humor of the "Bottom." A slavemaster, not wanting to part with good land he had promised his slave, gave him hilly, rocky ground and called it "the bottom of heaven." Reversing the truth, that this "good bottom land" was, in fact, the rocky, hilly top, is a typical white man's distorted truth. The land is beset by heat and cold, wind and rain, and like the main character, Sula, it symbolizes for the community the evil side of nature. But because the community members realize neither their own vulnerability nor that of the land, they do not survive. Morrison deeply believes that the future of the people and the future of the land are inextricably related.[25]

The Marduk/Tiamat epic does not represent the remnants of prelapsarian harmony but is a document of political conflict that may resonate more fully with the black woman fiction writer's approach to nature as conflicted. For the black woman writer, philosopher, ethicist or theologian, however, this conflict is not couched in the same framework recognized by many Latin American and American black male theologians. For the latter, Marxist theory has provided the analytical tools for examining the conflicts with the land that characterize, for example, the Latin American agrarian experience. Some black women, such as Angela Davis, have found classical Marxist theory instructive in their thinking on conflict. Others, such as Morrison, embrace conflict but are by no means strict philosophical Marxists. The writing of black women from Davis to Morrison, however, posits a more African communitarianism and animist sense of nature's independence than does classical Marxist theory, which has influenced Latin Americans (and to some extent black North American men such as James Cone).

Classical Marxist theory, I believe, carries with it the dualistic views of the white, Western Enlightenment and its oppositionalist treatment of nature. Cultural theories such as Marxism, which have influenced some womanists and white feminists, have ignored the fact that nature may not be reduced to culture.

Nature and Marxism

In the first volume of *Das Kapital*, Karl Marx defined labor "as a process in which both the human being and nature participate, and in which the human through its action mediates, regulates and controls its metabolism with nature."[26] Human beings act through labor to create environment with the material reality at hand. The critique of Marxism that can be raised is that it regards the material world, nature, as thoroughly desacralized and the object of human endeavor. It is by extension, therefore, markedly anthropocentric.

Karl Marx hoped to overcome the subject/object dualism with which philosophy had until then dealt with the relationship of the human being and nature. According to Marx, dialectical materialism not only overcomes human alienation but also the alienation of nature from the human. For this reason he calls his work "realized naturalism."

> Only here has his natural existence become his human existence; and nature become man for him. Society is therefore the perfected unity in essence of man with nature, the true resurrection of nature, the realized naturalism of man and the realized humanism of nature.[27]

Human beings can become human when private property is eliminated: They cease being objects and become subjects in history. Likewise, as human beings become more "natural," i.e., subjects, they discover the "humanism of nature." Later in the same passage, Marx equates naturalism and humanism "as fully developed humanism equals naturalism" where all "the conflict between man and nature" is resolved.[28] But what is discovered is only the independence of the human subject; nature is not permitted its own independent subjectivity.

In Marx's later writings even this elementary concern for nature as "resurrected" disappears, and nature is "subjugated" through massive technological advances which "subdue[s] the play of natural forces."[29] In modern scientific technology the human being is the subject and nature the object; nature is the object on which the human subject works. Nature has no ends of its own (see Merchant).

In effect, what Marxists do is to deny contingency, openness, and potentiality to nature but appropriate them for humanity. In Marxist thought, therefore, nature takes on the character of what is timeless, static, and continually recurring, while history becomes the location of innovation and change. This is strikingly evident in the writings of the Latin American liberation theologians and black American liberation theologians who posit creation as "the first political act," in which the liberator God, like the human being, is taken to be first, and most important, an actor in history.[30]

As a result, the Marxist can only conceive of a practical relationship to nature, that of work. Under the rubric of work, the Marxist continues the humanocentric, object relation with nature as the raw material of human civilization.

The ecological crisis has precipitated some changes in orthodox Marxist thinking, however. In the second edition of his well-known book on the concept of nature in Marx, Alfred Schmidt added a postscript in which he noted that the earlier Marxist concept of the "resurrection of nature" had better be resurrected in Marxist thinking or humanity may not arrive "at a reasonable condition—or indeed survive[s] at all."[31]

In his discussion of "The Metabolic Mediation: Labor as 'Creatio Continua,'" Vitor Westhelle, a Latin American liberation theologian, tries to equate alienation in labor with "the destruction of metabolism," by which he means the ecological crisis. Westhelle, however, recognizes that Marxism runs the continual risk of being "an anthropocentric concept."[32] His concern with the "diabolic" possibilities of humanocentrism notwithstanding, Westhelle never does acknowledge purpose and independence for creation apart from the creator and the creator's imago.

Black Women Writers, Nature and History

Angela Davis is the most explicitly Marxist of the black women writers whose works have been consulted for this book. In her autobiography she writes that "the *Communist Manifesto* hit me like a bolt of lightning." The oft-repeated phrase in the white women's movement, the personal is the political, also seems a description of what Marxist analysis has provided for Davis.

What had seemed a personal hatred of me, an inexplicable refusal of Southern whites to confront their own emotions, and a stubborn willingness of Blacks to acquiesce, became the inevitable consequence of a ruthless system which kept itself alive and well by encouraging spite, competition and the oppression of one group by another. Profit was the word: the cold and constant motive for the behavior, the contempt and the despair I had seen.[33]

Davis's life goal became the economic liberation of her people through political means, and Marxism was and has remained a means to that end.

In Davis's autobiography, however, there is a strikingly Morrison-esque passage in which she describes her move as a child from the projects of Birmingham to the country.

In 1948 we moved out of the projects in Birmingham, Alabama, to the large wooden house on Center Street. My parents still live there. Because of its steeples and gables and peeling paint, the house was said to be haunted. There were wild woods in back with fig trees, blackberry patches and great wild cherry trees. On one side of the house was a huge Cigar tree. There was space here and no cement. The street itself was a strip of orange-red Alabama clay.[34]

The reader is therefore not surprised to discover that Morrison was Davis's editor at Random House. Davis is a philosopher, Morrison a writer of fiction; yet both chose to focus on an analysis of the deformations of racism and sexism on the social conditions of their people. The haunted houses of Morrison and Davis lean out from the pages of their books as a metaphor for the way in which black history seeps spectrally into contemporary black life.[35] "Nature is a disorderly process"[36] on which housing is imposed. The housing reflects its inhabitants' ease or dis-ease with disorder. Throughout her autobiography, it is clear that Davis's family has a high tolerance (though obviously not without strain) for the disorder her political imprisonment and defense bring into their lives.

Of Toni Morrison's character Guitar Baines in *Sula,* Barbara Christian has written that "like the earth, which is turned soggy by the blood of racism, he is maimed."[37] For me this phrase captures the difference race makes when one approaches the category of nature. For the black woman, nature as she finds it has not escaped the deformations of racism. Therefore no assumptions of human capacity, of women's capacity, to relate to their "sister," the earth, can be made without considering the factor of race in a racist culture. It is not that black women's approach to nature has no parallels in the works of white women. On the contrary, the sense of nature as an independent character with her own teleology is strikingly parallel. Christian points out the significant role "the elements" of fire, air, and water play in Morrison's novels, the same elements that provide the infrastructure of Mary Daly's metaphysics of reality.[38] But the powerful spiritual forces the elements represent are deranged in complex patterns by race, sex, and class; and these derangements and displacements cannot be overcome by sheer mental process.

"Why Women Need the War God"

Karen Brown, a white feminist anthropologist and ethicist, has been researching Vodou in Haiti and in the Haitian community in New York City since 1973. Responding to injustice in her own life, Brown chose to direct her anger at injustice and, in fact, to "marry" this anger in a Vodou ceremony in which she married the war god Ogou. She describes her study of Vodou and the difference it has made in her work as a white feminist in a chapter entitled "Why Women Need the War God." This chapter, which appears alongside Carol Christ's chapter, "Feminist Liberation Theology and Yahweh as Holy Warrior: An Analysis of Symbol" appears in the volume *Women's Spirit Bonding* and represents the dilemma I am addressing here. What is a white feminist analysis of tragedy in human life? What capacity is there in white feminist theory for anger at injustice? How do we understand tragedy and rage in light of our commitments to peace with justice? To ecological justice?

What I have learned from Carol Christ is to be wary of even the patriarchal dimensions of liberation theologies, as these identify with the violence of Yahweh as Holy Warrior.[39] Seeking to develop a feminist theory that is "conceptually unstable" (Harding), however, I have learned from Karen Brown that it is a mistake for me as a white feminist to reject aggression, war, and hierarchy out of hand. Perhaps *the* mistake that white female slave owners, white female abolitionists, and suffragists made is that they turned away from their own anger at what the slave system accomplished *in them,* and in their own lives. They believed in an ideal world, a world before the Fall, and because they did, they lived in a willed ignorance of their own capacity for violence. As a modern white feminist, when I retreat to the harmonies of nature, I will my own blindness to the racial conflicts among women.

Brown's story, which she relates in the afore-mentioned chapter of *Women's Spirit Bonding,* goes like this: Originally out of anthropological curiosity, Brown studied Haitian Vodou for ten years. But gradually, as her study progressed, she gave up Western academic methods and

allowed Vodou rituals to "speak to me in their own language." Since
her marriage of eleven years was breaking up and she was, at the same
time, involved in a tenure battle at the university where she taught, she
decided to stop trying to get rid of her anger, her rage at her husband
and her institution. "One day I found myself saying, 'Karen, stop trying
to get rid of this anger. Marry it!' I telephoned a Vodou priestess I knew
in Brooklyn and said, 'I am ready.' And so I married Ogou. I stopped
trying to be good, to be understanding, to get over my anger, to be
superior to it. I claimed it as mine. It was a transformative experience."[40]

The god she married, Ogou, comes from the Yoruba culture of
Nigeria. Originally a spirit associated with iron workers who often had
to travel great distances in their work, he became the god of "the
mobile, the marginal and the isolated." The evolution of Ogou into a
god of war came about through his connection with things made
of metal, particularly weapons. In Nigeria this makes him the
god of change and assertiveness for Nigerians as they meet the challenge of industry. "Yet he also embodies the wisdom that the modes of
action so necessary for survival in the contemporary world, and so
beneficial in many ways, also contain seeds of destruction [the oil
industry in particular]. The Ogou cult in Nigeria has a trenchant ecological critique of modern technology and of what its ethos does to
people and the land on which they live."[41]

Ogou came to Haiti with Yoruban slaves during the eighteenth century and there has taken many faces. These faces are "all soldiers and
all male. . . . The different Ogou explore all aspects of hierarchy, war,
and anger; of the mentality of us-against-them; of the uses and abuses
of power, aggression, and self-assertion." The experience of the Haitian
people with the military is profoundly ambivalent: From Toussaint
L'Ouverture, the leader of the only successful slave rebellion in the
Western Hemisphere to the U.S. Marines, war makers in Haiti have
been "creative and destructive, liberating and oppressing." Rituals of
possession by Ogou follow the basic psychology of war making: "The
first stage is attack outward; the second threatens harm to the immediate community; the third threatens the self."[42]

Brown relates that many of her feminist friends were dismayed by her
decision to marry Ogou. "How can you have this relationship with—of
all things!—a male War God?" Brown's reply was, "It seems to me that
the Gods of war are necessary as long as there is anger in our hearts and
war in the world." Further, Brown contends that she does not believe
"humanity is ever going to do away with war, although I can imagine it
taking on quite different forms," i.e., non-nuclear. Brown is as active in

the peace movement as Carol Christ, for example. But she doubts that "we will ever have a world not characterized by some form of us-against-them thinking. . . ."[43]

But what is most exciting to me personally is that Brown is not *resigned* to violence; she is not, like some "Christian Realists" such as Reinhold Niebuhr, dividing up violence for some circumstances and not others. "I am *thankful* we will most likely *not have to live in a world without self-assertion, anger, and energy.*" For Brown, though she always acknowledges that this is not necessarily true for everyone, "the tragic vision is energizing."[44]

She contrasts this "tragic vision" with "idealistic" visions. "Women working with traditional Jewish and Christian models [here I would place the 'Creation theology' advocates], as well as those who have recently reclaimed the Goddess tradition, most often—although not always—speak from this idealistic, prophetic place," where the vision is a world without war, without aggression, without violence. But for Brown, while there are profound truths to this vision, which has come primarily from the victims of war, women, and women with dependent children, "it would be a mistake in a feminist critique of war to paint women as only nurturers, only creative, just as it can be dangerous to attribute only goodness and light to the realm of the spirit. If we go too far in that direction, we put the shadow behind us and put ourselves in a position to be grabbed from behind when we are least suspicious."[45]

What I have learned from Brown and, through her, from Vodou, is that as a white feminist, I have not sufficiently plumbed the depths of my own anger and capacity for violence and aggression and so, in my own unacknowledged racism, am "grabbed from behind." These capacities for covert and even overt violence exist within me whether I choose to own them or not, and they are more dangerous when unacknowledged. When white women's anger is unacknowledged it does not go away. It will find a channel. And it finds a channel similar to that structured throughout centuries of human civilization: Those with less social and political power are the objects, the victims of the aggressions of dominants. Nondominants, too, are aggressive; this is the so-called horizontal violence—black-on-black crime and so forth—of powerless people acting out their violence on other powerless people, it being too dangerous to attack the real cause of their powerlessness.

Vodou further teaches that the full range of human capabilities, the blinding flashes of violence as well as the dark, warm recesses of love and care, are sources of human creativity as well as destruction, and that sometimes creativity and destruction are not separate but one. This is a thesis that must be advanced with some care and trepidation, since the abuses of such an outlook are a live risk. Resignation to social evil is one risk, the abuse of power in the name of change is another. But whence comes the raging energy to substantively challenge the covert and overt violences of race, sex, and class if not from the raging chaos of the nature of things? This view is expressed with almost unbearable honesty in an interview given by Maya Angelou on evil.

Maya Angelou on Evil

In an interview that was part of a Bill Moyers's program, "Facing Evil," Maya Angelou related her experience of being raped at seven and a half years of age by a man who was well known to her family. This man was imprisoned and then released. The night he was released, he was found murdered. The police suspected that he had been kicked to death. Hearing this, Angelou the child stopped speaking for five years because she thought, with her child's view of things, that by speaking his name she had caused his death.

The sexual abuse of children is always evil, profound evil, we *must* say. During those five years of silence, the child Maya Angelou read everything she could find—every book in the black school library, every book in the white school library—from Langston Hughes to Shakespeare. Much of this literature she memorized. "When I decided to speak, I had a lot to say and a way to say it." The profound truth that Angelou relates is that one of the roots of her creativity is this horrible evil and its consequences. Out of the chaos of the violence perpetrated against her tumbled the poetry and prose that had named survival for her people and in naming survival helps to secure its beachhead in American society. Does this make for harmony? No. Does this mean that, as Job's foolish friend Eliphaz thought, every cloud has a silver lining? (Job 4:17) Again, no. It does mean that good and evil, creation and destruction, evil and good, destruction and creation, are more intertwined than I, as a white Christian feminist theologian, have so far allowed. It means that the chaos with which the female is identified in the Marduk/Tiamat epic is at once the origin of great creativity and great destructiveness. I now know that I need to spend more time coming to terms with the profound ambiguity of evil and to imbue my embrace of nature with a consciousness of its cultural interpretations.

Addenda

Very popular among white Christian feminists is a movement known as "creation theology" or "creation spirituality." This is a movement associated with the Institute in Culture and Creation Spirituality at Holy Names College in Oakland, California. The director is Matthew Fox, a Catholic Dominican.[46] On the faculty as well is Starhawk, a witch in the Wicca movement and a post-Jewish feminist.

In his work *Original Blessing,* Fox claims to have identified "two paradigms" within Christianity, the first, being "fall/redemption," the second being "creation-centered." Starhawk, in her new book *Truth or Dare,* identifies with Fox's work.[47]

In very general terms, Fox's main argument is that the "fall/redemption" paradigm contains aspects of Christian theology that emphasize suffering, death, sin, asceticism, dualism, and so on; the "creation-centered" paradigm, by contrast, centers on birthing, life, grace, hospitality, and integration.[48] However, some reviewers have argued persuasively that Fox's comparisons simply cover the fact that his theological perspective has some of the characteristics of a very traditional Christian doctrine of creation. "All of Fox's concerns are already contained in the Doctrine of Creation and Sanctification in traditional Christian spirituality."[49]

In fact, what Fox may have done is to eliminate some of the more creative aspects of Christian theology, especially for oppressed peoples. In playing the tune of the creation, a metaphor he uses constantly, Fox plays as one of the owners of creation, one for whom the created order poses no conflicts. "We (*sic*) are heirs to a promise. . . ."[50] In rejecting the Fall, Fox has given the oppressed about whom he frequently expressed concern *no tools for the rejection of their oppression as evil.*

According to Gustavo Gutiérrez, the discourse of "theologians of the developed world" who are concerned with the question of creation is reflective of a political naïveté that has "sapped most of their energy."[51] What passes for a theology of creation, says Vitor Westhelle, is often a defense of the status quo. "Not rarely, creation is interchangeable with 'the Created Order.'" In Latin America, order is not a positive concept because it is often a code word for repression, domination, and persecution. Westhelle cites the work of the Cuban writer Alejo Carpentier, who has described "the cultural dilemma of Latin America as the conflict between the sense of order and disposition that we have inherited from Europe and the effervescent spontaneity and marvelous anomaly of life as we experience it."[52]

The ideology of ordering as it appears in creation theology is perceived by the Latin Americans as an appeal to a cosmological justification for the "separation between the thing-out-there (where order is supposed to be found) and the observing subject." That is, the appeal to an underlying order in creation to which human beings are subject in fact eviscerates the human capacity to act, to become a subject in history, and by so acting to become *human*. Jacquelyn Grant has written that "black women are indeed becoming subjects. More and more they are resisting the objectification by those whose histories and herstories continue to render them invisible."[53]

Further, deviating from the created order (God's will, in Christian terms) is viewed from the dominant position, according to Westhelle, as "anomalous. . . . What lacks order, lacks goodness. Lack of order is evil." What Westhelle fears is that an appeal to the order of creation will, in fact, "in a modern and bourgeois world . . . be nothing but a freezing of a general set of relations of inequity that guarantees the oppression, submission and exploitation of those who are displaced."[54]

For Westhelle the alternative is to posit that there is "a close association between creation and novelty, so that the criterion to discern the process of 'creation' is to establish the dissonance with the old 'order.'"[55] This position on novelty strikingly resembles Audre Lorde, who repeatedly states that creativity is the emergence of novelty in conflict.[56] Latin American liberation theologians such as Westhelle, however, would do well to note the emphasis such writers as Lorde place on the distinctiveness of nature over creation.

5
The Self and Sin

I find my own
small person
a standing self
against the world
a quality of wills
I finally understand
    Alice Walker, *Good Night,*
    Willie Lee, I'll See You
    in the Morning

In my Introduction to Theology course last year, I had occasion to teach the by-now famous article by Valerie Saiving, "The Human Situation: A Feminine View." Saiving's essay, first printed in *The Journal of Religion* in 1960, is regarded by many women (*sic*) in religion as the beginning of modern feminist (*sic*) theology. Saiving wrote:

> I propose to criticize, from the viewpoint of feminine experience, the estimate of the human situation made by certain contemporary theologians. Although the views I shall outline receive their most uncompromising expression in the writings of Anders Nygren and Reinhold Niebuhr, I believe that they represent a widespread tendency in contemporary theology to describe man's predicament as rising from separateness and the anxiety occasioned by it and to identify sin with self-assertion and love with selflessness.[1]

Saiving proposed that what these two theologians represent as the universal human sins of prideful self-assertion are really the particular sins of certain male experiences of the world. Women (*sic*), by contrast, are not beset by the temptations of pride but rather, by those of "triviality, distractibility, and diffuseness; lack of an organizing center or focus, dependence on others for one's self-definition; tolerance at the expense of standards of excellence; inability to respect the boundaries of privacy . . . in short, underdevelopment or negation of the self."[2] This lack of a self was recognized but never developed by Reinhold

77

Niebuhr. He called it sensuality or, sometimes, sloth.[3] Therefore, what may be described as sin for male experience, namely self-assertion, is in fact not sin but grace in female experience.

I had not gotten too far into the presentation of Saiving's views—in fact, I had merely to utter the word "sloth" as representative of "women's sin" (*sic*)—when a black woman student jumped to her feet and explained to me in no uncertain terms that "sloth" could never be construed as the besetting sin of black women.

Now, on the one hand, I could say that this student was making the error many students of theology make when they read theology— namely, interpreting theological terms according to ordinary usage. What she may have heard me say was that Saiving was using "laziness" as the besetting sin of women; Saiving, of course, was referring to the failure to become a focused self. On the other hand, this student was also right. Saiving's analysis and those of white women who have followed her trenchant critique of Nygren and Niebuhr does not fit the experience of many black women, whose sin is neither sloth nor sensuality in the Niebuhrian sense.

Judith Plaskow developed Saiving's analysis in her marvelous book *Sex, Sin, and Grace: Women's Experience and the Theologies of Reinhold Niebuhr and Paul Tillich*. In this book Plaskow used the novels of Doris Lessing to put some women's flesh on the term "women's experience" and juxtaposed this lively content to the notion of human life found in Tillich and Niebuhr. Needless to say, she found quite a contrast.

But Plaskow was not merely following Saiving. While Saiving began her article by asking how men and women experience themselves, her conception of the differences that distinguish male from female experience was drawn from biologically rooted conceptions of human difference. Plaskow argues for "a definition of women's experience as the interrelation between cultural expectations and their internalization. . . ."[4] Because she relies on a culturally mediated notion of experience, Plaskow's definition of "women's experience" lacks the universalistic bias of Saiving and others who have made a similar argument. This enables Plaskow to be very specific about her own "experience." She acknowledges that her view is "modern, white, western, middle-class" and that this is appropriately used to contradict Tillich and Niebuhr, both of whom are also "modern, white, western, middle-class," as well as male.[5]

Because, as Plaskow argues, "the experiences of women in the course of a history" are "never free from cultural role definitions,"[6] I believe the role definitions of black women in a racist society will inevitably have great impact on "experience" as a category for study. In rereading the history of slavery, I have found that the prevailing logic has been to keep black and white women separate by dividing their cultural role definitions (black women as the body and sensuality; white women as the soul and spirituality). Hence for black women the term "experience" has a different interpretive matrix than it has for white women, despite their common female biology.[7] The protest of the female black student is totally valid: Without a historically accurate definition of what it means to be female in different racial, class, and sexual role definitions, Saiving's contribution to understanding "sin for women" is misleading.

The Truths of Black Women's Experience: Defining the Self

Black women writers use the category of truth extensively. Below I discuss Katie Cannon's use of "Quiet Grace as Truth" in her ethical writings. The truth claims of black women's experience of themselves have more than particular validity. Some of this claim to greater universality comes from the simple fact that to survive as oppressed people, black women had to know white reality as well as black reality. Dominant groups such as whites or males have no need to learn the nondominant position because it has no power to affect them. Further, I believe that some forms of experience *do more truth than others.*[8]

Truth as Quiet Grace

Black Womanist Ethics by Katie Cannon is a constructive ethic of the moral situation of black women based on the work of Zora Neale Hurston. Cannon begins her study from a critically conscious rejection of the dominant ethical theories that predicate the existence of freedom and choice for the ethical agent. Given their moral situation in slavery and in the twentieth century, this assumption of freedom of choice is wholly inadequate to the moral decision making of black women. The focus of Cannon's work, therefore, "is to show how Black women live out a moral wisdom in their real-lived context that does not appeal to the fixed rules or absolute principles of the white-oriented, male structured society."[9]

The literary history of black women forms the "richly stocked pantry" (described earlier) to which the black female ethical agent today can go to find a larder of experiences. To understand this chapter, it is critical to recognize that the "experiences" laid down in this literature are neither exclusively those of individual black women nor those of black women as a group separate from black men. As Cannon puts it, "The Black women's literary tradition parallels Black history."[10] "The majority of Black women who engage in literary composition hold themselves accountable to the collective values that underlie Black history and culture." Cannon also quotes Dexter Fisher, who contends that "to be totally *centered on the self* would be to forget one's history, the kinship of a shared community of experience, the crucial continuity between past and present that must be maintained to insure the future."[11]

Zora Neale Hurston's fiction presents characters, both male and female, who are moral agents. They are connected to the ongoing life of the black community. For Hurston it is certainly true that self-assertion, or pride, is not sin. The communitarian basis of the protagonists' sense of self as described by Cannon means that there is, however, a basis for the analysis of sin other than that taken by Saiving. Saiving's view, as recently discussed, is that "sin for women" (*sic*) is the failure to be a self. As Cannon states in quoting Karla Holloway, each of Hurston's novels "in different fashion, enjoins a search for truth. Usually the search ends in some internal recognition of sin or weakness. The search can end in a fulfillment after rectifying this weakness."[12]

In Hurston's fiction the moral wisdom of the black community is conveyed as the ways and means the community has evolved to meet the life-destroying environment of racism. This body of knowledge is passed from one generation to the next primarily in an oral culture in which the hands-on training in surviving as a black person in the United States with some of the self intact is tantamount to a folk art. Hurston's characters are not losers, the defeated in this struggle for survival. They are the ones who "with a quality of irresistible efficacy . . . adopt and accept their lot in life, while simultaneously embracing the external energy of replenishing help, which makes easier the realization of limits imposed on them."[13]

"Zora Neale Hurston's basic assumption in all of her fiction was that quiet grace is manifested in the search for truth."[14] As the community-mediated experiences come to her characters, they discover the truth of life in the possible options. The truths of their experience are not static; characters who cannot adapt to "the relativity of truth" are destroyed.[15] Hurston particularly valued her own unerring eye for the truths of experience, her ability "to hit a straight lick with a crooked stick."[16]

One of the novels Cannon uses to describe how "Quiet Grace as Truth" functions is Hurston's *Their Eyes Were Watching God* (1937). The novel is in many ways strikingly similar to Lessing's quest series.

The main character, Janie Crawford, spends thirty years struggling on many fronts to find self-actualization. She has to grapple with racism, with patriarchy, and finally with the emptiness of white middle-class consumerism in order to become a living, breathing human being.

It is in *Their Eyes Were Watching God* that Hurston's oft-quoted line that the black woman is "de mule uh de world" appears. It is uttered by Nanny, Janie's grandmother. Nanny had been born into slavery and she tries to communicate to Janie some of the truth of what she knows about the world and some of the quiet grace that has enabled her, Nanny, not only to endure but to prevail.

Nanny had been raped by the white slave owner, and the resulting baby looked so much like him that his wife attacked Nanny. She threatened to have Nanny beaten "with one hundred lashes of raw hide on her bare back, 'until the blood run down yo' heels.' " In this passage Nanny is holding her new baby.

> "You better git dat kivver offa dat yougun and dat quick!" she clashed at me. "Look lak you don't know who is Mistis on dis plantation, Madam. But Ah aims to show you. . . . Nigger, whut's yo' baby doin' wid gray eyes and yaller hair?" She begin tuh slap mah jaws ever which a 'way. Ah never felt the fust ones 'cause Ah wuz too busy gittin de kivver back over mah chile. But dem last lick burnt me lak fire. Ah had too many feelin's tu tell which one tuh follow so Ah didn't cry and Ah didn't do nothing else. But then she kept astin me how come mah baby look white. She asted me dat maybe twenty-five or thirty times. . . . So Ah told her, "Ah don't know nothin' but what Ah'm told tuh do, 'cause Ah ain't nothin' but uh nigger and uh slave."[17]

The slavemistress has no outlet for her own anger at her husband's behavior, so she takes it out on someone more powerless than she. Nanny runs away to the swamp to get away from a situation in which her baby will be sold from her if she stays: She exhibits the quiet grace of courage as, not fully healed from the birth, she hides in a hostile environment.

But Nanny's longed-for values of legal husband and financial security do not yet provide Janie with enough grist to build a life of truth. What Janie has gotten from her grandmother, however, is the ability to discern the truth when she sees it. This stands her in good stead when she again faces violence, not from a slavemistress this time but from her own husband, Jody, who beats her because she spoiled the dinner. Like the authenticity of Nanny's story as she tells of being beaten for having been sexually abused, so I found tremendous authenticity in the words of Hurston as she describes Janie's experience of battering. I have heard

these words from female survivors of sexual and domestic violence as
they finally break the cycle of violence. Jody slaps Janie for the burned
dinner and leaves.

> Janie stood where he left her for unmeasured time and thought. She
> stood there until something fell off the shelf inside her. Then she went
> inside to see what it was. It was her image of Jody tumbled down and
> shattered. But looking at it she saw it never was the flesh and blood figure
> of her dreams. Just something she had grabbed up to drape her dreams
> over. In a way she turned her back upon the image where it lay and looked
> further. . . . She found that she had a host of thoughts she had never
> expressed to him, and numerous emotions she had never let Jody know
> about. Things packed up and put away in parts of her heart where he
> could never find them. She was saving up feelings for some man she had
> never seen.[18]

When her self-esteem, her self-worth, are based on illusions and self-
alienating values, Janie sins. She begins to understand her sin when she
gains "a deeper sense of community"[19] than she had before achieved in
her life. For the black woman, Cannon tells me through Hurston's work,
sin is being outside the community and the life-sustaining bread of
survival that this community bakes and passes from one generation to
the next. There are truths to the black woman's experience that can be
named and in their naming be returned to the community, even as
Hurston sought to return to her community the harvest of what had
been sown in her. It seems she did succeed: Cannon quotes June Jordan
in this passage:

> But the book [*Their Eyes Were Watching God*] gives us more: the story
> unrolls a fabulous, written-film of Blacklife freed from the constraints of
> oppression; here we may learn Black possibilities of ourselves if we could
> ever escape the hateful and alien context that has so deeply disturbed and
> mutilated our rightful efflorescence—*as people*.[20]

In Love and in Trouble: The Contrary Women of Alice Walker

In some ways Alice Walker's writing is much like that of other black
women writers—Toni Morrison, June Jordan, Paule Marshall—in that
all of these writers find that the black woman's quest for herself and her
self-knowledge is pursued *through* the black community and its survival, not in spite of or outside it. But Barbara Christian points out that
it is the contrariness of Alice Walker's female characters, what I might

call their orneriness, that so distinguishes her work. The self of the black woman is achieved through the community, all right, but sometimes by challenging its dominant convictions when these convictions are not life-giving.

In my view this is nowhere better expressed than in Walker's novel *Meridian*. In Chapter Three I have already discussed the manner in which the main character, Meridian, redefines motherhood in her life in order to challenge the stifling, personality-destroying aspects of the legacy of black motherhood. Meridian gives her son away in order to save him from her own guilt and self-doubt. In Walker's view some white feminists are convinced that motherhood in general is a dead end for women. Walker, however, in *Meridian* and elsewhere pursues the theme that children represent the sacred, the continuity of life.

As I wrote in the article that appeared in *Christianity and Crisis*, the novel *Meridian* is Walker's exploration of the spiritual truth of her conviction that for black women, the source of creativity of life and the wellspring of change reside in their connection with the heritage of all black women.[21] This theme reappears constantly; certainly it is the direction pursued in *In Search of Our Mother's Gardens*.

Meridian seeks her identity through the legacy left her and other black women in the lives of, for example, Sojourner Truth and Ida B. Wells. Meridian believes in the sacredness and continuity of life, and in the African spirituality of animism—the spirit that inhabits all life. She discovers, against impossible odds, the societal forces that, in a perverted and distorted racist society, inhibit the natural growth of the living creation toward freedom. She learns that "this existence extended beyond herself to those around her because, in fact, the years in America had created them One Life."[22]

Walker's conviction that life itself is sacred is manifested in the contrariness of the character Meridian as she resists the fashionable revolutionary violence embraced by some in the civil rights movement. In *Meridian* Walker is saying that those who take up the struggle to change society will have to do so by struggling to change themselves. And unless they defeat in themselves what they seek to defeat in society, their own revolution will come to naught.[23] Early in the novel someone says of Meridian, "She thinks she's God." It may be more accurate to say that for Walker it is life that is divine, and the self-loving, self-respecting black woman who allies herself with life can embody its divinity.

Because of her intense focus on the integrity of black women's selves, Walker has been labeled a feminist. Yet she has distinctly objected to

the content of this definition as it has been articulated by white feminists and has actually coined a new word, "womanist," to describe her
vision of the wholeness of black women's selves.

In a critical essay on Walker's *In Love and Trouble,* Christian draws
attention to the two quotations with which Walker begins this collection of short stories. The first, by the West African writer Elechi Amadi,
describes the contrary spirit of a young African girl whose society so
constricts her life that she has been betrothed since she was eight days
old. The other quotation Walker uses is from the poet Rainer Maria
Rilke.

> People have (with the help of conventions) oriented all their solutions
> toward the easy and toward the easiest side of the easy; but it is clear that
> we must hold to what is difficult; everything in Nature grows and defends
> itself in its own way and is characteristically and spontaneously itself,
> seeks at all costs to be so and against all opposition.[24]

Later in this suggestive essay Christian says that "in order to defend
the selves they know they are, they must hold to what is difficult."[25]
The constraints of black women's lives are so numerous that to exist as
a self they are, by definition, in trouble. Much of the trouble, but by no
means all of it, comes from sexism; but this is always a sexism interpreted by race.

Of the many horrors depicted in these short stories, the violence
directed by the father toward "The Child Who Favored Daughter" was
the hardest for me to read. The Child and her Father are antagonists
because for the Father, the Child too much resembles his much-beloved
older sister. The Father believes, however, that this sister betrayed him
by having an affair with the white man "in whose cruel, hot, and lonely
fields he, her brother, worked." Despite the fact that "Daughter," the
sister's nickname, returns home insane from this "love" affair, he can
never forgive her. "He could not forgive her the love that knew nothing
of master and slave. For though her own wound was a bitter one and in
the end fatal, he bore a hurt throughout his life that slowly poisoned
him." So, when he finds proof of a similar betrayal by his own Child, the
Father beats and mutilates her. "In a world where innocence and guilt
became further complicated by questions of color and race, he felt
hesitant and weary of living, as though all the world were out to trick
him." Though Walker's work frequently portrays in agonizing veracity
the violence of black men against black women and children, she does
not allow the questions of "innocence and guilt" to be answered simply.
The complex warpings of human relationships that have been woven by

the "years in America" are each examined for their contributions to the sin and guilt, innocence and redemption of each character.

In the world defined by sexism, Walker's women are always "other." In the world defined by racism, Walker's women are always "other." And because they are always "other," they grow against the grain. This seems to be the logic of her use of the Rilke quotation: It is in the encounter with difficulty that the self grows and defines itself as over against.[26] The black woman may not wish for struggle; in fact, often Walker's characters explicitly embody her anger that things must be so tough for black women. But these women are not victims. Like the characters of Zora Neale Hurston, whose work Walker has done so much to redeem from the obscurity into which it risked being relegated, they are survivors, most of them, and sometimes, especially in such works as *The Color Purple,* they prevail against all odds.

The Difference Race Makes: Sin and the Self

The legacy of slavery bequeathed American women is made up of parts of selves: Black women have been cast as the body and nature, and have sought, in their quest for wholeness, the integrity found within culture, within the civilization the black community has forged as its bulwark against the dehumanizing elements of racism. For the black woman, then, to be a self is to be an "other" within the otherness of black people and to make a way out of no way. The besetting sin of black women consists in turning away from their community and their ancestors, in denying their heritage of social responsibility to their people and to oppressed women everywhere.

White middle-class women have been cast as the soul of culture, and, in their search for wholeness, have sought to recover their own embodiedness. This has taken many forms, from the nature-centered writings of Susan Griffin to the practical *Our Bodies, Ourselves*[27]; white women have sought to be a self in a body and to resist being cast as the island of civilization in the capitalist jungle. (Often, however, this economic aspect of their quest, arising from a social analysis of the peculiarly different oppressions of women according to race and class as well as sex, has not been made explicit.)

Valerie Saiving has taught me and, I believe, other white women, that for white middle-class women sin consists precisely in the diffusion of their selves that their role as "the feminine" in modern culture causes. Their diffusion into the spirit of home and hearth results in triviality and distractibility, sentimentality, and, interestingly, Saiving writes, an "inability to respect the boundaries of privacy."[28]

The question I now ask myself is whether I should not, therefore, include the desire to bond with black women under an *undifferentiated* label of "sisterhood" as sin—precisely in the same vein in which Saiving describes the besetting sin of white women as disrespect for the "boundaries."

Is this disrespect for the boundaries of cultural difference, racial differences, a good or bad thing? This may be a somewhat simplistic way of asking the question, but it was the subject of the exchange of letters between Carol Christ and myself in the pages of *Christianity and Crisis.*

Part of Christ's response to my article on the literature of black women and its articulation of difference was as follows:

> Confrontation with the African spirit world calls all of us to examine our own connections to the spirits of our ancestors and to the spirits of our land. I am not suggesting that honoring the spirits of our ancestors will exhaust for white women the significance of the African and Afro-American spirit worlds, but I do believe that it is one way to begin to learn what black women's lives and literatures can mean for us as white women. We need to be careful of universalizing, of course, and we need to resist the temptation to say that we have now defined the meaning of black women's literature. But unless we can move through awareness of difference to an understanding of connection within difference, we leave both black women and ourselves isolated from each other. I don't believe black women want that. I know I don't.[29]

My reply celebrated the gifts Carol Christ's writings have represented for white women. I wrote, however, that I stood by my central thesis: "As white women we must now live with and explore the *difference* color makes, because that is the agenda black womanists are setting."

It is the word "connection" that keeps returning in conversations with white women on this subject. Difference is fine and good, I hear, but how do I connect? Christ identifies some of the temptations of white women: universalizing, defining, and so on. But I believe connection is a temptation all its own. I feel it in myself as I write this book. I want nothing more than to "solve" this problem with black women and to connect with them; to bond with them and to share what is, for me, the genuine warmth and wonderfulness of what white feminists have been calling sisterhood.

I believe, however, that the desire to uncritically bond with black women without respecting the boundaries of difference is an extension of the Saiving/Plaskow insight on sin for women.[30] I would like to use the remainder of this chapter to turn, once again, to Catherine Keller's work on sexism, separation, and the self, and to apply the thesis that connection across cultural boundaries belongs to the temptations of white women and not only to their graces. Yet to paraphrase Walker, the questions of innocence and guilt are complicated by questions of sex and gender as well as by color and race.

Sexism, Separation, Connection, and the Self

I start from this assumption: that the history of black and white women in America *makes a difference* when we begin to talk about sin and the self in white feminist theology. On the basis of this primacy of difference I am assuming that connectedness may constitute sin for white women on some occasions—i.e., when cross-cultural, racial differences between women are encountered.

One of the sources of a theory of connectedness in white feminist theology today is process theology and its ancestor in the faith, Protestant liberalism.[31] It may be more accurate to say that rather than a *source* for white feminist theology, many feminists (*sic*) have found process theology to be largely congenial. Many aspects of process theology make sense to white middle-class women. Since women's (*sic*) experience has been denied as human experience, white feminist theology usually begins by claiming the validity of that experience and process theology has a framework that permits this claim. Further, the androgynous God concept of process theology is attractive to those who are tired of fighting the "God the Father" battles. Process theology's appreciation of relationality in human life and its significance for knowledge of God is another area of common work.[32]

But as Sandra Harding warns, patriarchal theories, no matter what their strengths, carry with them views that may prove undermining to the advance of feminist thought. I believe process theology imports into theological discourse a dualistic worldview under the guise of relationality. Dominant process perspectives in theology need to be critically reexamined because they sustain both an alienated picture of humanity and a dualistic worldview. This alienation manifests itself in an implicit identification of the *imago dei* in humanity with mental process, betraying its rationalist roots. The result is a split between the human self and the social order. Romanticism, too, is visible in the remnant (chastened by the twentieth century) progressive assumptions about human historical development. These views require white feminists (it is interesting to note that no black female theologian or ethicist has chosen a process perspective for her work) to be extremely wary of process theology as a benign face of patriarchy. It should be recalled that the black woman (and to a certain extent all nondominant peoples) symbolizes the body and materiality in American history; the white woman symbolizes the soul of culture; the white male continues to be the symbol of rationality.

One example from a prominent process theologian will suffice. John Cobb's *Process Theology as Political Theology* provides a telling example of God's working to offer us "God's future intention for the world" in the political process. His choice is listening to a good lecture in which "the ideas offered there are different from those which one had in advance. . . ."[33] This single quotation clearly reveals the fact that in process theology, ideas are where the action is. At the level of reason, all conflicts can be resolved into a harmonious system, or at least reduced to contrast. "Political theology favors, also in the political scale, the transformation of differences into contrasts. That means that diverse interests and *ideals* are to be united in a higher synthesis in the present."[34]

This higher synthesis also allows tremendous (mental) freedom. "In Whitehead's vision we are free to constitute ourselves *out of our world,* but what the world is, out of which we constitute ourselves, is given. We transcend that world, so that *we are responsible for what we make of ourselves,* but in the transcending we are still chiefly shaped by what we transcend."[35] Genuine difference is submerged in a higher mental synthesis that promises freedom. Failure to grasp this freedom is the problem of the particular individual.

But concretely, what might this mean for a poor woman? What might it mean for a battered woman? Is the poor woman capable of transcending her situation and achieving a higher mental synthesis? The battered woman, the survivor of rape or incest, the single mother, are they to blame if they do not choose to "act responsibly?" As Kate Cannon has so trenchantly pointed out, financial wherewithal clearly underlies white, Western male-dominated ethical theories of freedom and choice by the individual. Does this bode well for the importation of process viewpoints into white feminist theories?

The liberal tradition separates the knowledge of God from the physical and material situation of human beings and locates it in an artificially distorted version of human mental process. This is as inadequate in developing a trenchant critique of the social origins of sin, and the social sources of salvation, as is the theological perspective that places God outside the world and reduces God's capacity for self-revelation to dropping stones on us. Perhaps the former is even more inadequate because it succeeds in homogenizing judgment and reducing sin to maladjustment, eviscerating the capacity for a trenchant social criticism.

God's Fierce Whimsy, the analysis of Christian feminism and theological education by the Mudflower Collective, contains the line "we cannot be whole in only one area of our lives."[36] There is no way for me, as a white feminist, to be anything other than a "recovering racist." It is a characteristic of the liberal trajectory in theology, represented by the process critique above, to claim that we have gotten "beyond racism" and to note "how far we have come." In an exchange of letters between Carter Heyward, a white woman, and Kate Cannon that appears in the pages of *God's Fierce Whimsy,* Carter says the following:

> The problem with white liberalism (I don't know about black liberalism) is that liberal white men and women do not advocate real relation, not mutual relation, but rather a patronizing sort of relation based on hand-me-down affections. White liberals "love" black people; white liberal men "love" all women (white women and women of color)—as long as we're not threatening to change the name of the power game.[37]

The conflicts between white and black, female and male, are not accessible to transcendence. There is the history of slavery that lies behind us, the Jim Crow era between us, the economic apartheid before us. What then?

Kate writes to Carter, "You and I have shared with each other the experience of being molested as children."[38] Not abstract ideologies but real molestation forms part of the history of each of these theologians and ethicists as they both struggle with real relation that does not run away from its own history. Kate writes to Carter, "It's like I said in our discussion of *The Color Purple:* rebirth is only possible when we face terror face to face."[39]

Yet the role that white women have been dealt by American culture means that I have been socialized to connect across difference in order to provide the "cement of society" (This phrase was often used during the Constantinian era in discussions of the relationship between church and state.) Whereas the church once provided the cohesion that united societies internally so that they would be able to wage war externally, in nineteenth-century America the church was disestablished and that cohesive role fell to white women. This point is excellently made by Jean Bethke Elshtain in her study *Women and War.*[40] As a member of the white women's movement, I have not confronted the terror of difference. Instead, I have sought to obliterate it in "connections."

The point I have tried to convey in this latter section is that white women's selves have been forged by the dominant culture to provide the connections: This learning has its strengths, but in relation to cultural and racial difference, it should be defined as sin for white women.

It is striking how often the metaphor of webs and spinning appears in the writing of white women: *Reweaving the Web of Life, Feminism and Non-Violence, From a Broken Web: Separation, Sexism, and Self, Spinning a Sacred Yarn, Websters' New Intergalactic Wickedary of the English Language*. These and related metaphors, such as that of connection found in Beverly Harrison's *Making the Connections,* have prompted Keller to write, "The women's (*sic*) movement glistens with the mischief of Web and Weaver."[41]

In her book *From a Broken Web,* Keller's main argument is that patriarchal selves are formed by separation and alienation: "Only a self forged in the image of an impenetrable inner hardness, mistaken for integrity, could separate itself from the matrix of all life."[42] Feminism (*sic*) affirms the connectedness of self (her last chapter is entitled "The Spider's Genius"). Keller contends:

> We arise from the matrix; we redesign its elements; we are woven back into the matrix. This is the religious action of reconnecting. As the word itself tells us, matrix is always *mater,* mother. No inert matter here; there is no such thing. All beings come tied to the matrix of interconnection by what poet Judy Grahn calls "the one true cord,/the umbilical line/unwinding into meaning,/transformation,/web of thought and caring and connection."[43]

Yes, we can quote *The Color Purple* here, as does Keller and virtually every white feminist I know. But I find that I no longer want to merge uncritically with Celie's observation: "One day when I was sitting quiet and feeling like a motherless child, which I was, it come to me: that feeling of being part of everything, not separate at all. I knew that if I cut a tree, my arm would bleed."[44]

Why not? Sheer orneriness? No, because I must also separate since "Womanist is to feminist as purple is to lavender."[45] The selves of white women have been formed by connectivity. They have also been formed by the class prerogative of whiteness. It is telling that Keller relies so heavily on Whitehead for her articulation of the self and its formation. This quotation had particular meaning for me: "To *selve* this world is to *own* it: 'my process of being myself is my origination from my possession of the world.' "[46]

Unless white women can form selves capable of standing against the dominant culture sufficiently to actually *hear* the class prerogative of a line like that, I believe I and other white women will be ceaselessly seduced into uncritical acceptance of the white-assumed privilege of owning the world. Keller's is a complex book, and I have hardly done its valuable insights justice here. But it also illustrates Sandra Harding's point all too well. Patriarchal theories such as process theology carry enormous white, Western male freight that can sometimes be unconsciously imported into white feminism when we adopt these frameworks for our work.[47]

I should make it clear that I am beginning to believe that the jolts of traditional theological categories such as sin and evil are necessary in encountering the class bias of white feminism even as I believe there are experiential truths to the lived reality of white women's lives. Any patriarchal viewpoint will carry both resources and liabilities: One of the liabilities of the connectivities of theories such as process thought is its obliteration of differences between women. For white women the route to selfhood must lie both in claiming the truths of their lived experience and in being deeply suspicious of their connections to the dominant American culture and its class and race biases. Keller advocates a "hermeneutics of connection."[48] Along with Harding, I believe that white feminists need to be "conceptually unstable." We need to employ both a "hermeneutics of suspicion" and a "hermeneutics of connection." And I believe the order is important.

True, the *connections* are significant. But what I believe has been obscured in identifying connection with bonding is the fact that these connections may be like flint on tinder—they produce the sparks of creativity that have been kindled by conflict. But let me not coin too romantic an image that evokes the safety of hearth fires. These sparks that fly when the connections are made by facing the terror of real conflict can burn, and they can hurt.

In the foregoing chapters I have not spent much time articulating the differences between feminist or womanist viewpoints that are explicitly Christian and those that are not. There are good reasons for this: Many black womanists and white feminists do not believe these distinctions are central. It is more often patriarchal theologians who wish to divide women in this way. An extremely important exception to this is Christology. Jesus plays a very different role in the lives of black and white women.

6

Jesus and Christa

O God,
through the image of a woman*
crucified on the cross
I understand at last.

For over half of my life
I have been ashamed
of the scars I bear.
These scars tell an ugly story,
a common story,
about a girl who is the victim
when a man acts out his fantasies.

In the warmth, peace and sunlight of your presence
I was able to uncurl the tightly clenched fists.
For the first time
I felt your suffering presence with me
in that event.
I have known you as a vulnerable baby,
as a brother, and as a father.
Now I know you as a woman.
You were there with me
as the violated girl
caught in helpless suffering.

The chains of shame and fear
no longer bind my heart and body.
A slow fire of compassion and forgiveness
is kindled.
My tears fall now
for man as well as woman.

. . . .

*In a Toronto church the figure of a woman, arms outstretched as if crucified, was hung below the cross in the chancel.

You were not ashamed of your wounds.
You showed them to Thomas
as marks of your ordeal and death.
I will no longer hide these wounds of mine.
I will bear them gracefully.
They tell a resurrection story.

"By His Wounds You Have Been Healed"
1 Peter 2:24, anonymous[1]

In a class on "Women in Crisis" that I team-teach with Rosemary Ruether, a white woman related her experience of being raped at a deserted dump when she went to drop off some trash. "I lay there, wondering if he would come back and kill me," she recalled. As she lay on the heap of trash, injured and bleeding and wondering whether she was about to be killed, she had a vision of Jesus as a crucified woman who said to her from the cross, "You don't have to be ashamed, I know what you are suffering." After hearing this student's story I came across the poem above. I copied it and hung it on the door of my office. Few weeks go by in which some female student—ethnic and minority as well as white—does not stop by, read the poem, and tell me of how she has been abused.

When I first saw Edwina Sandys's sculpture "Christa" in the Cathedral of St. John the Divine in New York City, I was unsettled and disliked it intensely. The figure is of an unclothed woman crowned with thorns, arms outstretched in the form of a crucifix but without a cross behind it. I said to my companion, "Women are routinely crucified in contemporary society. This will tend to legitimate violence against them." Yet since then, because of the healing these statues seem to evoke in women who have survived sexual and domestic violence, I have revised my view. "Christa" is not experienced[2] by many women as legitimating violence against them but as identifying with their pain and freeing them from the guilt that somehow, because of the original sin of being female, they deserved what they got.

I relate this turn of events in order to do two things: to indicate that Christology is qualitatively different from the theological subjects discussed in the preceding chapters in terms of the emotional content of the debate it has inspired; and to turn the subject of Christology and the difference race makes from the limitations of the "Can a Male Savior Save Women?" discussion it has centered on for so long. The objections of Daly and other post-Christian feminists to a male savior figure are well known; they will not be exhaustively reported here. During the late eighties, as Christian feminism defines itself, the debate has moved elsewhere. If one has chosen to remain a Christian, then one must deal with the central figure of that tradition, Jesus the Christ.

Some additional considerations: Black women have already noted the different role Jesus plays in the black community and their disagreements with many white feminist Christologies.[3] But in the recent past, black and white women who do Christology have been radically redefining that task once they have chosen to do it. Whereas several years ago the difference race made in Christology might have been limited to the question of whether or not one regarded Christology as central, today the differences are more subtle. The Christological ground is shifting. This is due in part to the contributions of both women theologians of the two-thirds world and black American women who have come to see the Christological problem in a new light. It is also due to dialogue among white feminists.

A Short History of Some Problems in White Feminist Christology

Just as the contemporary white feminist reflection on sin can be said to date from Valerie Saiving's essay, so the modern Christological reflection can be said to date from the "Jesus was a feminist" writings of the early 1970s.[4] The basis for this assertion is what is regarded as Jesus' remarkably egalitarian, at times even preferential, treatment of women. Virginia Mollenkott argues that despite his knowledge of the rabbinical customs of his time, Jesus intentionally violated these customs—especially in regard to their restrictions on women. Examples of this behavior often cited are the Samaritan woman, the hemorrhaging woman, the adulterous woman, the mistaken woman, and others.[5]

In the fall of 1978, Judith Plaskow published a significant dissent from this type of argument entitled "Christian Feminism and Anti-Judaism." In the main Plaskow objected both to an uncritical lumping together of all patriarchal attitudes onto "rabbis," when the rabbinate became an institution only after the fall of Jerusalem, and to the identification of all Jewish attitudes toward women with only a comparatively few misogynist statements. She charged that "Feminist research projects onto Judaism the failure of the Christian tradition unambiguously to renounce sexism" and points to this as another example of the type of anti-Semitism that has enabled Christians to avoid taking responsibility for their own sins for two millennia. In short, the price for Jesus the feminist was yet another slam at the Jews, hardly a dissent from traditional patriarchal theology.[6]

Because the "Jesus was a feminist" position needed a foil for dramatically presenting Jesus' objections to patriarchy, white feminism set up first-century Judaism as unrelievedly patriarchal. Christian patriarchalism is instead projected back onto Judaism. Plaskow notes, "The 'Other' who is the recipient of these projections is, of course, the same Other who has received the shadow side of the Christian self since the beginnings of the Christian tradition. Feminists should know better!"[7]

That, of course, is what we are exploring here: White feminists are only just beginning to explore the ways of changing their theoretical underpinnings to respect the "otherness" of other women.[8] In 1987 Plaskow updated her original piece with "Christian Feminist Anti-Judaism: Some New Considerations." These new considerations can be broadly described as the nuances that ten years of living with this sensitivity has and has not brought. On the one hand, Plaskow warns Jewish women not to see anti-Semitism in every criticism of Jewish patriarchalism; on the other hand, she cautions that many white feminists "have not found a consistent way to talk about Jesus that is in harmony with their concerns about Jewish-Christian relations."[9]

In my response to Plaskow, in the same journal, I raised the same methodological point in relation to anti-Semitism that this book is raising in relation to racism; it is a point that is an extension of precisely what Plaskow claims about the context in which Christian feminists do Christology. I wrote, "I am always, to paraphrase Mary Pellauer, a 'recovering anti-Semite.' . . . I must be aware of the thousands of ways the inheritance of anti-Semitism will impact my thought and action, and I must work to bring these to consciousness in order to recover from this bias."[10] What I advocated is the "hermeneutic of suspicion" applied to one's own work, the suspicion that in a society that is structurally anti-Semitic, *bias is inevitable*. We must therefore structure white Christian feminist theology with that premise in mind. Despite my legitimate experience of a female oppression, I will inevitably carry with me the class, race, and sex biases of my culture—they permeate it like the air we breathe. The best I can do is work to divest myself of these biases by subjecting them to critical consciousness.

As is well known, white Christian feminist reflection on Jesus as the Christ has gone far beyond the first steps of "Jesus' feminism." Rosemary Ruether's well-known essay "Can a Male Savior Save Women?" answered the Christology problem for white feminism by arguing that the fact that God in Christ became male is inseparable from the type of male he became. By his liberating praxis, Jesus empties the patriarchalism of God the Father and reemerges as the "prophetic, iconoclastic Christ."[11]

This view of Jesus the liberator, identifying with "the poor, the downtrodden, those who hunger and thirst,"[12] is a more dynamic Christology and one that is closely related to the position Latin American liberation theologians have taken on the person and work of Jesus. (Parenthetically, it should be noted that this approach to Christology also has marked influence among black American liberation theologians, both male and female.) Yet, in a more subtle fashion, this liberation Christology still depends on contrast with the surrounding Judaism for its effect, as "Christ is seen as critic rather than vindicator of the present hierarchical social order."[13] Plaskow observes that in subsequent books Ruether has retreated from the startling insights into Christian anti-Semitism that she offered in her early *Faith and Fratricide* (1974).[14]

Another trend within more recent white feminist Christology has been the so-called "relational Christology" of feminists such as Carter Heyward. Heyward's *Redemption of God* (1982) and later *Our Passion for Justice* (1984) propose that Christology comes about through human relationality. Human beings bring God into the world.[15] Heyward quotes a poem by Dorothee Soelle:

> and what will David do without Jonathan
> and Karl Marx without Engels
> and Mary without Elizabeth
> and Ché Guevara without Fidel
> and Jesus without John
> and Dietrich without Eberhard?

"And what," continues Heyward, "will I do without you?"[16] Relational Christologies shift the weight of Christological reflection onto the Pentecostal community and its struggle for the justice of God. It avoids Christocentrism, what Soelle has called Christofascism.[17]

In *Metaphors for the Contemporary Church,* I indicated my adherence to a Christology of relation. In "A Christ for the Body," I asserted that "a Christology of Relation insists emphatically that we are all, and this includes God, in this together. God has chosen to give human beings responsibility, and it is our fault if we do not take it. Likewise, it is to our credit if we do."[18] But despite both Heyward's and my effort to do a Christology that avoids anti-Semitism (Heyward's *Redemption of God* includes a powerful chapter on the theological insights of Elie Wiesel, and the *Metaphors'* chapter on Christology begins with a discussion of Christian chauvinism in relation to Jesus the Jew), this Christology still relies, to some degree, on contrasting Jesus with his Jewish milieu. Plaskow points this out in relation to a line from Heyward's *Our Passion for Justice*. She quotes Heyward, " 'Jesus . . . seemed to perceive that his work would involve a radical shift in consciousness . . . from an emphasis, for example, on ritual to right-relationship.' I don't believe that Heyward believes that Judaism is unconcerned with right-relationship—she wrote her dissertation, after all, on right-relationship in Elie Wiesel—but it is difficult to read this sentence in any other way.[19]

This sentence startled me into the realization that the method of difference makes a Christology of relation impossible. Relationality without the shock of recognition of the uniqueness and difference of the "other" results in a Christology that obliterates the history of the Jews, as it will also obliterate the difference between the Jesus of the black community and any configuration of a white feminist Christ.[20]

"Who Do You Say That I Am?"

In her book *Faith, Feminism, and the Christ,* Patricia Wilson-Kastner begins her Christology with this question. Wilson-Kastner's answer is that Christ is "the agent of wholeness and reconciler of fragmentation in the world."[21] Wilson-Kastner has decided that the universe is moving toward "wholeness" (there is a strong process influence in her work)[22] and therefore anything that disrupts wholeness is to be rejected: "Ultimately, I would insist on a basic assumption that everything must mean something, and find its significance and fulfillment in unity with all that is. Everything makes sense as part of a whole, or it makes no sense at all; all unites and grows as a whole, or there is no real growth and life at all, merely a passing illusion."[23]

What happened in the incarnation is that "Jesus became flesh so as to show forth the love of God among us, a love which is not merely an expression of good will, but the power of an energy which is the heart, core, and cohesive force of the universe."[24] Wilson-Kastner's liberal feminism leads her to the belief that feminism is a quest for "wholeness." Her feminist Christology, therefore, is a type of "New Adam" universalized.

> In Christ we see something of how a divinely renewed humanity acts in the world. Christ is not simply the new male person, but one who shows all persons how to live. . . . Only within such a context, with such concerns, can a feminist Christology emerge. Such a Christology will be feminist not in the sense of making Christ into a female, or merely

attributing feminine characteristics to him, but in understanding the significance of Christ as embodying values and ideals which also are sought for and valued by feminists.[25]

Feminism equals wholeness equals bonding equals connection equals relationality.

Wilson-Kastner is not unaware of the tension between the particulars of experience and the notion of the universal in theology that she asserts. She counters that an adequate theology must include the particulars by subordinating them to the entire human community. "To gain new insights today, one needs to take into account a variety of perspectives, and find a firmer, more plausible base for theology. That base must involve both the whole human community, not just a part of that community, and the God who is the source of that whole."[26] She acknowledges that "respecting individual diversity" is a complex task. Yet she deliberately makes the concrete particulars of human experience secondary and finally renders them dysfunctional. She discounts the particularity of "women's experience, or blacks', or Native Americans', or white males,'" rendering them ancillary to "human community." In a parallel fashion, she asserts the concrete particularity of Jesus but subordinates the individual Jesus of Nazareth to the Christ who overcomes all dualisms and merges, at his Resurrection, into the church. So rather than a real person, the Christ is the one exception, the only one who is whole.[27]

Like most liberals, Wilson-Kastner sees difference, diversity, and otherness as being uniformly evil. The result is that any particulars that contribute to the reality of difference are uniformly to be subsumed under the universal, abstract ALL. Christ becomes the vehicle for the realization of that ALL.

> Because of the unity of divinity and humanity in the crucified Christ, the God who is self-giving and receiving accepts the fragmented human condition into the divine life for healing, and the humanity of Christ gathers into himself all the forces of alienation and destruction active in his own death. *All the dualisms which divide, separate, cause pain, and support oppression and lack of communion with the other* are all gathered together at the crucifixion, and Christ receives them. . . . Everything converges in him, and in his person and activity everything finds wholeness and meaning.[28]

There is no clash, no conflict, no energy, no passion in this Christology that finds Jesus the least offensive of these. As such I find it inadequate to meet the rigors of feminist theology in a suffering world where to be poor, to be abused, to be black, and to be female cannot be universalized.

"Who Do You Say That I Am?" Continued

Classical Christology describes white theological dilemmas; when you're poor and black Jesus is "all one needs!"[29] Jesus was so much all she needed that Sojourner Truth never had to read the Bible—couldn't, in fact: "Can't read a letter." She had only one text: "My text is, 'When I found Jesus!' "[30] In *The Prayer Tradition of Black People,* Harold Carter records a prayer by a black slave woman who prayed to the Jesus who suffered along with her, who would not fail to come to her as another who knew what it was to endure.

> Come to we, dear Massa Jesus. De sun, he hot too much, de road am dat long and boggy (sandy) and we ain't got no buggy for send and fetch Ooner. But Massa, you 'member how you walked dat hard walk up Calvary and ain't weary but tink about we all dat way. We know you ain't weary for to come to we. We pick out de torns, de prickles, de brier, de backslidin' and de quarrel and de sin out of you path so dey shan't hurt Ooner pierce feet no more.[31]

Modern black women writers of fiction are not classical theologians. Like Hurston, many may not themselves be Christian, but they faithfully report the idiom of black people; and the religion of black people, a distinctive Christianity, is a syntax for this idiom. It was said of Emily Dickinson that "she used Christianity more than she let it use her." The same can be said of black women writers. Often the ironies of the contrast between white Christian belief and white Christian practice form a dramatic premise, as in Alice Walker's short story "The Welcome Table." Sometimes, as in *Moses, Man of the Mountain,* Hurston's allegorical satire on the similarities between Voudou and Christianity, the claims of black American experience on the Christian narratives are made. And, in *Jonah's Gourd Vine,* the lyric of black preaching is preserved. Of Reverend John Buddy Pearson, Hurston wrote that "I have tried to present a Negro preacher who is neither funny nor an imitation Puritan ram-rod in pants. Just the human being and poet that he must be to succeed in a Negro pulpit. . . ."[32]

The figure of the poor Jesus, perhaps "Massa" but also in need of a cup of water after the way up Calvary, as the way to approach Christology, is obviously not unknown to Alice Walker. Her short story "The Welcome Table" articulates these themes. But Walker also adds

her orneriness; in "The Welcome Table" the old black woman who
dares to worship at a white church is not a romantic figure of poverty,
and she may just have gone out of her mind.

An old black woman in her "withered," "rusty" "Sunday-go-to-
meeting clothes," "angular and lean and the color of poor gray Georgia
earth, beaten by king cotton and the extreme weather," shows up at a
white "sanctuary of Christian worship." She sits down; the white
minister kindly tries to get rid of her. So does an usher. "It was the
[white] ladies who finally did what to them had to be done. Daring their
burly indecisive husbands to throw the old colored woman out they
made their point. God, mother, country, earth, church. It involved all
that and well they knew it."[33]

How well Walker knows the compact a racist society has made with
white women. To be the soul of culture, the cement of society, white
women cannot be contaminated by the presence of the exploitable
body, the black woman.[34] So it is they who force their husbands to pick
up the offending body, smelling of "the fermenting scent of onionskins
and rotting greens" and toss her out "back under the cold blue sky."[35]

As she tries to get her bearings outside, who should come along but
Jesus, "wearing an immaculate white, long dress trimmed in gold
around the neck and hem, and a red, a bright red, cape." When he got
up close to the old woman, all he said was "Follow me." She starts to
tell Jesus "how many years she had cooked for them, cleaned for them,
nursed them." He nods, he smiles with a sad smile, but he does not
speak. They go on down the road until the old woman walks herself to
death. Those who had seen her "high-stepping down the highway" said
she was alone. They wondered where she was going. "They guessed
maybe she had relatives across the river, some miles away, but none of
them really knew."[36]

This may be the white Jesus, identical to the picture the old woman
had taken from the house of her white employer, but he's the one master
to whom even the white masters have to kowtow. In fact, he's no longer
even one of them. He's an outcast, too.

Layer upon layer of irony, of reversal. The white Jesus is passing by
the church, the pious white Christian women reject a poor black
woman, the church is not the church, Christianity may not even be
Christian. Walker faithfully portrays the faith of the black community in
"Massa Jesus," but no one really knows whether there's anybody
across that river.

Some black women, notably those who have chosen to work in
Christian theology and ethics, do know that there's somebody across
the river. Consistent with the communitarian base of black women's

definition of experience, this knowledge is linked to the history of black survival in white America. In her book *White Women's Christ and Black Women's Jesus,* Jacquelyn Grant identifies the inadequacies of white feminist Christologies for black women in the appeal to experience, which, as we have seen, has consistently been an appeal to white experience. "Slavery and segregation have created such a gulf between these women, that White feminists' common assumption that all women are in the same situation with respect to sexism is difficult to understand when history so clearly tells us a different story."[37] The reality of Jesus in the black community, so vividly portrayed by Walker, is part of that experience of difference.

White feminist theology is racist not merely because it uses only white sources, though consistent use of only white sources reveals ideological blindness (despite her claims to universalism, Wilson-Kastner does not cite a single black or ethnic woman in her sources for *Faith, Feminism, and the Christ*). White feminist theology is racist because it has assumed the prerogative of naming the world for black women on the basis of white women's definitions of experience. Grant quotes Joel Kovel's definition of racism as "the tendency of a society to degrade and do violence to people on the basis of race, and by whatever mediations may exist for this purpose."[38] What I believe I as a white woman have done in misnaming this movement "feminism" instead of "white feminism" is to assume the racist posture of the power to define all of reality. I know that I need to recall Kovel's definition of a racist society as one in which the dominant race has co-opted the power of definition and reduced the nondominant to an object.[39]

The role of Jesus differs profoundly in the womanist tradition from that in the white women's movement, both historically and on the contemporary scene. For womanists, Jesus is the one who came specifically on behalf of those whose cultural lot was cast as the world's beasts of burden (Hurston).

Yet it is also Grant's contention that black women should take seriously white feminist Christological analysis, especially with reference to the exclusive emphasis of the black church on Jesus' maleness and its relationship to exclusive practice with regard to women in ministry. Grant quotes the nineteenth-century womanist Jarena Lee, who claimed the right of women to preach because ". . . the Saviour died for the woman as well as for the man."[40] In an argument that seems to be quite similar to that made by Wilson-Kastner, Grant states, "If Christ is a Saviour of all, then it is the humanity—the wholeness—of Christ which is significant."[41]

But despite this common assertion of "wholeness," Grant does not relinquish the particularity of Jesus, especially his poverty, for a more universal Christ. For Grant, Jesus' birth among "the least" means that "the challenge . . . for contemporary Black women is to begin a serious analysis which addresses the structural nature of poverty."[42] A further challenge is to develop a constructive Christology based on womanist experience as it is in turn based in the entire black community.[43]

Jesus the Ancestor

Several black female seminarians have suggested to me that Jesus' significance for the black community goes even beyond his suffering and identification with poverty and may be related to African ancestor worship.[44] And one black writer, Toni Cade Bambara, has been particularly influential in helping me to understand the difference between black and white thought. In her novel/prose poem *The Salt Eaters,* Bambara is concerned with the healing of Velma Henry, the tireless worker for good causes who has just attempted suicide. Velma is sick because she has adapted to the linear progressions of Western society: "drugs, prisons, alcohol, the schools, rape, battered women, abused children . . . the nuclear power issue. . . ."[45] A different understanding of time produces a very different idea of Christianity.

Velma's healing takes place when she remembers and

> enters a region where time melds the dead, the living, and the unborn . . . where "Isis lifted the veil"; where Shango presides over the rites of transformation; where Ogun challenges chaos and forges transition; where Obatala shapes creation; where Damballah ensures continuity and renewal; where Anancy mediates the shapes of Brer Rabbit, Brer Bear, Brer Fox, Brer Terrapin, the Signifying' Monkey; where the griot memory of [hu]mankind mediates its reincarnation as the conjure woman, High John, John Henry, the Flying African, Shine, Stagolee, the Preacher, the blues singer, the jazz makers. . .

In her commentary on Bambara's work, Eleanor Traylor points out in this passage that time for Bambara is a fusion of the ancestors and the future.[46] When the community forgets this and enters into the linear progressions of Western society with its crisis-upon-crisis, it becomes separated from life and cannot renew itself.

It is this literature that has led me to understand the significance of time in understanding the difference race and culture make in pursuing theology. White, Western theology is oriented toward the future. Wilson-Kastner's liberal feminist Christology is also profoundly future-oriented. She consistently writes of the "dynamic movement *towards* wholeness."[47] She relates her work to de Chardin's "*Omega point*," the "divine center of convergence toward which all is evolving," and to the Christian Book of Revelation.[48] And, most telling, she often quotes Jürgen Moltmann's *Theology of Hope,* a most Western reading of Christian futurity, with great approval.[49] Here again, Sandra Harding's thesis on the conceptual instability of feminism is useful for understanding how feminist appropriations of seemingly useful aspects of patriarchal theology or philosophy often result in the uncritical importation of viewpoints uncongenial to feminism—this time white, Western linear thinking.

One role of ancestor worship is to connect the contemporary society to the flow of all life; to mitigate against seeing the future as someplace forward of the past. In her essay "Salvation Is the Issue," Bambara demonstrates that her narrative makes visible and hence accessible this essential connection between all life and the ancestors. It is this connection that "saves." Her point is that a sane life, a natural life, is living out the contracts, covenants, black Americans have with themselves, with the ancestors, and with God. Her phrase "the serpent's sting"[50] may be a reference to the invasions of white sin consciousness, the rejection of the wholeness of life lived in continuity with the ancestors and self.

In some Western commentaries on African art, the absence of proportion in the Africans' representation of the human body has been interpreted as evidence of "primitive eyes" unable to grasp the concept of proportion. African philosophers, however, have noted that when Westerners are portrayed in African art, the figures are quite realistic and proportional. But ancestor figures, with their big heads, large torsos, and disproportionately small legs, are infantile in character. These statues present both an infantile and an ancestral aspect, contradictory qualities that imply cosmological and theological assertions: namely, that the newborn are felt to be especially close to the ancestors and are only gradually weaned by ritual and time to human status. Further, there is a primary interest in the increase of life through fertility. A childlike representation signifies a desire for children. The figures, in fact, represent a different understanding of the relationship of ancestry to present life. The basis of African philosophy is the desire to increase the life force in humankind, in crops, animals, and livestock. The art thus represents the concentric circles of life's energy as it radiates out over time. It presents a striking contrast to Western linear notions of time.[51]

As close as the ground we walk on, because it is there that we have planted their bones, most often under the bones of the white settlers, are the ancestors of Native Americans. Before settlement, before slavery, before the nuclear age, tribal people on the North American continent lived out of many visions in a religious worldview as internally complex as any system known. As Paula Gunn Allen points out in her book *The Sacred Hoop: Recovering the Feminine in American Indian Traditions,*

> Indians endure—both in the sense of living through something so complete in its destructiveness that the mere presence of survivors is a testament to the human will to survive and in the sense of duration or longevity. Tribal systems have been operating in the "new world" for several hundred thousand years. It is unlikely that a few hundred years of colonization will see their undoing. . . . American Indians are not merely doomed victims of western imperialism or progress; they are also the carriers of the dream that most activist movements in the Americas claim to be seeking.[52]

Native American traditions are an important source for black women writers. The novels of Toni Cade Bambara and Alice Walker, in particular, contain central characters who are of both black and Indian ancestry. In the novel *Meridian,* the main character, Meridian, has a father whose grandmother was called Feather Mae. Feather Mae is said to have been mad, insane, because she fought with her husband to save a sacred Indian burial mound. Meridian's father has continued to tend the mound, planting cabbages and tomatoes up along the biggest coil of the mound, called the Sacred Serpent. He reasons, "That mound is full of dead Indians. Our food is made healthy from the iron and calcium from their bones."[53]

Standing in the pit made by the Serpent's coils, Meridian seeks to understand her crazy ancestor, her father, and why they both sought to protect the mound.

> From a spot at the back of her left leg there began a stinging sensation, which, had she not been standing so purposely calm and waiting, she might have dismissed as a sign of anxiety or fatigue. Then her right palm, and her left, began to feel as if someone had slapped them. But it was in her head that the lightness started. It was as if the walls of earth that enclosed her rushed outward, leveling themselves at a dizzying rate, and then spinning wildly, lifting her out of her body and giving her the feeling of flying. And in this movement she saw the faces of her family, the branches of trees, the wings of birds, the corners of houses, blades of grass and petals of flowers rush toward a central point high above her and she was drawn with them, as whirling, as bright, as free, as they. Then the

outward flow, the rush of images, returned to the center of the pit where
she stood, and what had left her at its going was returned. When she came
back to her body—and she felt sure she had left it—her eyes were
stretched wide open, and they were dry, because she found herself staring
directly into the sun.[54]

Her father claims that the pit was constructed to give the living a
foretaste of the sensation of death. Meridian has another view. "It
seemed to her that it was a way the living sought to expand the
consciousness of being alive, there where the ground about them was
filled with the dead."[55]

Meridian's father tries to give the deed he holds to the Serpent coil
burial mound to a Mr. Longknife, who has come from Oklahoma to
recover it. Instead, the federal government, claiming the deed is invalid,
turns the Sacred Serpent into Sacred Serpent Park, with the warning
that "now that it belonged to the public, (it) was of course not open to
colored."[56]

After the park is integrated, Meridian goes there seeking to recover
her communion with the Indian ancestors. "But there were people
shouting and laughing as they slid down the sides of the great Serpent's
coil. Others stood glumly by, attempting to study the meaning of what
had already and forever been lost."[57]

Community, it should be emphasized, includes those who have
died—i.e., the ancestors. This is how healing comes about. Since all
that exists is alive and changing, it can be manipulated under certain
conditions and according to certain laws. Neither magic nor ritual,
these conditions are described by the Sioux as "walking in a sacred
manner," by the Navajo as "standing in the center of the world," and
by the Pomo as "having a tradition."[58]

Along with the centrality of Jesus, the theme of ancestor worship
resonates strongly in the black tradition. Jesus is one of the community,
and there is no community without this connection to Jesus. Healing
from the distortions of white, Western society comes about when one
"walks with Jesus," to echo Walker's "The Welcome Table." In the
womanist writer's connection to ancestor worship I hear the resistance
of the African sense of time to Western linear notions. Jesus may be
that connection to the bones of the ancestors who define the strength
and continuity of the tradition.

Christ as Christa/Community

Rita Nakashima Brock's award-winning new book in Christology,
Journeys by Heart: A Christology of Erotic Power, welds together some

of the themes explored in this chapter: particularity and connection, race, passion, and the role of Christ in the community. Brock's Christology keeps the survivor of abuse central. Her book is an analysis of what is broken in the human condition.[59] I find it interesting that as an Asian–Puerto Rican feminist, Brock has chosen to build her Christology on themes found in the writing of both black and white women, as well as those found in the works of Asian women and Latinas.

The heart metaphor found in the title and throughout the book is an unsentimentalized image for the joining center that unites body, spirit, reason, and passion through heart knowledge, the deepest and fullest knowing. For we know best "by heart."[60] The self, according to Brock and the feminist psychologists on whom she relies, is inherently relational. Particularly from the Swiss psychiatrist Alice Miller, Brock draws an analysis of the way patriarchy "crushes heart" and damages the human capacity for relationality. Heart is healed through the erotic, the power of human beings to love with their whole selves.

According to Brock, traditional Christology has mirrored the patriarchal family and, far from being a source of healing, has been an extension of brokenheartedness. She considers both Wilson-Kastner and Ruether. Her critique of Wilson-Kastner closely parallels the one made in this chapter. She notes Wilson-Kastner's obliteration of the particularity of Jesus in favor of an undifferentiated "wholeness." But in contrast to Ruether, neither is Brock advocating the liberator Jesus.

> Christ is what I am calling Christa/Community. Jesus participates centrally in this Christa/Community, but he neither brings erotic power into being nor controls it. Christa/Community is a lived reality expressed in relational images. Hence Christa/Community is described in the images of events in which erotic power is made manifest.[61]

Brock's view of Christa obviously avoids the anti-Semitic problems of the feminist or liberator Jesus.

The striking reference to the erotic power of Christa/Community is clearly based on Audre Lorde's "Uses of the Erotic: the Erotic as Power." Brock cites Lorde and maintains "that the erotic is the basis of being itself as the power of relationship and that all existence comes to be by virtue of connectedness, from atoms to the cosmos."[62] This is the basis of Brock's grounding in "existence-as-a-relational-process."[63]

How, if at all, does this differ from Wilson-Kastner's conviction that "wholeness" is the movement of the universe? I find Brock's critique of Wilson-Kastner extremely insightful. Her criticism is that Wilson-Kastner has taken the "physical, psychological, political, economic, and sociological connotations" of "wholeness" and transposed them into the abstract, philosophical categories of unity, "thereby confusing unity with connectedness."[64] Brock therefore wants to hold to both the uniqueness of concrete particularity *and* connectedness. "We do not experience ourselves or other persons as abstract principles or as general human beings, but as concretely present—as black tall man, Latin old woman, Korean small newborn."[65]

This is a definite gain: Concrete particularity need not preclude connectedness. Yet I believe the method of difference from which I began, positing an ontology of struggle, is quite distinct from Brock's premise. Brock finds connectedness everywhere—from atoms to the cosmos; I find struggle and conflict. When the atom is split, the raging energy stored there is released—for evil and for good. On the ambiguity of destructiveness, however, keep in mind, that more human lives have been saved through the splitting of the atom than were lost in Hiroshima and Nagasaki. By this I do not mean the "American Lives Saved Because We Dropped the Bomb," an argument that denies to Asian lives the same value accorded American lives. Rather, the research and treatment of cancer and related disorders that atomic energy makes possible is also a consequence of the destructiveness of the nuclear age. I believe there is *both* connection and destruction, creativity and evil at the heart of the cosmos.

A White Feminist Christology of Difference

Jesus was a Semite, a male, a practicing Jew. What do I encounter when I encounter this history? As a white feminist I encounter the differences of race, of gender, of time. I am shocked out of my assumption that I know who Jesus is by virtue of forty years of white, Western patriarchal Christianity seeping into my ears, eyes, nose, and mouth.

I am moved to anger by Jesus' death as another sufferer created by political tyranny. It should not be. I know that this suffering deserves my passionate denial—it must not be so forever.

Jesus is not my ancestor, however. However much I may wish to divest myself of Western notions of time, they are too deeply ingrained. I encounter ancestor worship with the shock of difference—this is not my ancestor; he belongs to others. His bones are not buried under my feet.

Have I a white church I can call Christa—owning at least the history of the Jesus movement (Schüssler Fiorenza)? Here, too, is the shock of the complicity of the white church in the occurrence of systemic evil from witch hunts through American slavery to the Holocaust.

What have I learned from these shocking encounters? Over the years I have learned that if Jesus rose anywhere for me, he rose in the survivors of abuse. This is what resurrection means to me—as the words that make up the acronym VOICES state: Victims of Incest Can Emerge Survivors. It is to those abused through sexual and domestic violence that I turn in compassion and rage, and say it shall not be. And I know my rage is claiming healing even as it respects the bones of the ancestors of others, the rights of others to say who is the Messiah of Israel, the claim of others that "your experience is not my experience." This is my encounter with the struggle to survive and to prevail.

7

God the Father, God the Mother, and the Goddess

He'll be your mother, when you're motherless;
He's your father, when you're fatherless;
He's your sister, when you're sisterless;
He's a brother, when you're brotherless.
Herbert Brewster, "Surely Our God is Able"[1]

In 1983 I appeared on the *Phil Donahue* show to discuss a translation project called *An Inclusive Language Lectionary,* in which I had participated for the National Council of the Churches of Christ. One of the most controversial changes we made in this experimental translation of portions of the Revised Standard Version of the Bible was to translate the Greek for "God the Father" as "God the [*Mother and*] Father."[2] The addition of "Mother" to the text, though in italics and in brackets for optional use, was loudly protested.[3] When Donahue asked members of the audience how they reacted to this change, one black woman quoted the Gospel song above and in effect said that in the black tradition there are many female as well as male terms for God. For this reason she did not find the ILL change objectionable.

Many people have found this change objectionable, however. The issue of whether male language should be used to refer to God continues to be an area of great controversy in Christian churches, both Protestant and Catholic. Among seminary students, many black women object to white feminist guidelines on inclusive language, particularly for chapel use, and continue to use Father language in reference to God, much to the consternation of white feminists. In my travels around the country I have found this to be uniformly the case: The use of Father language for God is an area of great conflict—both overt and covert—among black and white women.[4]

Given the increasing interests of white feminists—both pagan and

Christian—in Goddess traditions and the experimentation by white women writers with female language for God or God/ess, this conflict is widening. Many black women are concerned that eliminating Father language has become a litmus test for one's commitment to ending sexism.

Let me stress again that this is not an issue I mean to solve—i.e., to find a way to bridge the differences between black and white women in regard to God language to find a common term, a lowest common denominator. Rather, I hope to make the differences more apparent by exploring them from an unconventional angle, that of the political history of doctrine.

One thing I have learned from years of Bible study with abused women from very conservative religious backgrounds—including women whose religious language was completely different from my own—is that people have a right to their own religious beliefs. Respecting the integrity of that other belief system is a feminist issue.[5] Confronting the difference race makes is a white feminist issue.

God as Reliable Father

Many white feminist theologians regard the doctrine of God as Father as a projection of patriarchal family relationships. Mary Daly's warning that "if God is male, then the male is God"[6] is taken as a normative description of the function of all God language. Whether interpreted as positive or negative, theological assertions about God's nature are regarded as thinly veiled declarations about human relationships.

When Diane Tennis asks, *Is God the Only Reliable Father?* she answers that women *(sic)* need the Father God because the "biblical God" is "reliable," whereas earthly fathers are often not reliable.[7] Tennis does not agree with Daly that human relationships dictate God language. She argues the reverse—that God language can inform human relationships, in this case be a model for better "fathering." Tennis does not address the question of why it is that in two millennia of almost exclusive use of Father imagery for God, fathering has not been markedly aided by this metaphor.

To establish her case for the need of positive divine images for fathers, Tennis details the ways in which earthly fathers have exhibited unreliability. She particularly stresses the "absence of fathers" and the "survival responsibilities" of black women in the black community. She does not examine the black community and its religious mores except in relation to poverty and the absence of fathers.[8]

The dangerously superficial interpretation one can draw from Tennis's thesis in regard to black women's use of Father language is a kind of Moynihan theology.[9] In other words, the claim has been made that black women's attachment to Father language is due to the unreliability of real black fathers.

Tennis also seems to blithely equate the Goddess writings of someone like Carol Christ with God the Mother, reducing thealogy to theology and identifying both approaches with a mere gender change for God. She believes that mother and goddess (largely the same divine designation) are hazardous for women *(sic)* because they tend to aggravate women's already skewed sense of their responsibility for nurture and care. When she writes that "we *(sic)* need to disconnect the images of Idealized Mother and Mother Goddess from [unconditional] love so as to discourage women from abusive behavior against ourselves *(sic)* and others by presuming *our (sic)* infinity and *their* infantilism," she exhibits the reversals that make her book so appealing to patriarchal theology and so unhelpful to black and white women. The Goddess figures of which Christ and others write are not the all-embracing Earth Mothers who have been made transcendent.[10] Likewise, God as Mother is explicitly a model of relationality, not one of dominant parent, submissive child. Sallie McFague, for example, juxtaposes the models of Mother, Lover, and friend as bespeaking a different power relationship in God's connection with the world.[11]

Tennis's thesis does not hold up for white women in the twentieth century. One of the most important encounters of this century has been the theological reflections engendered by the Holocaust. How can we breeze through an assertion of God's reliability in the face of the extermination of six million Jews? This is a question Jewish theologians have asked since 1948. Does it not do violence to this Jewish history to assert, as Christians, that the biblical God is reliable? The conclusion that in the twentieth century God chose not to be reliable for the chosen people is unacceptable.[12] How, then, is it possible not to view Tennis's thesis as Christian chauvinism served up in another guise?

Or where is the reliability of God for Tamar? For Hagar? For the Daughter of Jephthah? In her introduction to a literary-feminist reading of these *Texts of Terror*, Phyllis Trible writes

Choice and change inspire my telling these particular tales: hearing a black woman describe herself as a daughter of Hagar outside the covenant; seeing an abused woman on the streets of New York with a sign, "My name is Tamar"; reading news reports of the dismembered body of a woman found in a trash can; attending worship services in memory of nameless women and wrestling with the *silence, absence, and opposition of God*.[13]

The witness of these texts that terrorize women mock the reliability thesis.

God as the Unreliable Father

I believe that the use of Father language in reference to God is a particularly key anchor for white Western patriarchy. In my own history, a dawning feminism brought a simultaneous consciousness of my father's violence against my mother and me and a profound silencing of meaning in the use of Father language for God. Carol Christ has written powerfully of the ways in which Father language can be pathological for many white women.[14] I have not traveled back to meaningful language for God through personal imagery, but rather, through spirit-centered appellations, primarily of presence and justice.

I am becoming increasingly convinced that much of white women's anger at God the Father is due to the high incidence of father/daughter incest in white families. This is an unscientific impression based on the white female seminarians who come through my office and share with me their experience of being sexually molested as children by their fathers and of their anger at God the Father. In the same breath. But it is also true that many of these survivors of incest are in seminary to become ministers precisely to please the father figure—a common response to childhood sexual abuse.

Alice Miller, on whose work Rita Brock has drawn so heavily, has made this connection as well. Miller finds God the Father "easily offended, jealous, and basically insecure; He therefore demands obedience and conformity in the expression of ideas, tolerates no graven images and—since 'graven images' included works of art for the Hebrew God—no creativity either."[15] Fear of the censure of this Father God figure caused Freud to deny the evidence of his own eyes and ears when his patients, particularly his female patients, told him of childhood sexual encounters with their parents (fathers). Freud turned their recollections into the drive theory that has dominated psychoanalysis for so long. The punitive religious tradition from which he came made Freud so emotionally captive that "he was forced to abandon his great discovery concerning traumatization in early childhood."[16]

Relegating these memories of early childhood sexual abuse to the "fantasy" level postulated by the drive theory enabled Freud to talk about the effects of sexual abuse without acknowledging its true cause. This has been a long-developed pattern for human dealings with the abuses of childhood: They become the stuff of fantasy from the Brothers Grimm to psychoanalysis. Miller wonders when it will be that

humankind "stops regarding the knowledge stored up in the unconscious as immaterial, as pathological fantasies of the insane or of
eccentric poets and comes to see it for what it really is: a perception of
reality." Given the work of Maya Angelou discussed in Chapter Four, it
is striking that Miller regards the reality of the sexual abuse of children
as an origin of human creativity, acceptable as story or fairy tale when
"legitimized as pure imagination. . . ." Humanity takes pride in "this
cultural heritage, of its wisdom, of 'the knowledge of good and evil' we
possess, but we do not have to let it affect us deeply unless we happen
to be poets or insane ourselves."[17]

Relegating the reality of childhood abuse to the level of fantasy
results in a distancing from the reality of cruelty in human life. Creative
writers, however, are precisely those who are able to take the suffering
inflicted on others and on themselves and translate it into constructive
narrative. Society has regarded the creative as exceptions when in fact
the "knowledge of good and evil" that is the source of the writer's
creativity is all too common. Miller warns that if writers reveal this
source, "if writers begin to describe their childhood, as has been
happening more and more frequently in the past decade, then they will
soon be confronted with the hostility of society, which sees the customs
and rights it has enjoyed for thousands of years threatened."[18] Com-
mentators on Maya Angelou's work do point to her as "exceptional"[19]
rather than acknowledging the reality of what she is saying about the
life of black children.

In examining the creative potential of "the knowledge of good and
evil" in a writer's imagination, I am not saying that this abuse is in any
sense good and should not be immediately and always stopped. What I
am saying, once again, is that the complex interrelationship of good and
evil is central to feminist theology. I believe that as a feminist theologian
I must work after the Fall, after the knowledge of good and evil, not in
the garden.

Is the sexual abuse of children the fault of God the Father? What
Miller is saying is that the pattern of victimization of children cannot be
broken until the silence about this violence is broken. Just as Angelou
broke her silence with a flood of words in her writing, so, too, must
survivors of sexual violence confront the fear of the father if they are to
be healed. The divine anchor for the power of the fathers in God the
Father is a powerful tool for keeping the silence. When images of God
the Father are allied with imperatives to obey, to be ignorant of good
and evil, then this image itself becomes violently abusive and must be
abandoned. I have worked with too many survivors of sexual and
domestic violence not to know that this is one of the ways in which God

the Father has functioned, and continues to function, in our society. Given the internal evidence of the biblical texts, however, this was not its original content. For me, in my work with these survivors, it does not fundamentally matter. The entire history of Western abuse of children, particularly of girl children by fathers,[20] stands between us and those texts; and no amount of ahistoricism can change that fact.

A poem by Judy Grahn vividly depicts this legacy of white Christianity to Western culture:

> This is the legacy of the white race
> that I will remember long after my death:
> that it beats its children
> that it blunts itself with alcohol
> that its women suffer from a blight: passivity
> that it carries a gun.
>
> This is the legacy of the white rose
> that I will remember long after my death:
> that its beaten children beat their children
> that it calls alcohol "spirits"
> that its women offer their passivity to their families
> like a whip.[21]

Black Christianity

Originally I began this chapter with a preconceived thesis (violating my epistemological premise to Sojourn before I find the Truth) that the persistence of Father language for God among black female seminarians was due to the absence of fathers in the black community. I had named the chapter "God the Father, the Family, and Poverty" and planned to draw on some of the sociological analyses of poverty in the black community—among them William Julius Wilson's *The Truly Disadvantaged: The Inner City, the Underclass, and Public Policy*.[22] In the course of examining the literature written by black women, however, I was confronted with the fact that black women writers of fiction, poets, theologians, and ethicists are not writing on God the Father.

In considering why this might be so, I was struck by the possibility that black Christianity may not be understood by studying white Christianity. The centrality of God the Father in the analysis of white-dominated Western society done by white feminists is not germane to black Christianity. God the Father is not all that central to black Christianity. Furthermore, the treatment of God the Father as a problem in white feminism is not the response that black women writers would, in any case, make.

In her essay "My Words Will Be There," Audre Lorde writes of the Africanism of Afro-American literature that it "deals with life as an experience to be lived. In many respects, it is much like the Eastern philosophies in that we see ourselves as a part of a life force; we are joined, for instance, to the air, to the earth. We are part of the whole life process. We live in accordance with, in a kind of correspondence with, the rest of the world as a whole. And therefore, *living becomes an experience, rather than a problem,* no matter how bad or how painful it may be. Change will rise endemically from the experience fully lived and responded to."[23] Much of the powerful Afro-American literature embodies this approach to dealing with pain, with difficulties, with the evils of life.

It is not that black girl children have not experienced sexual molestation by their fathers. Although other women writers—black and white—have depicted this violation, it is Alice Walker in *The Color Purple* who sliced public silence with the blade of these children's pain as told in Celie's own voice, her letters to God.

There are many lines in *The Color Purple* that are often quoted by white feminists, several of which I have already mentioned. In support of the need to reimage God, white feminists have often quoted Walker's words on Shug's lips that

> my first step from the old white man was trees. Then air. Then birds. Then other people. But one day when I was sitting quiet and feeling like a motherless child, which I was, it come to me: that feeling of being part of everything, not separate at all. I knew that if I cut a tree, my arm would bleed. And I laughed and I cried and I run all around the house. I knew just what it was. In fact, when it happen, you can't miss it. It sort of like you know what, she say, grinning and rubbing high up on my thigh.[24]

A difference race makes, however, is that Shug is claiming she left the "old *white* man" who looks just like white folks, "only bigger." No white ever listened "to anything colored say." The God in church is the God of the white Bible; the God Shug finds within, who's not a he or a she but an it, comes into the world with the humans born into it. "You come into the world with God. But only them that search for it inside find it. And sometimes it just manifest itself even if you not looking, or don't know what you looking for. Trouble do it for most folks, I think. Sorrow, lord."[25]

To my knowledge, no white feminist who has quoted this passage from *The Color Purple* has ever remarked on the rejection of the whiteness of God. But this, in fact, is the preoccupation of the passage, and it is taken to much greater length than the theme of distancing from God's maleness. The letting go of all personal imagery is the only other time that God as He is really an issue. Furthermore, God as She is also rejected.

But it is the appeal to the *Lord* during times of trouble that really marks the difference. Living the pain, as Lorde writes, is really living in Jesus. *Lord* in the black tradition can only mean one person, and that person is Jesus. Between Jesus and the Spirit, God the Father comes a close third, and for this reason preoccupation with Father-dominated language is likewise tertiary in the religious consciousness of black women.

In the course of the translation project *An Inclusive Language Lectionary,* the committee changed the Greek word *kurios,* translated in the Revised Standard Version of the bible as "Lord," to *Sovereign.* Lord is a male-identified term; it is also hierarchical. In the Appendix the committee wrote: "*Lord* is clearly a biased translation when used to refer to God, who is beyond sexual identification." It is, of course, more appropriate to the earthly Jesus, but again problematic for the risen Christ.[26] An unacknowledged assumption of these words, however, is the white Christian tradition, where Lord can be either God or Jesus. In the black religious tradition, the Lord is quintessentially Jesus and Jesus is not above but on behalf of the troubled, like God "a mother to the motherless, a father to the fatherless."[27]

As the committee's "Readings for Year A" circulated, we had many responses from churches. Many black Christians—both clergy and lay—supporters of the intent of the inclusive language translation, pointed out to us that we could really do what we liked with the God language, but that we'd best leave the language for the Lord alone. *Lord* has an entirely different connotation in the black Christian tradition than it does in white churches. In subsequent editions the committee on *An Inclusive Language Lectionary* has offered a choice of "Sovereign" or "Lord" in the text. We changed our approach not because of the ridicule of our enemies but out of respect for the difference of our friends.

What I did not understand during the years of the translation project, however, was the significance the King James translation had for black Christianity. Cheryl Townsend Gilkes's paper, " 'Mother to the Motherless, Father to the Fatherless': Power, Gender, and Community in an Afrocentric Biblical Tradition," uses Houston Baker's "vernacular theory" of the "distinctive culturally specific aspects of Afro-American literature and culture."[28] Gilkes's paper suggests to me that the pattern of repetition so characteristic of the King James translation is similar to the blues, the complex repetitive structure of the distinctive Afro-American musical tradition. This repetition, particularly of pronouns, found in the King James Bible is not sustained in the Revised Standard Version, the translation on which *An Inclusive Language Lectionary* is based. In fact, the committee decided not to put more pronouns into the text. In commenting on this practice I wrote:

> The English language's heavy reliance upon pronouns coupled with the notion that male terms can be understood generically to include women means that the hearers of the scripture are constantly bombarded with long strings of male pronouns. The committee has addressed this problem in several ways—by altering sentence construction to avoid excessive use of pronouns, substituting nouns for the repetition of pronouns, using "one" as the generic pronoun, and "they" and "their" as pronouns referring back to "each," "everyone," etc.[29]

The practice of the committee was, in truth, to extend the movement of the Revised Standard Version translation away from the rhythmic structure that so characterizes the King James Bible. This is an important factor in the underuse of *An Inclusive Language Lectionary* in the black churches. The biblical language of Fatherhood used in the King James Bible is therefore routine in the experience of black worship. I have concluded that this usage should not be overly interpreted as an exclusivist focus on God as Father.

Furthermore, God the Father has not preoccupied black women writers to the extent that it has been a focus for white feminists because black churches put so much emphasis on both the Spirit and the Lord that appeal to God as Father is always already mediated. The black tradition is profoundly trinitarian. This is established by Audre Lorde's 1960s poem entitled "Father, Son, and Holy Ghost," in which she lives through the pain of the life and death of her father. The poem is a reaching out to the spirit of the father and an admission of the conflicted emotions that effort brings. But even in this intense focus on the real father, Lorde adopts the trinitarian language of black churches for the title of her poem.[30]

The Eagle Stirreth Her Nest

Cheryl Gilkes argues that "both black and white Christian women identify problems in their churches and in society, but they define those problems differently, and they allocate their time, energies, and passions in distinctive, sometimes divergent, directions."[31] The question of gender and language is a key example of this difference that Gilkes notes. In the "four pillars" of the Afro-Christian worship experience—preaching, praying, singing, and testifying[32]—a diversity of gender imagery may be found. Much of this inclusive gender imagery, though not all, comes from the lips of black women, who, while they have been almost completely excluded from the pulpit, preach from the floor, pray virtually unceasingly, sing, and testify in much greater numbers than do their brothers.

But even within the masculinist traditions of black preaching, the influence of women is felt. In the black tradition preaching is a response to the community's needs that is made audible and visible in the worship experience. Since black churches are primarily women's communities, black preaching has had to gain their assent. And because black women are so strikingly the leaders of the prayer tradition, the singers of gospel music, and those who stand to testify, a preacher who did not reach out to the heights and depths of these women's theological response to life's pain and graces would not long remain in his pulpit.

Gilkes notes that "one of the most vivid examples of the tendency to emphasize God as mother in black preaching is [the late Rev. Clarence LaVaughn] Franklin's sermon, 'The Eagle Stirreth Her Nest.'" This classic sermon, with roots deep in the black biblical tradition, details in marvelous profusion all the ways in which God moves in human life as a mother. Though the pronouns for God remain masculine in Franklin's sermon, the details of female power in the ability of the community to come through suffering are vivid. The theme of the sermon is "human suffering as a way of creating a mature Christian." The divine providence shoves humanity out of the nest but does not abandon them in life's trials.

One of the most lively of contemporary black women preachers today is Rev. Yvonne Delk, head of the United Church of Christ Office for Church in Society. Delk's grandmother, Julia Anna Delk, founded the First Holy Temple United Holiness Church in America in Norfolk, Virginia, during the twenties. Delk credits her authority as an ordained minister and her spirit-filled preaching to this ancestor. During her struggles to claim ordination during the late sixties and early seventies, Delk recalls that she used the text "The Eagle Stirreth Her Nest" in a children's sermon at Freeman Avenue United Church of Christ in Cincinnati, Ohio. The "sense of femaleness" of the text mirrored for her the fact that "my nest was being stirred." After hearing a male minister preach this text in the older black idiom, she was jolted into remembering that notes for a sermon on this text were among the papers left her by Julia Anna Delk. Since then Delk has preached this sermon many times, and the stirring of the eagle has become a symbol for her, and for other black women, of the leadership role black women play in black churches, stirring them up and calling them to Christian maturity in recognizing women's right to ordained ministry.[33]

Gilkes observes that while the black church is not generally an egalitarian institution, the omnipresence of racial oppression *and* the legacy of the African religious tradition has generated a wealth of gender-inclusive imagery. In addition to "mother to the motherless, father to the fatherless," there is the expression "some mother's son and some father's daughter" used historically by black preachers to replace "man," "somebody," or "someone."[34] Because the lives of black women form much of the stuff out of which black religious knowledge is formed, the symbol system that has emerged from that matrix is more gender-inclusive than the religious symbolism common in white churches. It is not wholly inclusive, but "there exists an important foundation for change and inclusion."[35]

Mother to the Motherless, Father to the Fatherless

In fact, the older linguistic tradition of the black idiom is demonstrably more inclusive. The movement from the tradition of "some mother's son and some father's daughter" to the "black man" of the 1960s was not a step forward linguistically. Gilkes writes that black women felt included in "Negro," but during the 1960s, when the change to "black" was almost always allied to "man," they did not. The black power movement was "one of the most unfortunate contradictions of black liberation" in that it employed a masculinist rhetoric. Gilkes notes that some black preachers, such as C. L. Franklin, admonished black leadership for this hypermasculine tendency, but they were clearly exceptional.[36]

In her chapter "Some Mother's Son, Some Father's Daughter," Gilkes points to the many resources in the history of Afro-Christian churches for guidance in recasting the language of black worship. This is a thesis she extends in her paper "Mother to the Motherless, Father to the Fatherless." While slave peoples may have employed the missionaries' Bible, they applied a radically different hermeneutic, an interpretive posture that "incorporates the events that are central to the black experience and affirms the dignity of the African personality in the face of the forces of degradation; such a reading rejects the use of the Bible as an apology for oppression and it is quick to point out the categorical inclusion of Africans." This means the text can be expanded, bent and molded to include folk texts such as the Brewster gospel text. The phrase "father to the fatherless" is actually found only in Psalm 68. It is Gilkes's contention that the addition of "mother to the motherless" in the folk text is a way of claiming the greater gender inclusivity of African traditions, while at the same time drawing attention to the irony of this naming in view of the existential situation of real black mothers, and those thus rendered "motherless." "By connecting motherlessness and fatherlessness, the Afro-Christian tradition provided a comprehensive portrait of powerlessness."[37] For those who have African ancestors, the most acute human tragedy is not to be fatherless but to be motherless.[38] This makes neither the black church nor its ancestral African societies less sexist, but it does make them *sexist in a way that differs from the sexism of white, Western society.*[39]

The plethora of means of relating to God that exists in black churches is due in great part to the Afrocentric approach of augmenting the text, which resists the "theocentric monotheizing hermeneutic" that James A. Sanders has identified as such a "consistent" motive force in the construction of the biblical theological view.[40]

The preoccupation of white feminists with God as Father is due, at least in part, to the hegemony of the "theocentric monotheizing hermeneutic" in white, Western Christianity. It seems to me that if the role of God as "mother to the motherless, father to the fatherless" in Afro-Christian traditions is best understood by a sociohistorical approach, something of this nature might illuminate the different location of God as father in the social and political context of white Christianity.

The Politics of Divine Oneness

The encounter with sin for black women forced me to an awareness that greater difference exists than I had previously assumed—i.e., that sin for white women may, in fact, consist in asserting connection, sisterhood, bonding, whereas what is needed is respect for cultural difference. So, too, the encounter with God in the black Christian tradition has caused me to look not only interpersonally, at incest, but also politically. There are profound political differences between white, Western Christianity and black American Christianity. The examination of God the Father as a form of psychological support of patriarchy is critical; but all too frequently white feminists stop with interpersonal self-examination and fail to move on to political and economic analyses. If hegemony of God the Father is a particular cultural legacy of Western

Christianity, a white feminist analysis of that fact should include a systemic analysis of its social and political origins.

Theologians throughout Christian history have rarely understood the power of God as solidarity. God's power has been dependent on God's unity, a power that is threatened by sharing even within the Godhead itself. The most common model of God's power in Christian history is the absolute violence of the One Against All. Hannah Arendt has written: "The extreme form of power is All against One, the extreme form of violence is One against All."[41]

This understanding of God's power as the absolute of the One Against All was drawn from the context of Christianity's intellectual growth during the expansion of imperial Rome. Christian thinkers found their social models for God's activity in the Roman understanding of the essential relationship of power and unity. As all roads led to Rome, so Christian theologians began to believe that all power was God's and developed the conception of God's being as one of absolute oneness.

The religiopolitical structures of imperial Rome gave rise to the necessary challenge "Jesus Christ is Lord," which meant that Caesar was not Lord. This social and political necessity fit easily with the concept in Greek philosophy of God as absolute ruler and Father of the World (Plato's "Maker and Father of the Universe," *Timaeus* 28C) and provided the unifying link. God the Father possesses all authority over heaven and earth.

Evident in this point of view is a monarchy that makes God as supreme "Father" superior to the "Son" and the "Spirit," a logical consequence of abandoning the Trinity. Furthermore, monotheistic monarchism goes hand in hand with political ideologies of oppression. As Jürgen Moltmann points out, "The fundamental notion behind the universal is uniform religion: One god—one Logos—one humanity, and in the Roman Empire it was bound to be seen as a persuasive solution for any problems of a multi-national and multi-religious society. The universal ruler in Rome had only to be the image and correspondence of the universal ruler in heaven."[42]

The understanding of divine power in monarchical monotheism is one of absolute domination, the very definition of violence. God conceived as supreme ruler over all from whom other authorities take their cue is a theology of violence. Hierarchy introduces hierarchy: The absolute power of God legitimates the power of the father priest, the father of the country, the father in the family, and so on. Monotheistic monarchism has been a powerful weapon for both church and state in their efforts to legitimate the ultimate power of some over others. It is certainly a theological source for the justification of slavery.

The revolt of the Renaissance and the Reformation led to a radical change in some conceptions of divinity. Reflection on God since that watershed period is characterized by the modern emphasis on God as Absolute Subject. White moderns no longer need God to understand the substance of the world as the Neoplatonists had thought. God is needed to understand the self. Thus the experiencing self is the starting point for modern white, Western theological reflection.

But the emphasis on unity remains. Subject can only be considered an identical self, acting in different ways. This is the modern bourgeois concept of personality. The resistance to diversity, understood as a threat to the integrity of personality, can be noted in the lack of consideration given the Trinity in modern theology. Thus Schleiermacher made the doctrine of the Trinity the very last chapter in his *Christian Faith,* because the Trinity "is not a direct statement about Christian self-consciousness, but only a web of several such statements."[43]

While there has been a reversal in the direction of theological reflection and the ideal, bourgeois self, the personality, has become the center of theological reflection, the emphasis on unity remains intact. Schleiermacher wrote, "Christianity is a monotheistic mode of belief."[44] Unlike the older theologies, where the revelation of God's supreme rulership legitimated hierarchy in human community, in liberalism it is the social domination of a patriarchal bourgeois culture of personality that legitimates *divine* power. It should be recalled that Schleiermacher had some doubts whether non-Germans were capable of theological insight. He did not believe African people were capable of religion, period.[45]

Despite such reactions as Karl Barth's in the twentieth century, personality has inescapably become the subject of modern theology.[46] While the Renaissance discovered the human subject, it was not until the advent of those recently called "The Secular Magi"—Marx, Freud, and Nietzsche—that theology has been unable to escape from the human subject.[47] In attending to Nietzsche's critique of religion as the neurotic denial by humankind of their own power and the projection of that power onto divinity,[48] it is to Freud and not to Marx that theologians have turned to find answers for the modern age.

Influenced by Western naturalism, materialism, and psychologism, Nietzsche argued that humanity had placed all of its capacity for transcendence in a concept of God, projected that concept out of the world, and consequently had eviscerated true human capacity for world transformation. Of course, this also means that the symbols for God are determined by the human situation. In turning to Freud and not to Marx for explanations of this human situation, white North Atlantic theologians have never questioned the social arrangements prevalent during any period from imperial Rome to American slavery to Western post-industrial capitalism and everything in between for the possible sources of monarchical monotheism. Instead, deity conceived as absolute power has been understood (now from Freud) as a projection of human nature, itself innately power-hungry and consequently violent, a solitary combatant locked in struggle with other combatants.[49] That is the "nature of Man."

The Goddess and the Oneness of God

One of the least well understood aspects of thealogy, or reflection on "the Goddess," is that thealogians are not, in the majority, speaking of an external divine being. Mary Daly refers to "Goddess" as "the Self-affirming be-ing in women."[50] It is the political legacy of white Christianity that seeks to ally Goddess thealogies with God the Mother or the Great Mother, Earth Mother, or other such designations. But like other feminists, thealogians are not immune to the patriarchalisms of theories they have imported into feminist reflection.

In her chapter "Contemporary Goddess Thealogy: A Sympathetic Critique," Emily Culpepper notes how insidiously these influences can penetrate feminist reflection. She reflects on the fact that "Erich Neumann's book *The Great Mother* seems to fascinate many women to a detrimental degree." Archetypal theory in general seems to be particularly pernicious. Jungian theories are often the sources for feminist religious reflection because they at least take the female seriously as a symbol. "The illusion that Jungian theory is profemale causes too many feminists (both in women's studies and completely outside academia) to accept this work uncritically rather than take it as food for thought."[51] Culpepper's main objection is that these patriarchal theories are merely reified gender dualism that ignores the "rich diversity of living."[52]

This is a good lesson in the dangers of subjectification for both theologians and thealogians. Culpepper cries out with passion, a cry I have often echoed silently while reading my students' papers.

> I discovered I felt like yelling, yelling something like, "No! Not just THE GODDESS, not THE mother. Get out! Get out of Women's minds, Jung and Neumann!"[53]

What I find interesting in Culpepper's critique, sympathetic though it is, is her identification of the continuing tendency of white, Western culture toward oneness. I can do no better than to allow Culpepper to express this manifestation in her own words.

Here is a typical example of this problem. The feminist journal *Heresies*
announced that it would publish a special theme issue on the rapidly
growing and diverse phenomenon of feminist spirituality. By the time the
issue appeared, it had become "The Great Goddess Issue." There is
much that is valuable in this issue, but it exemplifies the problem I am
addressing. Gloria Orenstein's article, "The Reemergence of the Archetype of the Great Goddess in Art by Contemporary Women," illustrates
this unfortunate distortion of emphasis. . . . In her analysis, the archetype often seems *more real* than the actual women artists or their specific
works. . . . [The women] hold second place to an idea. *This is a familiar
patriarchal position.* Ultimately it is not liberating.[54]

In Western society there is a deeply entrenched intolerance to diversity that manifests itself in many forms. This is no less true in white
Christian feminism and white pagan feminism than in more explicitly
patriarchal constructions of reality. This, I believe, is a political institu-
tionalization of unity in Western society and its thought forms, and *it*
must be the focus of white feminist critique, to borrow a line from Mary
Daly, "beyond God the Father." A more complex, but I believe ultimately more precise way to articulate the differences between black
and white women on the subject of God language is to take into account
the relative tolerance of each for diversity within the system of divine
symbol. Insofar as Goddess religion is pressing white Christian feminists toward diversity, it is of enormous help in this project.

A White Feminist Political Theology

Diane Tennis couched her analysis of the "need" for God the Father
in interpersonal terms. Women *(sic)* need reliable fathers; women *(sic)*
don't need to burden ourselves *(sic)* with any more pressures to nurture.

My original objections to God the Father were limited to the real
violence patriarchy has inflicted on women. But both Tennis and I had
missed the fact that white Christianity is a social and political as well as
a psychological construct. The alliance with the psychological bent of
modern theology has not boded well for feminists interested in class
and race analysis. The similarity of the sexual violence perpetrated on
women of different classes and races must not be allowed to obscure
the different religiosocial contexts in which these acts of violence
should be interpreted. It may be that many white women object to the
use of Father language in referring to God because of the abuses of
Fathers against daughters. It may be that Tennis knows white women
who like Father language because they need to compensate for the lack

of reliable earthly fathers. This does not mean that the similarity of violence or absence can be equated with a similarity of social context or, for that matter, of theological insight drawn from these contexts. Without a broader contextual analysis of the social and political differences between black and white Christianity, these disparities are lost.

Black Christianity, or better, to adopt Gilkes's terminology, Afro-Christianity, is more tolerant of diversity within the system of divine symbol than is white Christianity. This does not mean Afro-Christianity is not sexist but merely that it is sexist in a way that is different from the sexism of white Christianity. I have no business trying to address the sexism of black churches. What I have learned from the encounter with this difference, however, is that the philosophical and political unity of white Christianity's approach to doctrine must be separated (as Rita Brock insightfully pointed out in regard to Wilson-Kastner's collapse of feminist political alliances into philosophical unity) from women's *(sic)* knowledge of human interdependence. In contrast to Brock, however, I believe that the particularity of cultural difference must be prior even to political alliance. The weight of white, Western Christianity is too heavily on the side of "all roads lead to Rome" for these assertions of bonding not to slide easily into cultural imperialism. When even Goddess feminists are tempted toward unity in the articulation of divinity, I know that this imperialistic bent of white, Western culture is very strong and very hard to resist.

I must be careful to take this analysis of the temptations of cultural imperialism into the final chapter, an analysis of violence. Sexual and domestic violence is a difference that black and white women hold in common.

8
A Difference in Common: Violence

every 3 minutes a woman is beaten
every five minutes a
woman is raped/every ten minutes
a little girl is molested
yet I rode the subway today
I sat next to an old man who
may have beaten his old wife
3 minutes ago or 3 days/30 years ago
he might have sodomized his
daughter but I sat there
cuz the men on the train
might beat some young women
later in the day or tomorrow
I might not shut my door fast
enough push hard enough
every 3 minutes it happens
some woman's innocence
rushes to her cheeks/pours from her mouth

like the betsy wetsy dolls have been torn
apart/their mouths
menses red split/every
three minutes a shoulder
is jammed through plaster and the
oven door/
chairs push thru the rib cage/hot
water or
boiling sperm decorate her body
I rode the subway today
and bought a paper from an
east Indian man who might
have held his old lady onto
a hot pressing iron/I didn't know

maybe he catches little girls in the
parks and rips open their behinds
with steel rods/I can not decide
what he might have done I only
know every 3 minutes
every 5 minutes every 10 minutes
I bought the paper
looking for the announcement
there has to be an announcement
of the women's bodies found

yesterday the missing little girl
I sat in a restaurant with my
paper looking for the announcement
a young man served me coffee
I wondered did he pour the boiling
coffee on the woman because she was stupid
did he put the infant girl in
the coffee pot because she cried too much
what exactly did he do with hot coffee
I looked for the announcement
the discovery of the dismembered
woman's body
victims have not all been
identified today they are
naked and death/some refuse to
testify one girl out of 10's not
coherent/I took the coffee
and spit it up I found an
announcement/not the woman's
bloated body in the river floating
not the child bleeding in the
59th street corridor/not the baby
broken on the floor

"there is some concern
that alleged battered women
might start to murder their
husbands and lovers with no immediate cause"
I spit up I vomit I am screaming
we all have immediate cause
every 3 minutes
every 5 minutes
every 10 minutes
every day
women's bodies are found

sin alleys and bedrooms/at the top of the stairs
before I ride the subway/buy a paper or drink
coffee from your hands I must know
have you hurt a woman today
did you beat a woman today
throw a child cross a room are the
little girls pants in your pocket
did you hurt a woman today
I have to ask these obscene questions
I must know you see
the authorities require us to
establish

immediate cause
every three minutes
every five minutes
every ten minutes
every day
> Ntozake Shange, "with no immediate cause"
> *Nappy Edges*[1]

Much of my adult life has been devoted to ending violence against women. Year after year, week after week, day after day, minute after minute they come through my office, through the Bible studies I conduct,[2] through workshops and groups, after speeches and panels—old and young, black, white, Latina, Asian, Native American. All women all day long every day participate in the structures of violence against women that are part of this society. I say all women because if a particular woman has not experienced this violence firsthand, she is still subject to the litany of violence reported in other women's lives: the newspaper and magazine headlines, the screams muted on the television news. To be female in this society is to have internalized a whole series of don'ts: don't go here, don't go there, don't go alone, don't hitch, don't-don't-don't. But it's still your fault when something happens. What did you do to provoke him? He's just frustrated from problems at work. It's the alcohol. The drugs. Not him, not him, not him. It's you.

Many women have learned the politics of silence about the violence that surrounds them every day. They have so silenced themselves that often they find it intolerable to bring these acts of violence to consciousness. The origins of the modern white women's movement are found in the small groups of women who began meeting during the early 1970s and going around the circle telling the story of their lives. At first shamefully and hesitantly because each was convinced that she was the only one to have suffered this abuse, then more surely and confidently as the story was repeated with different details by each woman in the circle. These stories of violence (and not, I believe, "boredom," Betty Friedan to the contrary) are the genesis of the modern white women's movement.

In her chapter "Moral Callousness and Moral Sensitivity: Violence Against Women," Mary Pellauer begins her discussion of ethics and violence against women with a personal story that demonstrates how it is that the connections between stories produce the critical consciousness that makes up the real content of white feminism.

> More than a decade ago I was a graduate student in social ethics, living in Chicago, newly married, in the early days of the women's movement. During this period, feminists in the area began to discuss something new and deeply disturbing: rape and battered women. . . .
> I heard stories about battered women for months before something odd and eerie happened. I saw flickering and confused images in the back of my mind, images of my father picking up a butcher knife and going after my mother . . . her picking up a frying pan to fend him off . . . him with a baseball bat . . . her running away.[3]

This echoes my own experience of sexual and domestic violence. It was long after I became a pastor and had been listening to the stories of violence related by women parishioners who came to me for counseling that I permitted the scenes of my father's violence against my mother and me to come to consciousness. In coming to me for help, these survivors of sexual and domestic violence allowed me to acknowledge at last my own personal contact with battering.[4] It was and always will be the repetitious *pattern* of these stories, despite their wide individual differences, that awakens me to the fact that violence against women is planned and indeed sanctioned.

Nonviolence

Joining the peace movement and becoming a pacifist was a logical extension of my commitment to end violence against women. A major contribution of feminist theology and thealogy to the peace movement is an analysis of patriarchy and its inevitable ties to militarism.

In an essay entitled "Patriarchy and Death," Mary Caudren identifies the origins of patriarchy in the male discovery of the biological fact of fatherhood and the experience of alienation this often evokes. She quotes Mary O'Brien, who, in *The Politics of Reproduction,* has argued that paternity is a social construct because the male has only social relations to ensure the biology of his paternity. Motherhood, by contrast, is physiologically based. This social construction of paternity is a "real triumph over the ambiguities of nature." From this analysis, Caudren concludes that the extension of paternity into the cosmic realm is a "compensatory activity for the many inadequacies of physical paternity. . . . God the Father and the 'Holy Father' are perfect metaphors for this enterprise."[5]

The many characteristics of patriarchy are shown to stem from this basic alienation: the elevation of mind over body; the preoccupation with immortality; the concern with absolutes in ethics; and certainly the subordination of the female.

It is only as a result of my encounter with the difference race makes that I have begun to recognize some of the limitations of this particular approach of white feminism to analyzing patriarchy and violence.

Slavery

Writing Chapter Two of this book was a profoundly troubling experience. I had always assumed that beyond the few white female abolitionists, white women had been caught in the system of slavery because of an imperative to obey their husbands. In other words, when I considered it at all, it seemed to me that their racism was merely an extension of white male sexism and therefore not really their fault. The real need of white women to get free of the white patriarchal message that they are to blame tends to preclude a nuanced approach to the question of white women's complicity in slavery.

Since the rejection of violence has been so central to my life's work, I almost ended up not writing Chapter Two. I still believe it would have been better to bring the history chapter more into the twentieth century. In order to write it at all, however, it was necessary for me to maintain some distance.

White female slave owners not only cooperated in the system of slavery, they were often the ones who perpetrated its immediate violence. The division of black and white women into exploitable body and exploitable soul does not free white women from responsibility for the violence they perpetuated (and continue to perpetuate in cooperation with modern American economic apartheid).[6]

Some of the legacy of violence that stands between black and white women can be addressed analytically; that is, the failure to see the source of their real anger at slavery and to change in light of that insight was due, in part, to white abolitionists' theoretical assumptions about human beings and society. By abandoning the assumptions of liberalism, white feminists can find theoretical underpinnings that are more in tune with the need to encounter the real differences between the situations of black and white women and the energy to change in light of these differences. For contemporary American society, this resides in an exploration of the nature of power as internalized by the entire society's experience of slavery.

Further, a change must take place in white women's understanding of themselves. I believe we must come to an ownership of the violence within. This theme is explored in great detail in Walker's *Meridian,* in her insights about black and white people, black and white women, and social change. An insight from that book that will be explored is the notion that if those who take up the struggle to change society want to do so only externally, they will defeat their own revolution. That which they seek to destroy in society will resurrect itself in their own psyches. The violence within must be defeated along with the violence without.

The Nature of Violence

> I know violence *is* as American as cherry pie.
> Alice Walker, *Meridian*

Despite the high incidence of violence—particularly against women and children[7]—in American society, most Americans regard themselves as a peace-loving people—a "free" society of rational citizens who value democracy. Much of the blindness of Americans to their own violence, especially toward the most vulnerable, is due to ignorance of the historical conditions of the formation of American society and a superficial understanding of the nature of violence.

Violence has often been defined as unjust coercive power. Karl von Clausewitz, the famous theorist of war, defined war as "an act of violence to compel the opponent to do as we wish."[8] But this definition betrays the common assumption that violence is always physical force. The term *violence* can be applied equally to overt physical force or to covert structures of repression. What is common to both, however, is compulsion.

The existence of covert structures of violence is a fairly recent insight generated primarily through the struggles of oppressed groups who have tried to understand their situations. Sexism, racism, and classism are now identified as violent because they exercise a kind of prior restraint that is coercive but does not necessarily, in the moment of being exercised, employ overt physical force. (The threat of physical force, however, is almost always present.)

Violence understood as unjust coercive power, exercised either covertly or overtly, depends upon an unequal distribution of power for its existence. In the previous chapter, I quoted Hannah Arendt, who has argued that the "extreme form of violence is One against All."[9] She also observed that

> even the most despotic domination we know of, the rule of masters over slaves, who always outnumbered him, did not rest on superior means of coercion as such, but on a superior organization of power—that is, on the organized solidarity of the masters.[10]

Thus we understand how it is possible for an elite minority of whites to maintain the violence of apartheid in South Africa. Theirs is a superior organization of power as domination that is consequently violent whether that violence is exercised covertly or overtly. The more power is organized unequally, the more violence results until, to recapitulate, the extreme of violence becomes One against All.

When power is understood and defended as control or domination, physical violence often results when that control is threatened. Hence violence has more recently been defined as a response of *powerlessness,* of what has been called "resourcelessness." From the struggles of the peace movement has come a definition of violence as the fear of a loss of control. Jo Vellacott, a Quaker peace activist, relates the following scenarios as an illustration of violence as resourcelessness.

> I am a member of an oppressed minority; I have no way of making you listen to me; I turn to terrorism. I am a dictator, yet I cannot force you to think as I want you to; I fling you in jail, starve your children, torture you. I am a woman in a conventional marriage situation; I feel helpless and inferior and powerless against my husband's constant undermining; so I in turn undermine him, manipulate him, make him look foolish in the eyes of his children. Or, I am a child unable to prevent her parents' constant quarrelling and to defend herself against her mother's sudden outbursts of rage. I smash something precious and run away, or I take to thieving, or I may even kill myself.[11]

By contrast, nonviolence can be construed as a response of resourcefulness. Herbert Marcuse is quoted by Vellacott as saying, "The success of the system is to make unthinkable the possibility of alternatives."[12] Nonviolence depends on a notion of power as pooling resources. While the masters in Arendt's analysis had some notion of solidarity, it was a solidarity dictated by the necessity to exclude the majority from participation in power. Power, however, may be conceived precisely as solidarity with the outsider, with the ones "out of power." It is a perspective that offers alternatives. Nonviolence can sound like a dependent term. The word means the absence of violence. Catherine Reid, an activist and writer from Vermont, states:

> I am often frustrated by the term non-violence as it seems to convey false assumptions of submission, passivity. "Non-violent" is only a fraction of its definition. Gandhi's term "satyagraha" seems much more useful. It means truth force. "Force" implies a more assertive, positive stand than does non-violence—that we rely on the strength of truth rather than on physical force.[13]

Obviously, then, understanding both violence and nonviolence requires an analysis of power. Power conceived as domination, especially in its extreme as the One dominating the All, depends upon terror for its maintenance and all-out physical force when challenged. Inevitably, it is either covertly or overtly violent.

A Slave Society and Violence

Alice Miller's work has demonstrated extensively that violence is not "innate" in the "nature of man," but rather is learned. If statistically Americans are an extremely violent society, especially toward those deemed socially powerless, where have they learned this violence?

One source of Americans' conviction that unjust coercion is an acceptable, even desirable exercise of power may be the more than two hundred years of legally institutionalized violence represented by slavery and Jim Crowism. The greater part of American history has seen the legal defense of both covert and overt structures of violence—including massive sexual violence—in the history of racial relations.

One might suppose that the Enlightenment ideals of faith in human rationality, the ontological identity of men and women, human beings as isolated individuals, and the natural rights doctrine would be in conflict with the system of slavery. Slavery as systemic brutalization, division of humanity into classes with distinctly different rights and the absence of certain rights held to be "self-evident" is not, at first glance, compatible with these Enlightenment ideals.

Yet from the time the New World was settled, conflict has been endemic in the American self-understanding. On the one hand, the New World is regarded by philosopher and trader alike as an Eden unsullied by Old World guilts. On the other, the wilderness is *also* feared as a place of unchecked license, the chaos that precedes civilization, and hence must be subdued. Some of this conflict is symbolically attributed to women—black and white. The slave woman takes on the character of the chaotic, untamed aspects of the wilderness; the white woman is Eve before the Fall, the remnant of the unsoiled soul in the midst of a sinful world. This division is also generalized to explain slavery in a society ordered by "self-evident truths." The slave represents the chaos of nature that must be subdued if civilization is to emerge.

The "natural law" doctrine is pressed into service to explain the existence of slavery. Thomas Reade Roots Cobb, one of the foremost legal scholars of the first half of the nineteenth century, offered the natural law doctrine as a major justification of the vast inequities in the system of laws in a slave-owning society. Cobb argued that "negro slavery is in no wise opposed to the law of nature," since American Negro slaves had been "found" in a condition of slavery in their native land. Continuing that slavery in the United States therefore leaves their natural condition unchanged.[14] As both person and property, the slave has different aspects of that condition protected under the law in different ways. As to person, the slave's person is protected in regard to "existence." Other rights are protected only to the extent that "are necessary to protect that existence." Hence, the penalties for rape would not and should not, "by such implication be made to extend to carnal forcible knowledge of a slave, *the offence not affecting the existence of the slave,* and that existence being the extent of the right which implication of the law grants."[15]

Cobb is in some doubt as to whether lawmakers should even concern themselves with rape as a problem in slavery. There was some legal consideration of "whether the offense of rape, committed upon a female slave, should not be indictable; and whether, when committed by the master, there should not be superadded the sale of the slave to some other master." Cobb questions the wisdom of such legal niceties, since "the occurrence of such an offence is almost unheard of; and the *known lasciviousness of the negro, renders the possibility of its occurrence very remote.*" Still, the law must be forced to consider all possibilities, no matter how remote. "Yet, for the honor of the statute book, if it does occur, there should be an adequate punishment."[16]

According to the above reasoning, the slave woman is regarded as the carnal aspect of this society. The connotation of lasciviousness as bestiality, sensuality, or uncontrolled salaciousness says much about the sources of slavery in natural law doctrine. The rational principle will always rule over the carnal principle in nature. The fact that Cobb is blind to the frequency with which slave women were brutally raped is demonstrated by his barely disguised revulsion at miscegenation, which is camouflaged as the "honor of the statute book."

It is instructive that Cobb himself appears to be offended by the fact of slavery, though he believes its existence "natural" and indeed necessary. He declares a conflict between "dictates of conscience enlightened by Christianity" and the law itself. "Pure slavery," at least, that which he assumes exists in Africa, has now, in a Christian society, at least been limited by law and so is mitigating "the power of the master [which] was absolute" in other cultures.[17] It is clear, as Arendt has argued, that the violence of slavery is predicated on the organized power of the masters. This is not limited by United States law, as Cobb fondly believes, but is in fact institutionalized into the very fabric of the American legal system.

Cobb adduces biblical arguments to support his contention that in a case of battery against a slave by the master, "there would be no redress whatever, for the reason given in Exodus 21:21, 'for he is his money.' "[18] But the master's "private interest" in preserving his property is all the protection the slave needs, in any case.

This biblically based argument for the priority of the slave's status as property over that of person provides the economic link without which these legal contortions would make no sense whatsoever. In the case of slavery, the natural law doctrine is captive to the economic service the slave provided to an agricultural economy. As with white female abolitionists, economic motive is not regarded by Cobb and other apologists for slavery as influencing their Enlightenment principles. If anything, the slave system is held to be the "natural order of things" from which the agricultural economy has grown.

Leaping forward slightly more than one hundred years, another apology for slavery entitled *Time on the Cross: The Economics of American Negro Slavery* by Fogel and Engerman, published in 1974, made the controversial argument that new methods of historical research called "cliometrics" had "revealed" that the institution of slavery was far more benign than previously thought, and economically extremely efficient.[19] The researchers' argument is that the aggressive and dynamic capitalism of the slave system had so improved the agricultural South that it had improved the standard of living for both slave and free. As their economic condition improved, slaves were converted to the benefits of the productive system of slavery and became "more ambitious." They learned the work ethic of their Victorian masters in a way free workers did not.

This volume produced a storm of reaction.[20] What is interesting for the purposes of this argument is the rampant and unexamined assumption, an assumption not targeted even by the most earnest critics, that human beings are rational and act in accordance with "enlightened interest." This book could be briefly summarized as "Ayn Rand meets the slave system." The slave masters, uniformly described as male, are said to have preferred not to resort to the physical punishment of slaves, as this would disturb their productivity, but rather relied on economic and work incentives to manage "their Negroes."

Numerous critics disputed the interpretation of the data offered to support this contention of the owner's restraint of physical brutality. Closer examination of records on whipping, for example, reveal that on the Barrow plantation, where records of whipping were kept, "a male was whipped every 6 days, and a female once every 12 days." During one twenty-three-month period, 175 whippings were recorded. Twelve female cotton pickers gave birth to fourteen children and seven of the mothers were whipped, two of them twice, and a third no fewer than four times.[21] Is this to be interpreted, according to Fogel and Engerman, as restraint? A whipping every four days indicates a visible, institutionalized physical terrorism that was augmented, these same records show, within the same two-year time frame, with jailing, chaining, beating with a stick, threats, shots, head raking, and public humiliation.[22]

Public whipping of women is sexual violence, yet the Fogel/Engerman volume argued that sexual exploitation of slave women was rare. The careful and sustained criticism of another publication, *Reckoning with Slavery*, details the unsupported and contradictory claims of *Time on the Cross*. It also exposes the contradiction between the picture of slavemasters as concerned that

> any attempt to interfere sexually in the lives of the slaves ultimately "might undermine slave morale and discipline." "Distraught and disgruntled slaves," we are told, "did not make good field hands."[23]

The slave owner as objective, profit-maximizing capitalist is similarly portrayed as preserving the "sanctity of the slave family."

> "Victorian attitudes predominated in the planting class," and these beliefs helped to protect slave women from "sexual exploitation." Fogel and Engerman report that sexual intercourse, whether forced or voluntary, between white men and slave women resulted in "only a very small percentage of the slaves born in any given year." They go on to claim that "racism" reduced the "demand of white males for black sexual partners."[24]

The contradiction is, of course, that if profit was the slave owner's overriding motive, humane gestures and social conventions would be overridden by more "direct practices," such as arranged matings, encouragement of early sexual intercourse, and rape.[25]

The fact that knowledgeable historians of American slavery could not afford to rely on the assumption that this monstrous book would simply be laughed at and disregarded, but had to write several extensive volumes refuting its claims, is testimony to the widespread American stereotypic view of slavery as an unfortunate but for the most part benign institution. What is particularly seductive about *Time on the Cross* is that it renovates the liberal doctrine of "man" as rational economic animal. The earlier version of this view of human nature as "rational man" was the one presumed by Cobb and other legal scholars who sought to order society according to natural laws, of which the inferiority of certain races was an unquestioned element.

The point I want to make here is that within the two most powerful systems ordering American life—law and economics—power is defended as control or domination according to race and sex. Hence in the major structures of American society—the legal and the economic—systemic violence is endemic. But these systems are not viewed as violent, but rather as rational and expedient means for ordering society.

The Violence of American Slavery and the Analysis of Patriarchy

Of the many studies of sexual and domestic violence that have emerged from the modern white women's movement, very few offer a political and economic context for interpreting male violence.[26] Feminists in the peace movement have likewise tended to analyze patriarchy monolithically, emphasizing the "natural" peacefulness of women— Mary Daly calls this "biophilia";[27] Helen Caldicott, women's "natural capacity for nurture";[28] and Mary Caudren, "women's nurturing instincts."[29]

Daly has argued that "patriarchy appears to be 'everywhere' . . . Even outer space and the future have been colonized."[30] Yet patriarchy *does not look the same everywhere*, which Daly seems to assume. She does not acknowledge the particular permutations of patriarchy in different social, political, and economic climates.

There are problems with defining patriarchy. It has been defined as "(1) a legalistic concept involving the historical period of father-right from antiquity to the demise of feudalism and (2) as an all encompassing view of human culture that spans recorded history to the present."[31]

These two definitions, as feminist theorist Zillah Eisenstein has pointed out, fail to acknowledge "the transformations patriarchy makes to accommodate the needs of particular economic systems without losing its original impetus to control the reproductive power of women and their place in the political structure."[32] A more comprehensive definition comes from Adrienne Rich.

> Patriarchy is the power of the fathers: a familial-social, ideological, political system in which men—by force, direct pressure, or through ritual, tradition, law and language, customs, etiquette, education and the division of labor, determine what part women shall or shall not play, and in which the female is everywhere subsumed under the male.[33]

The particular pattern of laws, customs, economics, etiquette, and tradition of American society is profoundly shaped by the American experience of slavery. This has therefore rendered American patriarchy inextricably interwoven with race and class as well as sex.

When white women employ a version of the natural law doctrine[34] to support claims for innate male aggressiveness and female peacefulness, what resources are offered in helping them to understand and confront their own history of violence toward black women? Further, how can this assumption provide a critical perspective on white women's current immersion in the structures of systemic racial and class violence?

Considering the bankruptcy of the modern, liberal "natural law" doctrine as it emerges in apologies for slavery both in the nineteenth and twentieth centuries, I believe as a white feminist I dare not allow my opposition to violence to reside only in women's (sic) natural peacefulness. I now contend that I must learn to talk about white women's violence.

Guilt and Atonement

While a perception of the relationship of white privilege and the history of American violence may be achieved by tinkering with analytical categories, the more difficult change is to encounter its internal contradictions to white women's understanding of themselves. It is more difficult, still, to encounter one's immersion in the systemic violence of racism and not be paralyzed by guilt. For it is equally true that most white women have already internalized blame to such a degree that they will seek to atone for the violent history of American racism without reservation and hence without insight. It is perfectly true that white women have cooperated in the history of American racism, but it is equally true that racism has helped bind white women to patriarchy by forcing their allegiance to white men over against black women and men.[35]

Black women, too, bear a disproportionate share of guilt for perpetuating social institutions that, in fact, hurt and destroy them. In *Meridian,* Alice Walker takes as her subject a black woman who in her own person tries to burn out the "consciousness of guilt" (p. 49), which she has carried around from the moment of her birth. Meridian's guilt is not only that she has stolen her mother's freedom, but that she has escaped her own unwilling childbearing, given her son away. Although she believes that in giving her child away "she had saved a small person's life" (p. 91), she almost wastes into death until a teacher, whom she mistakes in her delirium for her mother, whispers, "I forgive you" (p. 125).

Meridian's suffering on behalf of black motherhood is extended to suffering on behalf of black people. The sickness she struggles with throughout the novel (p. 25) is the sickness of her own kind: black Americans sick with the poisons of racism that the revolutionary violence they romanticize cannot even begin to destroy. *Meridian* as a novel has as one of its sources Walker's questions about the fashionable revolutionary violence of the second wave of the Civil Rights Movement—the black power movement.

As a student, Meridian's revolutionary cell despairs of her because she cannot say that she will kill for the revolution. The new black revolutionary wars in her with "something from the past" (p. 27). This something from the past is the moral integrity, the "invisible dignity" (Cannon) that has been won through centuries of enduring unspeakable suffering. "If they committed murder—and to her even revolutionary murder was murder—*what would the music be like?*" (p. 28). It is not until she has gone backward, to the people and their past that holds her up, that she can go anywhere else.

The years Meridian has devoted to living through the pain enables her to face up to the fact that there is no forward or backward because the "years in America had created them One Life" (p. 200). It's not that she is incapable of killing to prevent injustice; in fact she comes to see that she is free even to face this because of her spiritual struggles. The understanding she has acquired is this: "that even the contemplation of murder required incredible delicacy as it required incredible spiritual work . . ." (p. 200). What she has suffered so long to realize is that the revolutionary violence (perhaps "correct" politics at the moment, but never "right") will destroy those who employ it. It then becomes Meridian's part "to walk behind the real revolutionaries—those who know they must spill blood in order to help the poor and the black and therefore go right ahead—and when they stop to wash off the blood and find their throats too choked with the smell of murdered flesh to sing, I will come forward and sing from memory songs they will need once more to hear. For it is the song of the people, transformed by the experiences of each generation, that holds them together, and if any part of it is lost the people suffer and are without soul" (p. 201). Without suffering through the pain, the soul of struggle is lost and revolutionary violence is just murder. This is what Truman Held begins to understand at the end of the novel (p. 220).

As a white person, I explore the issue of violence not from an academic perspective but as one who is both victim and beneficiary of the fact that "violence *is* as American as cherry pie!" (p. 31). The idea of white women as both victims and beneficiaries of American violence is also sensitively portrayed in *Meridian*. The white civil rights worker Lynne Rabinowitz, from an exclusive women's college in the North, romantically admires the black people of the South as "Art" (p. 130). She dates and then marries Truman Held, who, on a good day, looked "like Che Guevara" (p. 24).

Lynne is "guilty of whiteness" (p. 133) perhaps in her own eyes, but certainly in the eyes of Tommy Odds, who has been maimed for life by a gang of white men. Odds hates Lynne's whiteness and forces himself on her one day when Truman is away. Instead of pushing him away, she is overcome by pity: "She thought about the loss of his arm. She felt her own guilt . . . and before he left she told him she forgave him and she kissed his slick rounded stump that was the color of baked liver" (p. 159).

Interlocking layers of violence conspire against these people—both victims, both perpetrators of violence. Truman's black male friends are afraid of Lynne because a white woman "was a route to Death, pure and simple" (p. 137). But convinced, by the years of self-expression permitted her in her upbringing, that all things can be overcome by charm, Lynne does "make friends" with Truman's friends. But even she cannot overcome the scars of racial violence, the false accusations of rape, that led to lynchings and maimings. And she conspires in creating the conditions of her own sexual exploitation.

Lynne's sufferings, like Meridian's, transform even as they scar. After Truman leaves her, Lynne comes to realize that great as the pain has been, "I can never be as dumb as my mother was. Even if I practiced not knowing what the world is like, even if I lived in Scarsdale or some other weird place, and never had to eat welfare food in my life, I'd still *know*." One of the things she knows is how foolish is the life of an oppressor. "I don't like them [oppressors]; they make me feel guilty all the time. They're ugly and don't know poor people laugh at them and are just waiting to drag them out" (p. 181).

Life and its sufferings are not overcome, but living through the pain is *"instructional"* (p. 181). It is the knowledge of good and evil that comes from that instruction in living. Nobody gets it right all the time. Lynne and Meridian have an exchange that summarizes my argument in this book on the difference it makes to white women to encounter race.

> "Besides," she [Lynne] continued, "nobody's perfect."
> "Except white women," said Meridian, and winked.
> "Yes," said Lynne, "but their time will come" (p. 181).

White women do need to come to terms with the white privilege that has been conferred on them through the systemic violence of American racism. I am not, even by virtue of the injustices practiced on the bodies and minds of white women every day, freed from the necessity to include this systemic violence in my analyses. But I have barely scratched the surface of the change that is necessary when I alter my analytical categories to expose the systemic violence of arguments according to nature. I must acknowledge that women's nature *(sic)* is not inherently peaceful and benign but capable of tremendous violence, both overt and covert.

I will not allow this insight to once again trigger white women's sense of guilt and spend the rest of my days wallowing in atonement. I must come to a forthright knowledge of good and evil, and live through the pain with both a hermeneutic of suspicion of racial privilege and a hermeneutic of the truth of white women's suffering as my tools. I don't know whether this is the best time for all white women to give up being perfect but I do know it's high time I did.

Notes

Introduction

1. The substance of this book may be found in the article "God and Her Survival in a Nuclear Age," *Journal of Feminist Studies in Religion* 4, no. 1 (Spring 1988), pp. 73–88.

2. "Narrative and Connection," *Christianity and Crisis* (March 2, 1987), pp. 71–75.

3. See Carol Christ's letter responding to my article and my reply in "Connections with the World of the Spirit," *Christianity and Crisis* 47, no. 13 (September 28, 1987), p. 320.

4. Audre Lorde, "The Master's Tools Will Never Dismantle the Master's House," in *This Bridge Called My Back: Writings by Radical Women of Color,* ed. Cherríe Moraga and Gloria Anzaldúa (Watertown, MA: Persephone Press, 1981), p. 100.

5. Lorde, "Master's Tools," p. 99.

6. *God's Fierce Whimsy: Christian Feminism and Theological Education* (New York: Pilgrim Press, 1985), p. 36.

7. Shiva Naipul, "The 'Third World' Does Not Exist," *Global Perspectives: A Newsletter of the Center for Global Education* (March/April 1987), p. 1.

8. There are several good anthologies on black women's fiction. See especially Mari Evans, ed., *Black Women Writers (1950–1980): A Critical Evaluation* (Garden City, NY: Anchor Press, 1984). A general anthology, Richard A. Long and Eugenia W. Collier, eds., *Afro-American Writing: An Anthology of Prose and Poetry,* 2nd ed. (University Park, PA: Pennsylvania State University Press, 1985), contains some black women's writing from 1760 onward.

9. Some sociological studies have now emerged; see the section "Social Analysis" on p. 7.

10. See Mary Helen Washington, ed., *Invented Lives: Narratives of Black Women, 1860–1960* (Garden City, NY: Doubleday, 1978); also, Alice Walker, *In Search of Our Mothers' Gardens: Womanist Prose* (San Diego: Harcourt Brace Jovanovich, 1983).

11. "Poetry Is Not a Luxury," in *Sister Outsider: Essays and Speeches* (Trumansburg, NY: Crossing Press, 1984), pp. 36–39.

12. Katie G. Cannon, *Black Womanist Ethics* (Atlanta: Scholars Press, 1988).

13. Judith Plaskow, *Sex, Sin and Grace: Women's Experience and the Theologies of Reinhold Niebuhr and Paul Tillich* (Washington, DC: University Press of America, 1980), pp. 34ff.

14. Carol P. Christ, *Diving Deep and Surfacing* (Boston: Beacon Press, 1980).

15. Yet, as I contend below, this fiction does remain *fiction*. I believe that as a white feminist, given my temptations to interiority, I should employ the fields of sociology, anthropology, economics, and so forth to check and double check my interpretations of these works. See pp. 3–7, below.

16. Barbara Christian, *Black Women Novelists: The Development of a Tradition, 1892–1976* (Westport, CT: Greenwood Press, 1980), p. 144.

17. Gloria Wade-Gayles, *No Crystal Stair: Visions of Race and Sex in Black Women's Fiction* (New York: Pilgrim Press, 1984), p. 4.

18. Toni Cade Bambara, "Salvation Is the Issue," in *Black Women Writers*, ed. Evans, p. 47.

19. Carol P. Christ, "Why Women Need the Goddess: Phenomenological, Psychological, and Political Reflections," in *Womanspirit Rising: A Feminist Reader in Religion,* ed. Carol P. Christ and Judith Plaskow (San Francisco: Harper & Row, 1979), p. 273, quoting Ntozake Shange, "For Colored Girls Who Have Considered Suicide When the Rainbow is Enuf," from the original cast album, Buddah Records, 1976.

20. See Christ's lengthy discussion of *for colored girls who have considered suicide/when the rainbow is enuf* in Chap. 7 of *Diving Deep and Surfacing,* esp. pp. 97, 101, 103, 117, and *passim.*

21. *for colored girls who have considered suicide/when the rainbow is enuf* (New York: Bantam Books, 1986), p. 67.

22. Ibid., p. xxi.

23. See *Laughter of Aphrodite: Reflections on a Journey to the Goddess* (San Francisco: Harper & Row, 1987), pp. xv–xvi.

24. Hannah Arendt, *On Violence* (New York: Harcourt, Brace and World, 1969), pp. 64–65. This book is a curious amalgam of penetrating insights on a number of complex issues such as white liberal guilt and of strongly entrenched bias against the black liberation movement of the 1960s. See her critiques of Frantz Fanon, for example, pp. 12, 14, 20, 21n, 65, 67, 69, 71, 75, 90.

25. Alice Walker, *In Search of Our Mothers' Gardens,* pp. xi–xii. Walker continues her definition:

> From the black folk expression of mothers to female children, "You acting womanish," i.e., like a woman. Usually referring to outrageous, audacious, courageous or *willful* behavior. Wanting to know more and in greater depth than is considered "good" for one. . . . 2). *Also:* A woman who loves other women, sexually and/or nonsexually. . . . Committed to survival and wholeness of entire people, male *and* female . . . Traditionally capable, as in: "Mama, I'm walking to Canada and I'm taking you and a bunch of other slaves with me." Reply: "It wouldn't be the first time." 3). Loves music. Loves dance. Loves the moon. *Loves* the Spirit. Loves love and food and roundness. Loves struggle. *Loves* the folk. Loves herself. *Regardless.* 4). Womanist is to feminist as purple to lavender.

26. I have noted the unmodified use of the term "women" by the use of *(sic)* in order to call attention to its inappropriately universalized connotations. This remains my practice throughout the book.

27. Recently, groups of oppressed peoples throughout the world have proposed that the systematic exploitation of groups and individuals be called "systemic violence." Systemic violence is not, in the moment of its exercise, characterized by forms of overt, physical violence such as shooting, whipping, hitting, etc., but rather by the constriction of opportunity or the unjust exploitation of labor, for example. Systemic violence almost always, however, includes the threat of physical violence. The structural injustices that characterize systemic violence often require occasional physical force or terrorism for their maintenance. See Susan Brooks Thistlethwaite, *A Just Peace Church* (New York: Pilgrim Press, 1986), pp. 39–45. American slavery combined systemic violence in the very concept of a hierarchy of slave and master and was maintained by frequent use of physical violence. In the structurally violent relationship between slave-owning white woman and black women slaves, physical violence accompanied, indeed, was a necessary accompaniment to the maintenance of slavery. Defining black and white women as different species tended to facilitate the exercise of systemic as well as physical violence between them because dehumanization of black women rendered the structural inequalities less visible and removed the moral impediments to physical violence.

28. In Rosemary Radford Ruether's course "The Church and Social Systems," the students write a paper tracing the economic history of their family. Rosemary has often observed to me that those with patently working-class backgrounds still describe themselves as middle-class. As we discussed this topic, Mary Pellauer, a feminist ethicist, remarked that it was a black woman in New York who suggested that she study the Vikings in order to understand her Norwegian family and its stresses.

Chapter 1 / Experience in White Feminist Theory

1. Bell Hooks, *Feminist Theory: From Margin to Center* (Boston: South End Press, 1984), pp. 1ff. It is always important to me to point out, however, that the "problem that has no name" may not, in fact, have been accurately identified by Friedan even for white middle-class, college-educated women. Applying the 50 percent guideline on the frequency with which wife battering occurs, it is far more likely that white women sought to escape the home because of the incidence of abuse (one of its causes, economic dependency, is directly related to whether women work outside the home and have economic independence). See, for example, R. Emerson Dobash and Russell Dobash, *Violence Against Wives* (New York: The Free Press, 1979), esp. Chap. 4, "The Nuclear Family and the Chastisement of Wives," pp. 48–74. My discussion of the abuse of women is in Chapter Eight.

2. It should be noted that Friedan's new work on "postfeminism" suffers from the same myopia. See *The Second Stage* (New York: Summit Books, 1981).

3. Hooks, *Feminist Theory,* p. 3, quoting Rita Mae Brown, "The Last Straw," in *Class and Feminism,* ed. Charlotte Bunch and Nancy Myron (Baltimore: Diana Press, 1974), pp. 14–23.

4. Susan Brooks Thistlethwaite, *Metaphors for the Contemporary Church* (New York: Pilgrim Press, 1983), pp. 5–9. I wrote:

> Feminist theologians tend to begin with their experience. Because women's experience has so often been denied to be universally human, the beginning point for almost all feminist thought is a recovery of the specifics of women's experience. But this is not experience conceived only as reflection on the subjective self, but includes experience of objective forces within history.

5. Sheila Greeve Davaney, "The Limits of the Appeal to Women's Experience," presentation to the Women and Religion Section of the American Academy of Religion, November 1986. In addition to quoting Hooks, Davaney also notes Jacquelyn Grant, "A Black Response to Feminist Theology," in *Women's Spirit Bonding,* ed. Janet Kalven and Mary I. Buckley (New York: Pilgrim Press, 1984), pp. 117–24, and "Black Feminist Theology: Celebration in the Midst of Struggle," unpublished keynote address, Women's Inter-Seminary Conference, Denver, Colorado, 1986.

6. The term *thealogy* is used to describe feminist reflections on the Goddess. In Greek *thea* is the feminine of the word for the divine. See Carol P. Christ, *Laughter of Aphrodite: Reflections on a Journey to the Goddess* (San Francisco: Harper & Row, 1987), p. ix–xvii. Christ credits Naomi Goldenberg with coining this term. See p. ix, note 1.

7. The field currently called the "sociology of knowledge" has as its task the description of this approach to the nature of knowledge. See, for example, the ground-breaking epistemology outlined in Jürgen Habermas, *Knowledge and Human Interests,* trans. Jeremy L. Shapiro (Boston: Beacon Press, 1971).

8. See Susan Brooks Thistlethwaite, "Still Crazy After All These Years," in *Opening Closed Doors: Theological Education and Sexual and Domestic Violence,* ed. Carol Adams (n.d.).

9. I do not believe that anyone raised in a racist society ceases to be racist. I have adapted the term "recovering sexist" from Mary Pellauer (following the AA model) and noted that we are all *always* "recovering racists" in this society.

10. This is the same epistemological shift that is going on in the theologies of liberation. It is by now axiomatic that theologies of liberation have their analyses rooted in the social, political, and economic context of the situation these theological works address. Thus, Gustavo Gutiérrez's landmark study, *A Theology of Liberation: History, Politics, and Salvation* (Maryknoll, NY: Orbis, 1973), begins with a thorough discussion of development and a critique of developmentalism as it has been practiced in Latin America. Unless and until the false consciousness created by the illusion of development is addressed, the theological question cannot even be posed.

11. (Maryknoll, NY: Orbis, 1985).

12. Sheila Greeve Davaney, "The Limits of the Appeal to Experience," unpublished paper, 1986, pp. 2–3.

13. Ibid., p. 24.

14. Michel Foucault, *Power/Knowledge: Selected Interviews and Other Writings, 1972–1977,* trans. Colin Gordon et al., ed. Colin Gordon (New York: Pantheon Books, 1981), pp. 109–33.

15. Chris Weedon, *Feminist Practice and Poststructuralist Theory* (New York: Basil Blackwell, 1987), pp. 125f.

16. Ibid., pp. 117–25; see also Michel Foucault, *The History of Sexuality,* vol. 1, *An Introduction* (New York: Pantheon Books, 1978) and *The History of Sexuality,* vol. 2, *The Use of Pleasure* (New York: Pantheon Books, 1986).

17. Sandra Harding, "The Instability of the Analytical Categories of Feminist Theory," *Signs* 13, no. 3 (1988), p. 646.

18. Ibid., p. 657.

19. Poststructuralism is well interpreted for feminist theory in Weedon, *Feminist Practice and Poststructuralist Theory.* Weedon argues that "Poststructuralist theories of language, subjectivity, discourse and power seem to me to offer useful ways of understanding experience and relating it to social power" (p. vii).

20. Mary Daly, *Pure Lust: Elemental Feminist Philosophy* (Boston: Beacon Press, 1984), pp. 135–38. An excellent discussion of the early feminist existentialism of Simone de Beauvoir and its influence in later feminist theory may be found in Josephine Donovan, *Feminist Theory: The Intellectual Traditions of American Feminism* (New York: Ungar, 1985), pp. 117–40.

21. Mary Daly, *Gyn/Ecology: The Metaethics of Radical Feminism* (Boston: Beacon Press, 1978), p. 8; see also *Beyond God the Father: Toward a Philosophy of Women's Liberation* (Boston: Beacon Press, 1973), pp. 95–97.

22. See *Websters' First New Intergalactic Wickedary of the English Language,* "conjured by Mary Daly in Cahoots with Jane Caputi" (Boston: Beacon Press, 1987), "Word-Web Three, the inhabitants of the foreground, their activities and characteristics," pp. 183–235.

23. Joel Kovel, *White Racism: A Psychohistory* (New York: Columbia University Press, 1984), p. x.

24. Ibid.

25. Daly, *Pure Lust,* pp. 4–5.

26. Ibid., p. 4.

27. Ibid., p. 5.

28. Ibid., p. 6.

29. Ibid., p. 293.

30. For example, Paul Tillich's theological perspective would need to be examined for its origins in European notions of "truth" and "beauty," categories that Cornel West has pointed out are deeply dependent, in white Western philosophy, on assumptions of racial superiority. See Cornel West, *Prophesy Deliverance! An Afro-American Revolutionary Christianity* (Philadelphia: Westminster, 1982), p. 48. See also Susan Brooks Thistlethwaite, "The Literature of Black Women and the Doctrine of Justification," in *Love: The Foundation of Hope: The Theology of Jürgen Moltmann and Elisabeth Moltmann-Wendel,* ed. Frederic B. Burnham et al. (San Francisco: Harper & Row, 1988), p. 132.

31. Audre Lorde, *Sister Outsider: Essays and Speeches* (Trumansburg, NY: Crossing Press, 1984), pp. 66–71.

32. Lorde, "Age, Race, Class, and Sex: Women Redefining Difference," in *Sister Outsider,* p. 115.

33. Ibid., p. 115.

34. Ibid., p. 116.

35. Rosemary Radford Ruether, *New Woman/New Earth: Sexist Ideologies and Human Liberation* (New York: Seabury, 1975), pp. 4, 195.

36. Paulo Freire, *Pedagogy of the Oppressed* (New York: Herder and Herder, 1970), p. 19. The term *conscientização* refers to "learning to perceive social, political, and economic contradictions, and to take action against the oppressive elements of reality."

37. David McLellan, *The Thought of Karl Marx: An Introduction* (New York: Harper & Row, 1971), p. 199.

38. William Lloyd Newell, *The Secular Magi: Marx, Freud, and Nietzsche on Religion* (New York: Pilgrim Press, 1986), pp. 147–55.

39. Peter Gay in H. Stuart Hughes, *Consciousness and Society: The Reorientation of European Social Thought, 1890–1930* (New York: Basic Books, 1977), p. 152, italics added. Gay's new biography is *Freud: A Life for Our Times* (New York: W. W. Norton, 1988).

40. See *Psychoanalysis and Women,* ed. Jean Baker Miller (New York: Bruner/Mazel, 1973); Juliet Mitchell, *Psychoanalysis and Feminism* (New York: Vintage, 1975); Nancy Chodorow, *The Reproduction of Mothering* (Berkeley: University of California Press, 1978); Dorothy Dinnerstein, *The Mermaid and the Minotaur: Sexual Arrangements and Human Malaise* (New York: Harper & Row, 1977); Naomi Goldenberg, *The Changing of the Gods: Feminism and the End of Traditional Religions* (Boston: Beacon Press, 1979). This does not even take into account the hegemony of psychology in such popular feminist writers as Anne Wilson Schaef.

41. See, for example, the many publications of Cheryl Gilkes, an ordained black woman in the National Baptist Convention U.S.A. with a Ph.D. in sociology from Northeastern. Among these are " 'If It Wasn't for the Women . . .': Social Change, Racial-Ethnic Women, and Their Community Work," in *Women of Color in America,* ed. Maxine Baca Zinn and Bonnie Thronton Dill (Philadelphia: Temple University Press, forthcoming); " 'Liberated to Work Like Dogs!': Labeling Black Women and their Work," in *The Experience and Meaning of Work for Women,* ed. Nia Lane Chester and Hildy Grossman (Hillsdale, NJ: Lawrence Earlbaum Assoc., forthcoming); "Discovering What 'Everybody Knows,' " in *Sociology,* ed. Beth B. Hess, Elizabeth W. Markson, and Peter J. Stein, 3rd ed. (New York: Macmillan, 1988), as well as the several other works cited in this book.

42. In an essay on her writing, Toni Cade Bambara has said that what informs her work is the question "Do we intend to have a future as sane, whole, governing people?" "Salvation Is the Issue," in *Black Women Writers (1950–1980): A Critical Evaluation* (Garden City, NY: Anchor Press, 1984), p. 47.

43. McLellan, *The Thought of Karl Marx,* p. 389.

44. Paraphrased from *The Main Enemy* in Michele Barrett, *Women's Oppression Today* (London: Verso, 1980), p. 18.

45. Zillah Eisenstein, "Developing a Theory of Capitalist Patriarchy," in Zillah Eisenstein, ed., *Capitalist Patriarchy and the Case for Socialist Feminism* (New York: Monthly Review Press, 1979), p. 11.

46. Susan Griffin, *Woman and Nature: The Roaring Inside Her* (New York: Harper & Row, 1978), p. 219. This is not to say that Griffin has no understanding of the violent conflict between what patriarchy says about woman and nature and that nature as it is experienced by *some women*. But as in Daly's works, the experience of women is here aligned with nature and ranged over against patriarchal violence and destruction; it is also undifferentiated. As evidence of this undifferentiation I offer the consistent use of the word "we" to describe women's *(sic)* experience, and the quotations of black women that are employed with no attention to the fact that their words may describe the different ways in which black and white women are regarded by patriarchal culture; or the different ways in which black women may regard their own experience and its relation to nature (p. 166).

47. As economically oppressed people, black women have been socialized to see existence in terms of struggle and conflict. This has made the possibility of bonding among black women very problematic. See Lorde, "Eye to Eye" in *Sister Outsider*, pp. 145–75.

48. Beverly Harrison, "The Power of Anger in the Work of Love," in *Making the Connections*, ed. Carol Robb (Boston: Beacon Press, 1985), pp. 9–14, italics added.

49. Lenore E. Walker, *The Battered Woman* (New York: Harper & Row, 1979), esp. pp. 69–70. Walker identifies the "cycle of violence" that exists in a battering relationship and notes the times during this cycle when battered women are more and less motivated to change the relationship.

50. Susan Schechter, *Women and Male Violence: The Struggles of the Battered Women's Movement* (Boston: South End Press, 1982). See esp. Chap. 2, "The Roots of the Battered Women's Movement: Personal and Political."

51. See Jennifer Baker Fleming, *Stopping Wife Abuse: A Guide to the Emotional, Psychological, and Legal Implications for the Abused Woman and Those Helping Her* (Garden City, NY: Anchor, 1979), pp. 18–19, 20, 23, 50, 59, 81–83, 87, 101, 120, 123–24, 143, 235, but esp. p. 81.

52. "Every Two Minutes: Battered Women and Biblical Interpretation," in *Feminist Interpretation of the Bible*, ed. Letty Russell (Philadelphia: Westminster, 1985), pp. 96–107; statistics cited in note 1.

53. Recorded in Alice Rossi, ed., *The Feminist Papers* (New York: Bantam Books, 1973), p. 428. I have changed the wording from the Francis Gage papers recorded in Rossi to conform to Bell Hook's rendering in *Ain't I a Woman? Black Women and Feminism* (Boston: South End Press, 1981), p. 160. Racist overtones are revealed in Gage's exaggerated spellings.

54. Keep in mind that the major male figures of poststructuralism include Ferdinand de Saussure and his structural linguistics, Emile Benveniste, Karl Marx, Louis Althusser and his theory of ideology, Sigmund Freud, and Jacques

Lacan. Jacques Derrida and his critique of the metaphysics of presence, as well as Michel Foucault's theory of discourse and power, are also included in this classification.

Chapter 2 / Slavery: A White Feminist History

1. See anthologies such as *Black Women Writers (1950–1980): A Critical Evaluation,* ed. Mari Evans (Garden City, NY: Anchor Press, 1984); *Black Women Writers at Work,* ed. Claudia Tate (New York: Continuum, 1986); and, of course, Barbara Christian, *Black Feminist Criticism: Perspectives on Black Women Writers* (New York: Pergamon, 1985).

2. Katie Geneva Cannon, *Black Womanist Ethics* (Atlanta: Scholars Press, 1988); Jacquelyn Grant, *White Women's Christ and Black Women's Jesus: White Feminist Christology and Womanist Response* (Atlanta: Scholars Press, 1989).

3. See Eleanor Flexner, *Century of Struggle: The Women's Rights Movement in the United States* (New York: Atheneum, 1972); Carol Ellen DuBois, *Feminism and Suffrage: The Emergence of an Independent Women's Movement in America, 1848–1869* (Ithaca, NY: Cornell University Press, 1978); William O'Neill, *Everyone Was Brave: The Rise and Fall of Feminism in America* (New York: Quadrangle, 1969); dissenting views are found in Pamela Allen, "Woman Suffrage: Feminism and White Supremacy," Chap. 5 in *Reluctant Reformers,* ed. Robert Allen (Washington, DC: Howard University Press, 1974), pp. 136ff.; and Gloria T. Hull, Patricia Bell Scott and Barbara Smith, eds., *But Some of Us Are Brave: Black Women's Studies* (Old Westbury, NY: Feminist Press, 1982).

4. Barbara Andolsen, *Daughters of Jefferson, Daughters of Bootblacks: Racism and American Feminism* (Macon, GA: Mercer University Press, 1986); Elizabeth Fox-Genovese, *Within the Plantation Household: Black and White Women of the Old South* (Chapel Hill, NC: University of North Carolina Press, 1988). The publication of these two studies indicates that there may be a trend developing among white women to reevaluate the role of white women in slavery.

5. Fox-Genovese, *Within the Plantation,* p. 192.

6. See, for example, Nancy F. Cott, *The Bonds of Womanhood: "Woman's Sphere" in New England, 1780–1835* (New Haven: Yale University Press, 1977); or Barbara Welter, *Dimity Convictions: The American Woman in the Nineteenth Century* (Athens: Ohio University Press, 1976). Cott specifies her area of investigation. Welter, however, uses the general label "American" to mean Northern, white, educated, middle-class women. Her sources are primarily from Boston and Philadelphia.

7. Gerda Lerner, *Black Women in White America: A Documentary History* (New York: Pantheon Books, 1972), p. 19.

8. Bell Hooks, *Ain't I a Woman? Black Women and Feminism* (Boston: South End Press, 1981), p. 37.

9. Ibid., pp. 37–39.

10. Andrew Sinclair, *The Emancipation of the American Woman* (New York: Harper-Colophon, 1965), quoted in Hooks, *Ain't I a Woman?,* p. 30.

11. Fox-Genovese, *Within the Plantation*, pp. 197–98.

12. Ibid., p. 199, citing William Harper, *Memoir on Slavery Read Before the Society for the Advancement of Learning at Its Annual Meeting in Columbia, 1837* (Charleston, SC, 1838), pp. 3, 4, 6, 7.

13. Susan Brownmiller, *Against Our Will: Men, Women and Rape* (New York: Bantam Books, 1975), p. 165 (see also pp. 166–88). Bell Hooks faults Brownmiller for "tend[ing] to see devaluation of black womanhood as occurring only in the context of slavery. In actuality, sexual exploitation of black women continued long after slavery ended and was institutionalized by other oppressive practices" (*Ain't I a Woman?*, p. 59).

14. Ann Douglas, *The Feminization of American Culture* (New York: Knopf, 1977), pp. 50–93.

15. Welter, *Dimity Convictions*, esp. Chap. 2, "The Cult of True Womanhood: 1800–1860," pp. 21–41.

16. Harriet Beecher Stowe, *Uncle Tom's Cabin* (New York: Macmillan, 1926).

17. The Fox-Genovese volume documents at some length the *resistance* of black women to slavery. *Within the Plantation*, pp. 16–17, 201, 308, 329, contains some examples. Her total references to slave women's resistance in revolts, murder, arson, running away, poisoning, psychological resistance, infanticide, abortion, and suicide number in the dozens.

18. Quoted in Hooks, *Ain't I a Woman?*, p. 28. See also Fox-Genovese, *Within the Plantation*, p. 363.

19. Sarah Grimké, *Letters on the Equality of the Sexes and the Condition of Woman* (1838) (New York: Burt Franklin, 1970), p. 60.

20. Ibid., p. 98.

21. Quoted from Alice S. Rossi, ed., *The Feminist Papers: From Adams to de Beauvoir* (New York: Bantam Books, 1974), pp. 305–6.

22. *Letters on the Equality of the Sexes*, quoted in Rossi, p. 314.

23. Ibid., pp. 314–15.

24. This type of apples and oranges comparison of black women's economic and social pain with white women's psychological pain occurs in contemporary feminist writing, as is obvious from the Ulanov or Washbourn writings quoted in the next chapter.

25. Angela Davis, *Women, Race and Class* (New York: Random House, 1981), p. 29.

26. Fox-Genovese, *Within the Plantation*, p. 329.

27. Quoted in Gerda Lerner, *The Grimké Sisters from South Carolina: Pioneers for Woman's Rights and Abolition* (New York: Schocken Books, 1973), pp. 161–62, italics added.

28. Elizabeth Cady Stanton, *The Woman's Bible*, 2 vols. (1895 and 1899) (New York: Arno, 1972), pp. 680–81. See also Catherine Stimpson, " 'Thy Neighbor's Wife, Thy Neighbor's Servants': Women's Liberation and Black Civil Rights," in *Woman in Sexist Society*, ed. Vivian Gornick and Barbara K. Moran (New York: Basic Books, 1971), pp. 453–79. A modern use of this analogy is found in Helen Mayer Hacker, "Women as a Minority Group" (Indianapolis: Bobbs-Merrill reprint, 1951).

29. Quoted in Rossi, ed., *Feminist Papers*, p. 428, spelling corrected following Hooks, *Ain't I a Woman?*, p. 160. See Chapter One, n. 53, above.

30. Hooks, *Ain't I a Woman?*, p. 4.

31. Susan Brooks Thistlethwaite, "Ephesians 5:21–33: Sex, Race and Class in Ephesians," published as "Missbrauch fuhrt zu Misshandlung," in *Feministisch gelesen: 32 ausgewahlte Bibeltexte für Gruppen, Gemeinden und Gottesdienste*, ed. Eva Renate Schmidt, Mieke Korenhof, and Renate Jost (Stuttgart: Kreuz-Verlag, 1988), pp. 253–59.

32. See H. Shelton Smith, *In His Image, But . . . Racism in Southern Religion* (Durham, NC: Duke University Press, 1972). See index of biblical texts cited by Smith.

33. Ralph Andreano, ed., *New Views on American Economic Development: A Selective Anthology of Recent Work* (Cambridge: Harvard University Press, 1965). See also Jean H. Baker, *Affairs of Party: The Political Culture of Northern Democrats in the Mid-Nineteenth Century* (Ithaca, NY: Cornell University Press, 1983).

34. Miriam Gurko, *The Ladies of Seneca Falls: The Birth of the Women's Rights Movement* (New York: Schocken Books, 1976), p. 213.

35. Elizabeth Cady Stanton, *Eighty Years and More: Reminiscences 1815–1897* (New York: Schocken Books, 1917), pp. 240–41.

36. Susan B. Anthony and Ida Husted Harper, eds., *History of Woman Suffrage* (Rochester, NY: Susan B. Anthony, 1902), vol. 2, pp. 94–95 (note).

37. Ibid., p. 245.

38. Gurko, *The Ladies*, p. 221; also Stanton, *Eighty Years*, p. 256.

39. Anthony and Harper, *History of Woman Suffrage*, vol. 2, p. 245.

40. Ibid., p. 189.

41. Rossi, ed., *Feminist Papers*, pp. 415ff, italics added. See also Fox-Genovese, *Within the Plantation*, p. 336. Fox-Genovese is one of the few white women to have considered class in relationship to this entire issue. She and Eugene Genovese, she notes, "will discuss these institutions in depth in our forthcoming book *The Mind of the Master Class* (title tentative)" (p. 436).

42. This is the subject of Katie G. Cannon's work *Black Womanist Ethics*. Cannon argues that "the cherished ethical ideas predicated upon the existence of freedom and a wide range of choices proved null and void in situations of oppression" (p. 2). This work will be discussed at length in Chapter Five.

43. Davis, *Sex, Race and Class*, p. 36.

44. Rosalyn Baxandall, Linda Gordon, Susan Reverby, eds., *America's Working Women: A Documentary History—1600 to the Present* (New York: Random House, 1976), p. 46.

45. Harriet H. Robinson, *Loom and Spindle or Life Among the Early Mill Girls* (Kailua, HI: Press Pacifica, 1976).

46. Barbara Wertheimer, *We Were There: The Story of Working Women in America* (New York: Pantheon Books, 1977), pp. 66ff.

47. Baxandall et al., *America's Working Women*, p. 66.

48. Wertheimer, *We Were There*, p. 103.

49. Lerner, *Grimké Sisters*, p. 335.

50. Robinson, *Loom and Spindle*, p. 51.

51. Ida B. Wells, *Crusade for Justice: The Autobiography of Ida B. Wells,* ed. Alfreda M. Duster (Chicago and London: University of Chicago Press, 1970), p. 230.

52. Ibid., p. 229.

53. Anthony and Harper, *History of Woman Suffrage,* vol. 4, p. 246.

54. Ibid., p. 216 (note).

55. Carolyn Merchant, *The Death of Nature: Women, Ecology, and the Scientific Revolution* (New York: Harper & Row, 1980), p. 27. It should be obvious that Merchant has been influenced by Sherry Ortner.

56. Ibid., p. 168.

57. Zillah Eisenstein, *The Radical Future of Liberal Feminism* (New York: Longman, 1981), p. 95, quoting Mary Wollstonecraft.

Chapter 3 / Class and Creation

1. Beatrice Royster, "The Ironic Vision of Four Black Women Novelists," Ph.D. dissertation, Emory University, 1975, p. 158, quoted in Gloria Wade-Gayles, *No Crystal Stair: Visions of Race and Sex in Black Women's Fiction* (New York: Pilgrim Press, 1984), p. 149.

2. Carol P. Christ, *Laughter of Aphrodite: Reflections on a Journey to the Goddess* (San Francisco: Harper & Row, 1987), p. ix.

3. "God and Her Survival in the Nuclear Age," *Journal of Feminist Studies in Religion* 4, no. 1 (Spring 1988), p. 87.

4. Vernon Lattin, "Ann Petry and the American Dream," *Black American Literature Forum* 15 (Summer 1978): 69. Analysis cited in Wade-Gayles, *No Crystal Stair,* p. 152.

5. In *Gather Together in My Name,* Maya Angelou writes:

> In my memory, Stamps [Arkansas] is a place of light, shadow, sounds and entranc-
> ing odors. The earth smell was pungent, spiced with the odor of cattle manure, the
> yellowish acid of the ponds and rivers, the deep pots of greens and beans cooking
> for hours with smoked or cured pork. Flowers added their heavy aroma. And
> above all, the atmosphere was pressed down with the smell of old fears, and hates,
> and guilt.

In Richard A. Long and Eugenia W. Collier, eds., *Afro-American Writing: An Anthology of Prose and Poetry,* 2nd ed. (University Park, PA: Pennsylvania State University Press, 1985) pp. 663–64.

6. Wade-Gayles, *No Crystal Stair,* pp. 3–4.

7. Dolores Williams, "Black Women's Literature and the Task of Feminist Theology," in *Immaculate and Powerful: The Female in Sacred Image and Social Reality,* ed. Clarissa W. Atkinson, Constance H. Buchanan, and Margaret R. Miles (Boston: Beacon Press, 1985), p. 102.

8. Bell Hooks, *Ain't I a Woman? Black Women and Feminism* (Boston: South End Press, 1981), p. 145.

9. In *Ain't I a Woman?* Bell Hooks emphasizes that the "systematic de-valuation of black womanhood was not simply a direct consequence of race hatred, it was a calculated method of social control," pp. 59–60.

10. The emphasis on "spirit" in the black religious tradition, while it cannot be reduced to this dynamic, is nevertheless, in my view, another effort to reject the reduction of black personhood to embodiment alone.

11. "The Combahee River Collective: A Black Feminist Statement," in Zillah Eisenstein, ed., *Capitalist Patriarchy and the Case for Socialist Feminism* (New York: Monthly Review Press, 1979), p. 365.

12. Gustavo Gutiérrez, personal communication, Boston College, 1983.

13. Quoted by Jo Vellacott, "Women, Peace and Power," in *Reweaving the Web of Life: Feminism and Nonviolence,* ed. Pam McAllister (Philadelphia: New Society Publishers, 1982), p. 38.

14. Barbara Christian, *Black Feminist Criticism: Perspectives on Black Women Writers* (New York: Pergamon, 1985), p. 71.

15. This is the subject of the first section of Chapter Two.

16. Angela Davis, *Women, Race and Class* (New York: Random House, 1981), pp. 223–24.

17. Ibid.

18. Ibid., p. 234.

19. Davis, *Women, Race and Class,* p. 5, citing W. E. B. DuBois, "The Damnation of Women," Chap. 7 of *Darkwater* (New York: Harcourt, Brace and Howe, 1920).

20. Jacqueline Jones, "Three Strands of History," *The Nation* (February 20, 1982), p. 214. Gloria Wade-Gayles, in another review (*Signs* 9 [1983–1984], p. 135), has the same dissenting view as Jones.

> Contrary to the evidence Davis presents, housework in and of itself need not be drudgery. Only its devaluation and its repetitiveness make it undesirable. . . . Similarly, rewards can be gained from having and raising children. From someone as analytically astute as Davis, the attempt to force facts into a specific political framework is disconcerting.

21. Madonna Kolhenschlag, *Kiss Sleeping Beauty Goodbye: Breaking the Spell of Feminine Myths and Models* (Garden City, NY: Doubleday, 1979). See Chap. 1, "Sleeping Beauty at Seventeen," pp. 7–31.

22. Kathryn A. Rabuzzi, *The Sacred and the Feminine: Toward a Theology of Housework* (New York: Seabury, 1982), p. 56. It is crucial to note feminist critiques of these three thinkers, something Rabuzzi does not do. Carol Christ and Ursula King discussed this issue at the American Academy of Religion Annual Meeting, November 21, 1988. Carol Christ's address was entitled "Mircea Eliade and the Origins of Western Religions: A Feminist Critical Reassessment." Ursula King gave a paper on the same panel entitled "A Question of Identity: Women Scholars and the Study of Religion."

23. Ibid., p. 99, quoting *National NOW Times,* December/January 1980–81, p. 2.

24. See Zillah Eisenstein, *The Radical Future of Liberal Feminism* (New York: Longman, 1981), pp. 177–200, "Friedan's Liberal 'Feminist Mystique' and the Changing Politics of NOW." Eisenstein quotes Friedan's view that it is

"the *right* of every woman in America to become all she is capable of becoming—on her own and/or in partnership with a man" (p. 179).

25. Ibid, pp. 96–97, citing Rilke from Gaston Bachelard, *The Poetics of Space,* trans. Maria Jolas (Boston: Beacon Press, 1969), pp. 70–71, italics added.

26. Ibid., pp. 94–95. The problem of the Fall in relation to the difference race makes is treated in the next subsection.

27. Cornel West, *Prophesy Deliverance! An Afro-American Revolutionary Christianity* (Philadelphia: Westminster, 1982), pp. 48ff.

28. Rabuzzi, *Sacred and Feminine,* p. 106.

29. Christian, *Black Feminist Criticism,* p. 74.

30. Zora Neale Hurston, *Their Eyes Were Watching God* (Philadelphia: Lippincott Co., 1937; repr. Urbana: University of Illinois Press, 1978), p. 29.

31. Toni Morrison, *The Bluest Eye* (New York: Washington Square Press, 1970), p. 159.

32. Alice Childress, *Like One of the Family: Conversations from a Domestic's Life* (Boston: Beacon Press, 1986), pp. 60–61.

33. Helen Caldicott, *Missile Envy: The Arms Race and Nuclear War* (Toronto: Bantam Books, 1984), p. 316.

34. Penelope Washbourn, *Becoming Woman: The Quest for Wholeness in Female Experience* (New York: Harper & Row, 1977), p. 1.

35. Ibid., p. 117, quoting Mary Daly, *The Church and the Second Sex* (New York: Harper & Row, 1968), p. 149.

36. Ibid., pp. 126–27.

37. Ann Belford Ulanov, *Receiving Woman: Studies in the Psychology and Theology of the Feminine* (Philadelphia: Westminster, 1981), p. 91, italics added.

38. Audre Lorde, *Sister Outsider: Essays and Speeches* (Trumansburg, NY: Crossing Press, 1984), p. 75.

39. Alice Walker, *Meridian* (New York: Washington Square Press, 1976), pp. 69–70.

40. Ibid., pp. 91f.

41. Christian, *Black Feminist Criticism,* pp. 238–39.

42. Walker, *Meridian,* pp. 121–25.

43. Susan Brooks Thistlethwaite, "Narrative and Connection," *Christianity and Crisis* (March 2, 1987), p. 73, italics added.

44. Walker, *Meridian,* p. 200.

45. Jacqueline Jones, *Labor of Love, Labor of Sorrow: Black Women, Work and Family from Slavery to the Present* (New York: Basic Books, 1985).

46. Rosemary Radford Ruether, *New Woman/New Earth: Sexist Ideologies and Human Liberation* (New York: Seabury, 1975), esp. pp. 194–95.

47. Mary Daly, *Beyond God the Father: Toward a Philosophy of Women's Liberation* (Boston: Beacon Press, 1973), pp. 114, 4.

48. Ibid., p. 39.

49. Mary Daly, *Pure Lust: Elemental Feminist Philosophy* (Boston: Beacon Press, 1984), p. 102.

50. Ibid.

51. Ibid., p. 28.

52. See Daly, *Pure Lust*, pp. 156–59. She critiques Tillich's "hairy claw view" of ontological reality, in which "ontological reason," or the mind, is presumed to dominate "technical reason," which it grasps and shapes. According to Daly, Tillich ends up picturing technical reason as a "sort of wayward wife who refused to meet the demands of her lord and master and finally not only threatened but actually obtained a divorce—in the middle of the nineteenth century." Not surprisingly, this is the period of the first wave of feminism. Tillich's project, then, is to reunite reality, but obviously under a sexist-inspired hierarchy.

53. Ibid., p. 405.

54. Adrienne Rich, *Of Woman Born* (New York: W. W. Norton, 1976), p. 285. Rich, like Sherry Ortner or Susan Griffin, observes that a nature/woman *(sic)* identification in patriarchal consciousness is driving women *(sic)* to explore culture. I have argued (p. 45) that the factor of slavery in this equation renders white women the "soul of culture" and black women as the exploited body or nature. Hence, white women seek to *claim* an identification with nature and the body that has been denied to them. Black women, by contrast, seek to be culture, that part of the dichotomy they have been refused. Yet, it is also true that it would be a practice of the patriarchal "politics of abstraction" not to make distinctions among women and to lump all females together. This is consistent with the practice of an abstractionist phrase like "Third World" where the North Atlantic society is regarded as the norm and the *majority* of the worlds peoples, a markedly diverse group, are given one label.

55. Daly, *Pure Lust*, p. 400, quoting Alice Walker, *The Color Purple* (New York: Harcourt Brace Jovanovich, 1982), p. 167.

56. Ibid., p. 400 (note).

57. Dolores Hines, "Racism Breeds Stereotypes," *The Witness* 65 (February 1982), p. 7.

58. Audre Lorde, "Eye to Eye: Black Women, Hatred, and Anger" in *Sister Outsider*, pp. 145–75.

Chapter 4 / Creating and Destroying Grace: Nature and the Fall

1. See studies of anorexia such as Joan Jacobs Brumberg, *Fasting Girls: The Emergence of Anorexia Nervosa as a Modern Disease* (Boston: Harvard University Press, 1988), p. 280, n. 14. Brumberg notes that there have been only eighteen reported cases of anorexia nervosa among blacks in the United States and Western Europe, and only two among African blacks. Brumberg quotes George Hsu ("Are Eating Disorders More Common in Blacks?" *International Journal of Eating Disorders* 6 [January 1987], pp. 113–24):

> The rarity among blacks of anorexia nervosa and bulimia is the result of cultural differences that protect young black women from the negative self-images and intense pressure for slimness that are part of the white middle-class experience. These data, if correct, are telling evidence of the separateness of black culture and white. . . .

2. Genia Pauli Haddon, *Body Metaphors: Releasing the God-Feminine in Us All* (New York: Crossroad, 1988). See especially Chap. 9.

3. In *Women, Culture and Society,* ed. Michelle Z. Rosaldo and Louise Lamphere (Stanford: Stanford University Press, 1974), pp. 67–87.

4. See especially the work of such process theologians as John Cobb.

5. Gustavo Gutiérrez, *A Theology of Liberation: History, Politics, and Salvation* (Maryknoll, NY: Orbis, 1973), p. 155.

6. Bruce Vawter, *On Genesis* (New York: Doubleday, 1977), pp. 86ff.

7. This is Jürgen Moltmann's view as represented especially in his work *God in Creation: A New Theology of Creation and the Spirit of God* (San Francisco: Harper & Row, 1985). The incursive nature of God is labeled "penetration," see p. 16 for example.

8. Carol P. Christ, *Laughter of Aphrodite: Reflections on a Journey to the Goddess* (San Francisco: Harper & Row, 1987), p. 88.

9. Rosemary Radford Ruether, *New Woman/New Earth: Sexist Ideologies and Human Liberation* (New York: Seabury, 1975), pp. 194–95.

10. Catherine Keller, *From a Broken Web: Separation, Sexism, and Self* (Boston: Beacon Press, 1986), p. 73.

11. Ibid., pp. 73–74.

12. Ibid., p. 74. Keller cites "uroboros" in Erich Neumann, *Origins and History of Consciousness* (Princeton: Princeton University Press, 1954), pp. 18ff.

13. For a discussion of the relationship of "resourcelessness" as violence, see Jo Vellacott, "Women, Peace, and Power," in *Reweaving the Web of Life: Feminism and Nonviolence,* ed. Pam McAllister (Philadelphia: New Society Publishers, 1982), p. 32.

14. Keller, *From a Broken Web,* p. 76, quoting the *Enuma Elish,* p. 102.

15. A related group of opposing themes may be seen in the conflicts between so-called "creation theologians" and their avocation of harmony in nature and the Latin American liberation theologians with their emphasis on social struggle. This difference is summarized in the addenda at the conclusion of this chapter.

16. Starhawk, *Truth or Dare: Encounters with Power, Authority and Mystery* (San Francisco: Harper & Row, 1987), p. 19.

17. Ibid., pp. 320–21.

18. Ibid., p. 141.

19. Ibid., p. 159.

20. Ibid., pp. 161ff.

21. Ibid., p. 6.

22. Ibid., p. 15.

23. Bell Hooks, *Feminist Theory: From Margin to Center* (Boston: South End Press, 1984), p. 163, italics added.

24. Toni Morrison, *Beloved* (New York: Knopf, 1987), p. 5.

25. See Barbara Christian's discussion of this issue in the novels of Toni Morrison in "Community and Nature: The Novels of Toni Morrison," in Barbara Christian, *Black Feminist Criticism: Perspectives on Black Women Writers* (New York: Pergamon, 1985), pp. 49–50.

26. Karl Marx, *Das Kapital*, 3 vols. (Berlin: Dietz, 1947), 1:192; see also 1:57, 3:723, 728ff.

27. Karl Marx, "Economic and Philosophical Manuscripts," *Early Writings* (Harmondsworth, England: Pelican Marx Library, 1975), pp. 349ff.

28. Ibid., p. 348.

29. Alfred Schmidt, *Der Begriff der Natur in der Lehre vom Marx* (Frankfurt, 1962, 1971), p. 159.

30. Gutiérrez, *A Theology of Liberation*, pp. 155ff.

31. Schmidt, *Der Begriff der Natur*, p. 211.

32. Vitor Westhelle, "The Metabolic Mediation: Labor as *Creatio Continua*," in *Lift Every Voice: Constructing Christian Theology from the Underside*, ed. Susan Brooks Thistlethwaite and Mary Potter Engel (San Francisco: Harper & Row, forthcoming).

33. Angela Davis, *An Autobiography* (New York: Random House, 1974), p. 110.

34. Ibid., p. 77.

35. It should be recalled that Davis extensively examines black history during slavery and the Jim Crow era for their impact on Marxist interpretations of present black economic and social conditions in *Women, Race and Class*.

36. Christian, *Black Feminist Criticism*, p. 152.

37. Ibid., p. 61.

38. Mary Daly explicitly maintains that nature has a telos, an end, of her own *Pure Lust: Elemental Feminist Philosophy* (Boston: Beacon Press, 1984), pp. 48, 148. In Morrison's writing fire, air, and water are powerful and independent forces that act and react and interact on, to, and with human actions.

39. Susan Brooks Thistlethwaite, " 'I am Become Death,' God in the Nuclear Age," in *Lift Every Voice*, ed. Thistlethwaite and Engel.

40. Karen Brown, "Why Women Need the War God," in *Women's Spirit Bonding*, ed. Janet Kalven and Mary I. Buckley (New York: Pilgrim Press, 1984), pp. 193–98.

41. Ibid., p. 195.

42. Ibid., pp. 195–97.

43. Ibid., p. 198.

44. Ibid., italics added.

45. Ibid., p. 199.

46. Matthew Fox, *Original Blessing: A Primer in Creation Spirituality* (Santa Fe, NM: Bear & Co., 1983); *On Becoming a Musical, Mystical Bear* (San Francisco: Harper & Row, 1972); *Whee! We Wee All the Way Home* (Santa Fe, NM: Bear & Co., 1981); and *A Spirituality Named Compassion* (Minneapolis: Winston Press, 1979).

47. Starhawk, *Truth or Dare*, p. 14 (note): "The Fall/Redemption model is not the only one in Christianity. In Christian theology, as in Judaism, a current of religious thought has always existed that stresses and celebrates the sacredness of creation. For a full discussion of the creation-centered tradition in Christianity, see Matthew Fox, *Original Blessing*." She also recommends, "for examples of earth-centered Jewish celebration," Arthur Waskow, *Seasons of Our Joy: A Celebration of Modern Jewish Renewal* (Toronto: Bantam, 1982).

48. See especially Appendix B, "Fall/Redemption and Creation-Centered Spiritualities Compared at a Glance," in Fox, *Original Blessing,* pp. 316ff.

49. Charles E. Hambrick-Stowe, "A Spiritual Vision for the United Church of Christ," *Historical Intelligencer* (New York: Historical Council of the United Church of Christ, 1986), p. 15.

50. Ibid., p. 237.

51. Gutiérrez, *A Theology of Liberation,* p. 173, quoted in Vitor Westhelle, "Creation Motifs in the Search for a Vital Space: A Latin American Perspective," in *Lift Every Voice,* ed. Thistlethwaite and Engel.

52. Ibid., citing *Tientos y Diferencias* (Buenos Aires: Calicanto, 1976).

53. Jacquelyn Grant, "Subjectification as a Requirement in Christological Construction," in *Lift Every Voice,* ed. Thistlethwaite and Engel.

54. Westhelle, "The Metabolic Mediation."

55. Ibid.

56. Audre Lorde, *Sister Outsider: Essays and Speeches* (Trumansburg, NY: Crossing Press, 1984), pp. 114–23.

Chapter 5 / The Self and Sin

1. "The Human Situation: A Feminine View," in *Womanspirit Rising: A Feminist Reader in Religion,* ed. Carol P. Christ and Judith Plaskow (San Francisco: Harper & Row, 1979), pp. 25–26, reprinted from *The Journal of Religion* (April 1960). Saiving originally published her article under the name Valerie Saiving Goldstein. She now uses Saiving alone.

2. Ibid., p. 37.

3. Reinhold Niebuhr, *The Nature and Destiny of Man,* vol. 1 (New York: Charles Scribner's Sons, 1964), pp. 179–85.

4. Judith Plaskow, *Sex, Sin, and Grace: Women's Experience and the Theologies of Reinhold Niebuhr and Paul Tillich* (Washington, DC: University Press of America, 1980), pp. 2–3.

5. Ibid., p. 6.

6. Ibid., p. 11.

7. Yet I do not want to fall into the culture/nature dichotomy that I was skirting in the last chapter. I am not saying that women's biology is irrelevant to their understanding of themselves—birth, lactation, vaginal penetration, lesbian sexual practice, menstruation, and menopause are all profound aspects of women's experience, but none floats free of cultural definition. See, for example, Adrienne Rich, *Of Woman Born* (New York: W. W. Norton, 1976).

8. It may be that I have so redefined the nature of truth here that Davaney and I ultimately agree. See Chap. 1, "Experience in White Feminist Theory," above. She writes, our values' " 'truth,' so to speak, lies not in how well they depict some ontological structure of reality, but in the forms of experience that commitment to such values engenders" ("The Limits of the Appeal to Experience," p. 30).

9. Katie G. Cannon, *Black Womanist Ethics* (Atlanta: Scholars Press, 1988), p. 4.

10. Ibid., p. 77.

11. Ibid., pp. 77–78, quoting Dexter Fisher, ed. *The Third Woman: Minority Women Writers of the United States* (Boston: Houghton Mifflin, 1980), p. 139, italics added.

12. Ibid., p. 127, quoting Karla Holloway, "A Critical Investigation of Literary and Linguistic Structure in the Fiction of Zora Neale Hurston," Ph.D. dissertation, Michigan State University, 1978.

13. Ibid., p. 127.

14. Ibid.

15. Ibid., p. 128.

16. Ibid.

17. Ibid., p. 133, quoting Zora Neale Hurston, *Their Eyes Were Watching God* (Philadelphia: Lippincott, 1937; repr. Urbana: University of Illinois Press, 1978), pp. 33–34.

18. Ibid., p. 135, quoting Hurston, *Their Eyes*, p. 49.

19. Ibid., p. 132.

20. Ibid., p. 136, quoting June Jordon, "On Richard Wright and Zora Neale Hurston: Notes Toward a Balancing of Love and Hatred," *Black World* 23 (April 1976), p. 6.

21. Susan Brooks Thistlethwaite, "Narrative and Connection," *Christianity and Crisis* (March 2, 1987), p. 73.

22. Ibid., quoting Alice Walker, *Meridian* (New York: Harcourt Brace Jovanovich, 1976), p. 204.

23. This point on the violence within and the violence without is expanded in Chapter Eight.

24. Barbara Christian, "The Contrary Women of Alice Walker," in *Black Feminist Criticism*, p. 32, quoting Alice Walker, *In Love and Trouble: Stories of Black Women* (New York: Harcourt Brace Jovanovich, 1973).

25. Ibid., p. 34.

26. Here we may see a tiny thread running between Walker and de Beauvoir in that this sense of the "over-againstness" of the self is a major theme of existentialism. Rilke was much influenced by existentialism. He translated Kierkegaard's works from the Danish. J. F. Hendry, *The Sacred Threshold: A Life of Rilke* (England: Carcanet Press, 1983).

27. The Boston Women's Health Book Collective, *Our Bodies, Ourselves* (New York: Simon and Schuster, 1973).

28. Saiving, "The Human Situation," in *Womanspirit Rising*, p. 37.

29. Carol P. Christ, "Connections with the World of the Spirit," *Christianity and Crisis* 47, no. 13 (September 28, 1987), p. 320.

30. It is important to acknowledge that pagan feminists such as Carol Christ now work outside the Christian framework, so categories such as sin are inappropriate to their work. It may also be that having freed herself from such Christian distinctions, it is appropriate for Christ to move in different directions. If I am to respect the differences of black women, I must also extend that respect to white pagan feminists and not invade their boundaries. I want to be heard, therefore, not as correcting Christ's work, but as sparking off (Daly) her insights to go in a different direction.

31. One can certainly argue the differences between Protestant liberalism and process philosophy, as do many interpreters. But insofar as Protestant liberalism has sought above all things to find God in the world and not apart from it, emphasizes the individual person as a source of good and not only sin, has a progressive view of history and relates religion to modern culture, to that extent liberal thought is obviously one of the contributors to contemporary process thinking. See, for example, John Dewey, *A Common Faith* (New Haven: Yale University Press, 1934). Process philosophy is most technically articulated in the works of Alfred North Whitehead; see especially *Process and Reality: An Essay in Cosmology*, ed. D. R. Griffin and D. W. Sherburne (New York: Free Press, 1978). Process *theology* has related process philosophy to the major theological problems of God and the world, the human person, sin and grace, and the church and the kingdom of God. See John Cobb and David Ray Griffin, *Process Theology: An Introductory Exposition* (Philadelphia: Westminster, 1976).

32. See Marjorie Suchocki, *God, Christ, Church: A Practical Guide to Process Theology* (New York: Crossroad, 1982); Penelope Washbourn, *Becoming Woman: The Quest for Wholeness in Female Experience* and also *Seasons of Woman: Song, Poetry, Ritual, Prayer, Myth, Story* (San Francisco: Harper & Row, 1979). See also *Feminism and Process Thought: The Harvard Divinity School/Claremont Center for Process Studies Symposium*, ed. Sheila Greeve Davaney (New York: E. Mellen Press, 1981).

33. John Cobb, *Process Theology as Political Theology* (Philadelphia: Westminster, 1982), p. 103.

34. Ibid., p. 105, italics added.

35. Ibid., p. 101, italics added.

36. *God's Fierce Whimsy* (New York: Pilgrim Press, 1985), p. 19.

37. Ibid., p. 50.

38. Ibid., p. 56.

39. Ibid., p. 57.

40. Jean Bethke Elshtain, *Women and War* (New York: Basic Books, 1987). A weakness, however, is that Elshtain brings no racial distinctions to her analysis of "women."

41. Catherine Keller, *From a Broken Web: Separation, Sexism, and Self* (Boston: Beacon Press, 1986), p. 217.

42. Ibid., p. 248.

43. Ibid., quoting Judy Grahn, "Helen you always were/the factory," in *The Queen of Words* (Trumansburg, NY: Crossing Press, 1982), p. 92.

44. Ibid., p. 222, quoting Alice Walker, *The Color Purple*, p. 167.

45. This is part of the definition of "womanist" in *In Search of Our Mothers' Gardens*, pp. xi–xii.

46. Keller, p. 236, quoting Alfred North Whitehead, *Process and Reality: An Essay in Cosmology*, p. 81.

47. The immense value and insight of Keller's book emerges from her intricate awareness of the myths that underlie the female and male in their sense of self. My critique here is largely of her work when she departs from these

insights gained in the women's movement and allies herself with the hidden patriarchalism of process thought.

48. Ibid., p. 218.

Chapter 6 / Jesus and Christa

1. I found this poem, handwritten, taped to a bulletin board at the Cathedral of St. John the Divine in New York during the exhibition of Edwina Sandys's sculpture "Christa." It appears in print in "Ecumenical Decade 1988–1998: Churches in Solidarity with Women," in *Women in a Changing World,* ed. Anna Karin Hammar and Anne-Marie Kappelli (Geneva: World Council of Churches, 1988), p. 23.

2. Note here the unmodified use of the word *experience;* I am exercising a hermeneutic of connection in regard to these women's knowledge that the violence perpetrated against them is wrong.

3. Jacquelyn Grant, *White Women's Christ and Black Women's Jesus: Feminist Christology and Womanist Response* (Atlanta: Scholars Press, 1989).

4. See Leonard Swidler, "Jesus Was a Feminist," *Southeast Asia Journal of Theology* 13 (1971), pp. 102–10. This article was widely quoted and circulated.

5. Virginia Ramey Mollenkott, *Women, Men and the Bible* (Nashville: Abingdon, 1977), p. 2.

6. Judith Plaskow, "Christian Feminism and Anti-Judaism," in *Cross Currents* (Fall 1978), reprinted by permission in "Dialogue Between Christians and Jews," *New Conversations* (Spring 1987), pp. 20–22.

7. Ibid., p. 21.

8. Virginia Mollenkott, in a new introduction to the revised edition of her widely read *Women, Men, and the Bible* (1976; New York: Crossroad, 1988), has written: "But after years of glimpsing the world from *various angles* shared with me by my Jewish sisters and friends, some of my previous wording seemed to me absolutely appalling. Although financial pressures have made a massive rewriting impossible—apart from the introduction and study guide, I had to stay within the original word limit—I have attempted to renuance my argument" (p. ix, italics added). That is, of course, the key issue: Some white feminists have begun to take account of the "various angles" in doing their work.

9. Plaskow, "Christian Feminist Anti-Judaism: Some New Considerations," p. 25.

10. Susan Brooks Thistlethwaite, "Response to Judith Plaskow," *New Conversations* (Spring 1987), p. 29. Mary Pellauer, in an address at the Lutheran School of Theology, in October 1987, used the AA model to argue that in a sexist society, we are all best described as "recovering sexists."

11. Rosemary Radford Ruether, "Christology and Feminism: Can a Male Savior Save Women?" in *To Change the World: Christology and Cultural Criticism* (New York: Crossroad, 1981), p. 53.

12. Ibid., p. 54.

13. Ibid., p. 55.

14. Rosemary Radford Ruether, *Faith and Fratricide* (New York: Seabury Press, 1974).

15. Carter Heyward, *The Redemption of God* (Washington, DC: University of America Press, 1982), p. 33. See also *Our Passion for Justice* (New York: Pilgrim Press, 1984).

16. Ibid., p. xv.

17. Dorothee Soelle, *Christ the Representative: An Essay in Theology after the Death of God,* trans. David Lewis (Philadelphia: Fortress Press, 1967).

18. Susan Brooks Thistlethwaite, *Metaphors for the Contemporary Church* (New York: Pilgrim Press, 1983), p. 99.

19. Plaskow, "Christian Feminist Anti-Judaism: Some New Considerations," p. 25.

20. Heyward herself is working on precisely these dilemmas by attempting to reconstruct the entire historical superstructure of the way Christology has traditionally been done, i.e., between the poles of the "Jesus of History" and the "Christ of Faith." She is critical of her work of ten years ago, in the "Christology from below" model of *Redemption of God,* which mires Christology in these types of historical comparisons to which Plaskow, and now also Heyward, objects. See "Doing Feminist Liberation Christology: Moving On Beyond 'Jesus of History' and 'Christ of Faith.'—A Methodological Inquiry," in *Lift Every Voice: Constructing Christian Theology from the Underside,* ed. Susan Brooks Thistlethwaite and Mary Potter Engel (San Francisco: Harper & Row, forthcoming).

21. Patricia Wilson-Kastner, *Faith, Feminism and the Christ* (Philadelphia: Fortress, 1983), p. 52.

22. Ibid., p. 53, n. 7. She writes in a note that "As is immediately obvious, the outline I am sketching is related to that general movement called 'process thought.' For an introduction to process thought and its journey from philosophy to theology, see Alfred North Whitehead, *Process and Reality.*" She notes, however, that her own constructive position will be closer to that of Pierre Teilhard de Chardin. This is due, I believe, to the anthropological base of de Chardin's thought and the anthropocentric character of Wilson-Kastner's approach to reality. See Patricia Wilson-Kastner, "Contemporary Feminism and the Christian Doctrine of the Human," *Word and World* 2 (Summer 1982), pp. 234–42.

23. Ibid., p. 52.

24. Ibid., p. 90.

25. Ibid., pp. 91–92.

26. Ibid., p. 65.

27. Ibid., pp. 100ff.

28. Ibid., p. 100, italics added.

29. Harold A. Carter, *The Prayer Tradition of Black People* (Valley Forge, PA: Judson Press, 1976), p. 50.

30. Olive Gilbert, *Sojourner Truth: Narrative and Book of Life* (1850 and 1975; repr. Chicago: Johnson Publishing, 1970).

31. Carter, *The Prayer Tradition*, p. 49.

32. Katie G. Cannon, *Black Womanist Ethics* (Atlanta: Scholars Press, 1988), p. 129, quoting Zora Neale Hurston to Johnson, April 1934, James Weldon Johnson collection, Yale University Library, New Haven.

33. Alice Walker, "The Welcome Table," in *In Love and Trouble: Stories of Black Women* (New York: Harcourt Brace Jovanovich, 1973), pp. 80–84.

34. See Elizabeth Fox-Genovese, *Within the Plantation Household: Black and White Women of the Old South* (Chapel Hill, NC: University of North Carolina Press, 1988), Chap. 4. "Gender Conventions," pp. 192–241. Fox-Genovese's complex presentation of this issue covers the extent to which slaveholding women did and did not oppose the definitions of their womanhood that were based on the degradation of black womanhood. She does summarize that slaveholding women, while sometimes covertly dissatisfied with their society's intermingling of gender definition and slave injustice, "rarely attacked frontally the standards to which their society tried to hold them" (p. 241).

35. Walker, "The Welcome Table," in *In Love and Trouble*, pp. 81–84.

36. Ibid., pp. 86–87.

37. Jacquelyn Grant, *White Women's Christ and Black Women's Jesus*, p. 199.

38. Ibid., p. 206, quoting Kovel, *White Racism: A Psychohistory* (New York: Columbia University Press, 1984), p. x.

39. Ibid., citing Kovel, *White Racism, passim*.

40. Ibid., pp. 230–31, quoting Jarena Less, *Religious Experiences and Journal of Mrs. Jarena Lee* (Philadelphia, 1849), pp. 15–16.

41. Ibid., p. 231.

42. Ibid., p. 232.

43. Ibid.

44. I especially want to thank Francina Parrett for sharing this insight.

45. Toni Cade Bambara, *The Salt Eaters* (New York: Vintage Books, 1981), pp. 25ff.

46. Eleanor Traylor, "Salvation Is the Issue," in *Black Women Writers (1950–1980): A Critical Evaluation* (Garden City, NY: Anchor Press, 1984), pp. 64–65.

47. Wilson-Kastner, *Faith, Feminism and the Christ*, p. 52, italics added.

48. Ibid., p. 110.

49. Ibid., pp. 97–98, 105–6, 121, 126–27, 130, 132, 137 are examples.

50. See quotation on p. 5, above.

51. Frank Willett, *African Art: An Introduction* (New York: Praeger Publishers, 1971), pp. 162, 200.

52. Paula Gunn Allen, *The Sacred Hoop: Recovering the Feminine in American Indian Traditions* (Boston: Beacon Press, 1986), p. 2.

53. Alice Walker, *Meridian* (New York: Washington Square Press, 1976), p. 54.

54. Ibid., p. 58.

55. Ibid., p. 59.

56. Ibid., p. 56.

57. Ibid., p. 59.

58. Allen, *The Sacred Hoop,* p. 69.

59. Rita Nakashima Brock, *Journeys by Heart: A Christology of Erotic Power* (New York: Crossroad, 1988), pp. 6–14.

60. Ibid., p. xiv.

61. Ibid., p. 52.

62. Ibid., p. 41.

63. Ibid.

64. Ibid., p. 62.

65. Ibid.

Chapter 7 / God the Father, God the Mother, and the Goddess

1. Anthony Heilbut, *The Gospel Sound: Good News and Bad Times* (New York: Simon and Schuster, 1975), p. 252.

2. See *An Inclusive Language Lectionary: Readings for Year A* (Atlanta: John Knox Press; New York: Pilgrim Press; Philadelphia: Westminster Press, 1983). Years B and C followed in 1984 and 1985, with a revised edition of Year A appearing in 1986.

3. Susan Brooks Thistlethwaite, "Opening the Mail Which Did Not Tick," *Review of Books and Religion* 12, no. 6 (March 1984), pp. 6ff.

4. I say "among" rather than between because many black women who wish to explore other usages feel that the strong emphasis on God as Father in black churches, coupled with the steadfast resistance to black female clergy, makes experimentation in this area well-nigh forbidden. Further, the inclusive language movement is widely regarded as a white feminist development, and there is very little womanist literature on the subject.

5. See Susan Brooks Thistlethwaite, "Every Two Minutes: Battered Women and Biblical Interpretation," in *Feminist Interpretation of the Bible,* ed. Letty Russell (Philadelphia: Westminster, 1985), pp. 96–107.

6. Mary Daly, *Beyond God the Father: Toward a Philosophy of Women's Liberation* (Boston: Beacon Press, 1973), p. 19; see also 7, 10, 13, 16, 18, 150, 193.

7. Diane Tennis, *Is God the Only Reliable Father?* (Philadelphia: Westminster, 1985), p. 9.

8. Ibid., pp. 35–41.

9. The so-called "Moynihan Report" is a study entitled *The Negro Family: The Case for National Action* from the Office of Policy Planning and Research of the Department of Labor. The report was completed in March 1965 by Daniel Patrick Moynihan, then Assistant Secretary of Labor, with his staff. See *The Moynihan Report and the Politics of Controversy* (Cambridge: M.I.T. Press), pp. 38–124. Moynihan interpreted statistics on black female heads of households—never more than 25 percent in any region of the United States according to the statistics quoted in the study—to be evidence of a black female "matriarchy" (p. 76), which he subsumed under the heading "pathology" (p. 75). Psychological studies were marshaled to show that children from these "disor-

ganized households" did poorly in school and were prone to violence (p. 85). This report popularized the myth of black matriarchy, a thesis widely disputed by black female sociologists, ethicists, and other analysts. See Hooks, *Ain't I a Woman?*, pp. 72ff. See also, Pauli Murray, "The Liberation of Black Women," in *Voices of the New Feminism*, ed. Mary L. Thompson (Boston: Beacon Press, 1970), pp. 354–55; "Jim Crow and Jane Crow," in *Black Women in White America*, ed. Gerda Lerner (New York: Random House, 1972), pp. 592–99; Cheryl Townsend Gilkes, " 'Some Mother's Son and Some Father's Daughter': Gender and Biblical Language in Afro-Christian Worship Tradition," in *Shaping New Visions: Gender and Values in American Culture*, ed. Clarissa W. Atkinson, Constance H. Buchanan, and Margaret Miles (Ann Arbor: U.M.I. Research Press, 1987), p. 9. Gilkes notes: "The [Moynihan] report engendered a sense of shame concerning black women's putative achievements in the political, economic, and cultural life of the black community." Gilkes also summarizes Murray's thesis that the "black power movement was a successful masculinist movement within the black community," occurring around the same time as this report.

10. Tennis, *Is God the Only Reliable Father?*, p. 68. See Christ's "Why Women Need the Goddess" for an explicit statement that women need the Goddess precisely to give up projecting all that is good in them outward, and to give up denying their own capacity for embodying divinity. In *Womanspirit Rising: A Feminist Reader in Religion*, ed. Carol Christ and Judith Plaskow (San Francisco: Harper & Row, 1979), pp. 273–87. Christ's healing insight is, in my experience, the aspect of pagan feminism most underappreciated (and misunderstood) by Christians.

11. Sallie McFague, *Models of God: Theology for an Ecological, Nuclear Age* (Philadelphia: Fortress, 1987), pp. ix ff.

12. Mark H. Ellis, *Toward a Jewish Theology of Liberation* (Maryknoll, NY: Orbis Books, 1987).

13. Phyllis Trible, *Texts of Terror: Literary-Feminist Readings of Biblical Narratives* (Philadelphia: Fortress, 1984), pp. 1–2, italics added.

14. Carol P. Christ, "A Daughter of the Father God," in *Laughter of Aphrodite: Reflections on a Journey to the Goddess* (San Francisco: Harper & Row), pp. 93–102.

15. Alice Miller, *Thou Shalt Not Be Aware: Society's Betrayal of the Child* (New York: Farrar, Straus and Giroux, 1984), p. 221.

16. Ibid., p. 222. Much of the Miller book is a history of how she came to doubt the validity of the drive theory and her exploration of how Freud denied his earliest belief that hysteria in eighteen cases was the "repression of sexual abuse by an adult or by an older sibling who had in turn previously been abused by adults" (pp. 109ff.). See also the Appendix, "Daughters Are Breaking Their Silence," pp. 319ff.

17. Ibid., p. 231.

18. Ibid., p. 232. In her appendix on "Daughters Are Breaking Their Silence," Miller notes that Virginia Woolf "was subject to schizophrenic episodes beginning at the age of twelve and took her own life in 1941 at the age of fifty-

nine, although she had no apparent grounds for doing so. From the time she was four until she reached puberty, she was sexually molested by her much older half brother, virtually on a daily basis, without being able to tell anyone about it. . . . [Her biographer Quentin] Bell, for example, writes that he doesn't know whether this trauma had any permanent effect on Virginia or not!" (p. 320).

19. In his interview with Maya Angelou, Moyers gives the clear impression that she is to be understood as an "exception." In his view, of course, this is a great compliment. Public Broadcasting System, "Understanding Evil—with Bill Moyers."

20. See the several sources for comprehensive statistics on this subject as cited in Marie Fortune, *Sexual Violence: The Unmentionable Sin* (New York: Pilgrim Press, 1983) pp. 163–75. Fortune has done ground-breaking work in identifying sexual and domestic violence as a *theological* problem.

21. Judy Grahn, *Descent to the Roses of the Family* (Iowa City: Common Lives/Lesbian Lives, 1986), pp. 2ff. Grahn subtitled this "Open Letter to my Brother on the Subject of Family Pride."

22. William Julius Wilson, *The Truly Disadvantaged: The Inner City, the Underclass, and Public Policy* (Chicago: University of Chicago Press, 1987).

23. Audre Lorde, "My Words Will Be There," in Mari Evans, ed., *Black Women Writers (1950–1980): A Critical Evaluation* (Garden City, NY: Anchor Press, 1984), p. 266, italics added.

24. Alice Walker, *The Color Purple* (New York: Washington Square Press, 1982), p. 178.

25. Ibid., p. 177.

26. *An Inclusive Language Lectionary: Readings for Year A*, Appendix, "Sovereign, God the *Sovereign One*," etc. (RSV Lord, *Lord*, etc.).

27. Gilkes, "Some Mother's Son," p. 89. Gilkes argues that this inclusive language used by Brewster was a recognition of the hegemony of black women in the song tradition of Afro-Christian churches.

28. Cheryl Townsend Gilkes, " 'Mother to the Motherless, Father to the Fatherless': Power, Gender, and Community in an Afrocentric Biblical Tradition," unpublished paper, an earlier version of which was presented to the American Academy of Religion Annual Meeting, December 7, 1987, quoting Houston A. Baker, Jr., *Blues, Ideology, and Afro-American Literature: A Vernacular Theory* (Chicago: University of Chicago Press, 1984), pp. 3–4.

29. Thistlethwaite, "Opening the Mail," p. 6.

30. Audre Lorde, "Father, Son, and Holy Ghost," in *Chosen Poems—Old and New* (New York: W. W. Norton, 1982), p. 9.

31. Gilkes, " 'Some Mother's Son,' " p. 73.

32. Gilkes has chosen to use Afro-Christian instead of black churches because of the diversity of the traditions from which she draws her examples, and because " 'Afro-Christian' recognizes that our African ancestors constructed a complex and dynamic tradition not only from the materials provided by the missionaries and other Europeans confronted in the nighttime of slavery, but also from the cultural imagination of their African background, in which women were essential to cultural and religious practice. Slaves did not forget about the

women priests and queen mothers in their ancestral societies" ("Some Mother's Son," pp. 78–79). See also Cheryl Townsend Gilkes, "The Roles of Church and Community Mothers; Ambivalent American Sexism or Fragmented African Familyhood?" *Journal of Feminist Studies in Religion* 2 (Spring 1986), pp. 41–59.

33. Yvonne Delk, personal communication, July 5, 1988.

34. Gilkes, "Some Mother's Son, p. 92.

35. Ibid., p. 92.

36. Ibid., pp. 93–94.

37. Ibid., pp. 4–15.

38. Ibid., p. 31.

39. Ibid., pp. 31ff.

40. Ibid., p. 37, quoting James A. Sanders, *From Sacred Story to Sacred Text: Canon as Paradigm* (Philadelphia: Fortress, 1987), p. 186.

41. Hannah Arendt, *On Violence* (New York: Harcourt Brace Jovanovich, 1969), p. 41.

42. Jürgen Moltmann, *The Trinity and the Kingdom* (San Francisco: Harper & Row, 1981), pp. 129–131.

43. Frederick Schleiermacher, *The Christian Faith* (Philadelphia: Fortress, 1976), p. 738.

44. Ibid., p. 37. Schleiermacher also believed that monotheism was the "highest" mode of religious belief. The Trinity therefore embarrassed him because the Three-in-One could be interpreted as a remnant of polytheism. See pp. 738ff.

45. Ibid., pp. 34ff.

46. Even Barth did not fundamentally challenge this shift. Barth's God is Absolute Subject, not absolute substance. He states, "God's Word is God in his revelation. God reveals himself as Lord. He alone is the revealer. He is wholly revelation" (*Dogmatics in Outline* [New York: Harper & Row, 1959], p. 126). Note that consistent with the tendency of white theology, the "Lord" is God, not Jesus.

47. William Lloyd Newell, *The Secular Magi: Marx, Freud, and Nietzsche on Religion* (New York: Pilgrim, 1986).

48. Ibid., pp. 147–55.

49. Freud himself responded to the nuclear age by relating it to the death-wish drive that he postulated drove humanity to self-destruction. See Paul E. Stepansky, *A History of Aggression in Freud* (New York: International Universities Press, 1977), esp. Chap. 1, "Thanatos and Aggression: The Strained Linkage. Eric Fromm, in *The Anatomy of Human Destructiveness* (New York: Holt, Rinehart and Winston, 1973), follows Freud in postulating that the source of human violence is "innate" drives. The significant work of Alice Miller is an important correction. Miller's several works, *Thou Shalt Not Be Aware: Society's Betrayal of the Child* (New York: Farrar, Straus and Giroux, 1984) and *For Your Own Good: Hidden Cruelty in Child-Rearing and the Roots of Violence* (New York: Farrar, Straus and Giroux, 1983), identify the origins of

human destructiveness in child abuse. According to Miller, destruction is *learned,* not innate.

50. Mary Daly, *Gyn/Ecology,* p. 111.

51. Emily Culpepper, "Contemporary Goddess Thealogy: A Sympathetic Critique," in *Shaping New Visions,* ed. Atkinson, Buchanan, and Miles, pp. 60–61.

52. Ibid., p. 60.

53. Ibid., p. 61.

54. Ibid., p. 62.

Chapter 8 / A Difference in Common: Violence

1. "with no immediate cause," *Nappy Edges* (New York: St. Martin's Press, 1972).

2. "Every Two Minutes: Battered Women and Biblical Interpretation," in *Feminist Interpretation of the Bible,* ed. Letty Russell (Philadelphia: Westminster, 1985).

3. Mary Pellauer, "Moral Callousness and Moral Sensitivity: Violence Against Women, in *Women's Consciousness, Women's Conscience,* ed. Barbara Hilkert Andolsen, Christine E. Gudorf, and Mary Pellauer (Minneapolis: Winston Press, 1985), pp. 34–35.

4. It was, however, Naomi Goldenberg who called me on my failure to use my own history as a survivor in the theological writings I have done on this subject. I would like to thank her for her honesty; as I wrote on the dust jacket of Carol Christ's *Laughter of Aphrodite,* "in the eyes of patriarchal theology all women are pagan." The differences between feminist theologians and thealogians are real, but they are not chasms. They are, for me, equally the source of creativity and change.

5. Mary Caudren, "Patriarchy and Death," in *Women's Spirit Bonding,* ed. Janet Kalven and Mary I. Buckley (New York: Pilgrim Press, 1984), pp. 175–76, quoting Mary O'Brien, *The Politics of Reproduction* (London: Routledge and Kegan Paul, 1981), p. 29.

6. In a similar fashion, Shange, Walker, and other black women writers do not let the black community off the hook for the violence perpetrated against black women and children by black men despite the real deformations of racism. See, for example, the Shange poem at the beginning of this chapter, her *for colored girls,* and Walker's *The Color Purple* or *The Third Life of Grange Copeland.*

7. Richard Gelles and Claire Pedrick Cornell, eds., *International Perspectives on Family Violence* (Lexington, MA: D. C. Heath and Co., 1983).

The accumulated evidence from both empirical studies and position papers in child abuse and spouse abuse is that child abuse and spouse abuse are probably most common in Western, industrialized, developed nations. Developing countries also seem to have problems of abuse and violence, but these are interpreted as being grounded in the social disorganization caused by modernization and the

resultant changes in family, clan, tribal, and social institutions. China is frequently
described as a society with little or no problem with child or wife abuse, as are the
Scandinavian countries. (p. 161)

The Gelles and Cornell volume makes the point that because definitions and
study methods vary from one country to another, true cross-cultural comparisons are difficult. But on the basis of their data, it seems that the United
States has a high incidence of wife and child abuse, as well as other forms of
violence—such as rape, robbery, and murder.

8. Quoted in Hannah Arendt, *On Violence* (New York: Harcourt, Brace and
World, 1969), p. 41.

9. Ibid., p. 42.

10. Ibid.

11. Jo Vellacott, "Women, Peace, and Power," in *Reweaving the Web of Life:
Feminism and Nonviolence,* ed. Pam McAllister (Philadelphia: New Society
Publishers, 1982), p. 32.

12. Ibid., p. 38.

13. Pam McAllister, "Introduction," in *Reweaving,* p. vi.

14. Thomas Reade Roots Cobb, *An Inquiry into the Law of Negro Slavery in
the United States of America* (Philadelphia: T. & J. W. Johnson & Co., 1858),
1:82–115, quoted in Willie Lee Rose, ed., *A Documentary History of Slavery in
North America* (New York: Oxford University Press, 1976), p. 197.

15. Ibid., p. 199, italics added.

16. Ibid., p. 204, italics added.

17. Ibid., pp. 198–99.

18. Ibid.

19. Robert William Fogel and Stanley L. Engerman, *Time on the Cross: The
Economics of American Negro Slavery* (Boston: Little, Brown and Company,
1974).

20. See Paul A. David and Peter Temin, "Slavery: The Progressive Institu-
tion?" *Journal of Economic History* 34 (September 1974), pp. 739–83; Paul A.
David and Peter Temin, "Capitalist Masters, Bourgeois Slaves," *Journal of
Interdisciplinary History* 5 (Winter 1974/75), pp. 445–57; Richard Sutch, "The
Treatment Received by American Slaves: A Critical Review of the Evidence
Presented in *Time on the Cross,*" *Explorations in Economic History* 12 (Oc-
tober 1975), pp. 335–438. See also Paul A. David, Herbert G. Gutman, Richard
Sutch, Peter Temin, and Gavin Wright, *Reckoning with Slavery* (New York:
Oxford University Press, 1976).

21. David et al., *Reckoning,* pp. 59–65.

22. Ibid., p. 63.

23. Ibid., p. 135, quoting *Time on the Cross,* vol. 1, pp. 78 and 84.

24. Ibid., p. 136, quoting *Time on the Cross,* vol. 1, pp. 129–35.

25. Ibid., p. 134.

26. Susan Schechter, *Women and Male Violence: The Struggles of The
Battered Women's Movement* (Boston: South End Press, 1982), lists several
racial breakdowns in her index, but racial differences is not central to her study.

27. Mary Daly, *Pure Lust: Elemental Feminist Philosophy* (Boston: Beacon Press, 1984), p. 28.

28. Helen Caldicott, *Missile Envy: The Arms Race and Nuclear War*, rev. ed. (New York: Bantam Books, 1986), p. 236.

29. Mary Caudren, "Patriarchy and Death," in *Women's Spirit*, p. 175.

30. Mary Daly, *Gyn/Ecology: The Metaethics of Radical Feminism* (Boston: Beacon Press, 1978), p. 1.

31. Zillah Eisenstein, *The Radical Future of Liberal Feminism* (New York: Longman, 1981), p. 18.

32. Ibid., p. 19.

33. Adrienne Rich, *Of Woman Born* (New York: W. W. Norton, 1976), p. 57.

34. Keep in mind that the whole natural law thesis in this chapter is difficult and complex. "Natural Law" or natural right is in its origins a Stoic doctrine that has undergone many modern alterations. The Lockean view is an influential modern reinterpretation of natural law. Locke's views that human beings emerge in a "state of nature" and achieve civilization only by the social contract was believed to have had great influence on nineteenth-century white feminists. But part and parcel of the Lockean view is its intellectual support for laissez-faire capitalism under the guise of protecting the individual and "his" rights. For a feminist critique of the pernicious influence of this Lockean natural-law perspective in white feminism, see Zillah Eisenstein, *The Radical Future of Liberal Feminism*, in which she explicitly connects Locke to such modern white feminists as Betty Friedan.

One change that more radical feminists such as Mary Daly have made from the Lockean perspective is an appeal to the remote past and the "state of nature" as a matriarchy. For white radical feminists, this tends to strengthen the romantic appeal of the entire category of "nature." When white feminists such as Sharon Welch or Sheila Greeve Davaney adopt a poststructuralist critique, they have done so precisely to correct this "naturalism" and its assertion of an essential female nature and experience.

35. See Elizabeth Fox-Genovese, *Within the Plantation Household: Black and White Women of the Old South* (Chapel Hill, NC: University of North Carolina Press, 1988), Chap. 4, "Gender Conventions," pp. 192–241.

Index